THE FIRST DECADENT

J. K. HUYSMANS

THE FIRST DECADENT

BEING THE STRANGE LIFE OF

J. K. HUYSMANS

BY

JAMES LAVER

CITADEL PRESS • NEW YORK

CONTENTS

ILLUSTRATIONS

———————— • ————————

7

CHAPTER ONE

THE FATHER OF THE MAN

———————————— ● ————————————

In the little town of Breda, in Holland, a family of artist-craftsmen had been settled for centuries. Its name was Huysmans, the exact equivalent of the English name Housman, and its traditional craft was the painting of missals. Some of its members, however, had been more ambitious, and had wandered from their native town. The dictionaries of artists have something to say of Jacob Huysmans, born in Antwerp, who died in London in 1696, and of Jean Baptiste Huysmans, also born in Antwerp and sufficiently important a painter to be Master of the Guild of St. Luke about the year 1676. He died in Antwerp in 1711. Cornelius Huysmans, born in Antwerp in 1684, is known as Huysmans 'of Malines', in which town he died in 1727. Examples of his work are in the Louvre.

Shortly after the Battle of Waterloo, there was born in Breda a child who was christened Godfried. When he was old enough he applied himself to the newly invented craft of lithography, but he had sufficient artistic talent not to be content with reproducing other men's work. He was himself a designer and, finding that his native place did not offer enough scope, he migrated in the early eighteen-forties to Paris, where there was beginning to be a ready market for the work he was able to do.

In 1845 he fell in love with a French girl whose name was

9

Elisabeth Malvina Badin, and when asking for her hand he described himself as a *dessinateur lithographe* earning 3000 francs a year and hoping shortly to earn more. His own name he gave in the French style as Victor Godefroy Jean Huysmans. He was then twenty-nine years old and his bride eighteen.

His wife also had an artistic tradition in her family. She was of Burgundian origin and her maternal grandfather was a sculptor who had gained the Prix de Rome and had assisted in the decoration of the Colonne Vendôme and of the Arc de Triomphe du Carrousel. Born in Paris in 1760, he had died some two years before his granddaughter's marriage. Her father had no such background of art. He was a cashier in the Ministry of the Interior, a fact which was not to be without significance in the life of the subject of the present volume.

We do not know where Godfried Huysmans lived before his marriage, but it was almost certainly on the left bank of the Seine. The Rive Gauche has in the course of nearly two thousand years of history undergone many vicissitudes. In Roman times it was the centre of Paris—the real Lutetia—as the recently excavated arena bears witness, but after the destruction of the town by the barbarians in the third century, the centre of gravity shifted to the other side of the river, and, in the Middle Ages, the Rive Gauche was occupied almost entirely by great monasteries such as the Abbey of St. Germain and the Abbey of St. Geneviève, and, later, by the University of Paris.

What we now call the Luxembourg Quarter, or the Sixth Arrondissement, is properly the old Bourg St. Germain, the little town which grew up round the Abbey of that name. Together with its suburb, the more famous Faubourg St. Germain (now the Seventh Arrondissement), it became, at the end of the seventeenth century, the chosen quarter of the

French aristocracy. Readers of Balzac will remember the distinction drawn between the *nouveaux riches* of the Faubourg St. Honoré on the right bank and the conservative aristocratic families of the Faubourg St. Germain. Some of them still remained at the end of the reign of Louis-Philippe but the Quarter was already beginning to lose its prestige. Further east along the Rive Gauche the decay had set in even earlier, and when Godfried and Elisabeth Huysmans were looking for a home in the neighbourhood of the Rue St. André-des-Arts, the district had decayed into something nearly resembling a slum. They found a lodging in the narrow little street which had just been re-baptised Rue Suger, having been formerly called the Rue du Cimetière-St. André. The street and indeed the whole district in which it stood was dirty, congested and airless, for Baron Haussmann had not yet driven his boulevard through it. But it had one compensating advantage. It was cheap.

Today the very centre of the *Quartier Latin* might be considered to be the spot where the Boulevard Saint-Michel crosses the Boulevard Saint-Germain. But the Boulevard Saint-Michel did not exist when Godfried Huysmans settled there. It was not completed until eight years later. It drove straight for the river, widened the old Place du Pont Saint-Michel into its own vast *Place*; it almost completely swept away the ancient Rue de la Harpe; but it left, almost untouched, the network of old streets bordered by the Seine, the Rue Dauphine, the Boulevard Saint-Germain and itself.

The Rue Saint-André des Arts,[1] with its eighteenth-century houses, from one of which Voltaire set out on his last triumphal drive through Paris, is now a street of clinics and pharmacies for the poor, and a considerable portion of its length has been swallowed up by the open square where the great church once stood.

[1] More correctly called Saint-André des Arcs.

The Father of the Man

If we cross this street and pass through the Rue d'Éperon—
where Racine once lived—we reach the Rue Suger, parallel
with the Rue Saint-André des Arts and ending in the same
Place. It is a narrow, curving, sombre little street. 'The
pavements, the walls, the windows seem melancholy and
hostile; two starved cats make their way across it and dis-
appear under one of the old seventeenth-century *portes
cochères* bristling with nails and still furnished with their
iron knockers.'[1]

No. 11 in the Rue Suger was no exception. It was described
in 1885 as 'an old house still in existence, with its ancient
round-headed double door painted green and studded with
enormous nails'.[2] It was here, on February 5th, 1848, that
the French wife of the Dutch immigrant gave birth to a son.[3]

He was baptised at the Church of Saint Séverin, and given
the names of Charles Marie Georges (it was not until he was
grown up that he reverted to the Dutch form of Joris Karl),
and as might have been expected in such surroundings, he
was frail, white-faced and undersized.

He had chosen a very unpropitious moment for his arrival.
The 'Hungry 'Forties' had been just as hungry in Paris as
elsewhere and the city, especially in its poorer quarters, had
not been spared by the terrible cholera epidemic; nor was this
all. To the horrors of pestilence and famine were added those
of civil war. All over Europe thrones were toppling and
monarchs in flight. To many it seemed like the end of the
world, as it was certainly the end of an epoch.

It is true that Louis-Philippe had departed with a mini-
mum of fuss, and it seemed for the moment as if the Revolu-

---

[1] Georges Cain, *Nouvelles Promenades dans Paris*, Paris (1908).

[2] By Huysmans, *En Marge*, p. 50.

[3] The modern visitor will find little remaining of the old Rue Suger,
but, on the south side between a school and what is now a great hole in
the ground a couple of houses remain. One of these is the No. 11 in
which Huysmans was born, but it has now been renumbered No. 9.

tion was in the hands of the idealists. Georges Charles Huysmans was three weeks old when Lamartine made his famous speech from the Hotel de Ville. Liberty, Equality and Fraternity seemed to have triumphed at last. There was a torchlight dance in front of the Arc de Triomphe and crowds paraded the streets shouting 'Long live the People', 'Long live the National Guard', 'Long live the Workers'; but this honeymoon was not destined to last very long. The men who had made the Revolution of 1848 found, like all revolutionaries, that they had to cope with their own Left Wing. They tried to deal with the situation by arresting the demagogue Raspail, and by organising a great fête in the Champs de Mars. It was all in vain. The mob invaded and threatened the Assembly; barricades sprang up all over Paris, and at one of these the Archbishop of Paris, attempting to mediate, was shot.

One of the most formidable of the barricades was erected in front of the Petit Pont, at the entrance to the Rue Saint Jacques, little more than a stone's throw from the house in the Rue Suger. Manned by a hundred and fifty men, nearly all of whom had seen service in the Garde Républicaine, and more than five hundred other insurgents, it was stoutly defended and had to be carried by assault. Noise of the battle must have sounded terrifyingly near to the young mother watching over her four months old child.

The other barricades did not survive much longer. Cavaignac occupied Paris with his troops, and the insurrection, not without a considerable amount of bloodshed, was finally put down. The Government breathed again and began to draw up schemes for a Constitution. Meanwhile Louis Napoleon Bonaparte, who had just been elected a Representative of the People, bided his time, ready when the moment arrived to make their labours unnecessary.

Of Godfried Huysmans' political opinions we know nothing.

Poor and a foreigner, he was not likely to visit the cafés and clubs in the Quarter, where the political affairs of the day were discussed. The little family, with its pious and artistic traditions, kept itself to itself, the father pursuing his trade as a lithographer and sometimes, more ambitious, getting out his canvases and brushes and painting for his own pleasure. We know that he copied a picture by Zurbaran and even painted a portrait of his wife. She, on her part, busied herself with the duties of the household and the care of her child. The household was modest but by no means poverty-stricken; relatives visited the young couple and there were even modest celebrations for birthdays and fêtes.

Perhaps because the apartment in the Rue Suger had become too small owing to the birth of his son, Godfried Huysmans, shortly afterwards, moved to No. 38 Rue St. Sulpice, a house overshadowed by the choir of the great church, and which had previously been used as a presbytery. In retrospect there seems almost a fatality in this choice of lodging, as if it had been pre-ordained that the young Huysmans should find himself surrounded from his earliest years by a suggestion of the ecclesiastical, and that the first important object to meet his infant eyes should be the church which was to play so important a part in his later development.

'All these streets and alleys around St. Sulpice', remark the authors of *Les Logis de Huysmans*[1] 'have a curious closed room atmosphere of Catholicism. They smell of the country curé. And indeed many of our good provincial abbés stay, when they are in Paris, in the hotels of the district. Many cassocks wander in the neighbourhood of the church, looking for those frightful images of St. Anthony, of the Immaculate Conception, of the Maid of Domrémy, and of the Sacred

[1] M. C. Poinsot and G. V. Lange, *Les Logis de Huysmans*, Paris, 1919, p. 30.

Heart which dishonour the sometimes charming churches in French villages and towns.' The good men little knew that, in the eyes of the child playing at their feet, their piety was to be, one day, no excuse for their bad taste.

Huysmans has very little to say about his early childhood, but we know that the religious atmosphere was not only a matter of living next door to a church in an apartment that had once been occupied by priests. Some of his relations were actually 'in religion', and he records[1] the impression they made upon him when he went, with his mother, to visit them in their convent parlours: 'cousins and aunts, grave and gentle women, white as wafers,[2] who alarmed him by their low voices, who troubled him by their looks, and asked if he were a good boy. He felt a sort of terror, and hid himself in his mother's skirts, trembling when, at parting, he was obliged to bend his brow to those colourless lips, and undergo the touch of a chilly kiss.' He remembered in later life the 'bare parlours with their faded scent of wainscotting and of wax and the convent gardens through which he had passed, gardens impregnated with the bitter salt scent of box, planted with clipped hedges, intermingled with trellises, whose green grapes never ripened, divided by benches of mouldering stone'.

The peaceful and almost cloistered existence of the little family was shortly, however, to be brought to an end. Before his son was nine years old, Godfried Huysmans died. He was buried on June 26th, 1856. We do not know how long the survivors continued to live in the Rue St. Sulpice, but very soon the young widow, who was under thirty when her husband died, married again.

The new husband's name was Og, which does not sound

---

[1] *En Route*, p. 17.

[2] The actual phrase is '*blanches comme des oublies*'. We have followed the happy translation of Mr. C. Kegan Paul.

very French. It is possible that he too was the descendant of Dutch immigrants. We know very little about him except that he had two daughters by Huysmans' mother, and that the family lived at No. 11 Rue de Sèvres, where they conducted an *atelier de brochage*.

Once again the atmosphere was ecclesiastical. No. 11 Rue de Sèvres was no ordinary house but the remains of a vast monastery of the Praemonstratensians commenced in the late seventeenth century and finished in the early eighteenth. With its garden and courtyards it filled the whole space between the Rue de Sèvres and the Rue du Cherche-Midi, and between the Rue de la Chaise and the Place de la Croix-Rouge. The monks were dispersed by the Revolution and the great church destroyed; but enough remained to enable Madame Og to find plenty of room for her work-rooms and her family too.

Huysmans himself has described it.[1] The great corridors, wide enough for a charge of cavalry, were still intact. All the doors of the cells opened into them, but a few of the rooms opened into one another and formed spacious apartments: too spacious for comfort, for they were extremely high and paved with tiles and, in winter, were desperately cold. Huysmans remembered a vast room on the first floor where he passed, he says, a 'frozen childhood'. The only method of heating the room was by means of a wood fire in the middle, and the family huddled round it, a screen behind them, their feet roasted and their backs frozen.

Below were magnificent cellars, with vaulted roofs like the crypt of a church. They came in useful for the whole neighbourhood when the Germans were bombarding Paris; and, in more peaceful times, they housed a stock of wine, old burgundies of the kind known as 'pélure d'oignon', which mellowed in the dry air, and perfumed the

[1] See *De Tout*, p. 19.

whole apartment when they were brought up and the cork drawn.

The ground floor was occupied by the workrooms which Huysmans was to describe later in *Les Sœurs Vâtard*. They must have been quite familiar to him even as a child, for he was one of those sharp little boys whose eye misses nothing. In the centre of the courtyard there was, in his early days, a stall where one could buy bowls of soup and portions of beef. But the proprietor went into bankruptcy and the calm of the cloister flowed back again into the deserted court.

The *quartier* itself was very different from what it is now, different even from what it was when Huysmans described it in his later years. The prolongation of the Boulevard Raspail had not yet engulfed part of the Rue de la Chaise and the Rue de Varennes. It was not until 1907 that it swallowed up the Convent of the Sœurs Hospitalières de St. Thomas de Ville-neuve, one of the few monastic institutions left intact by the French Revolution on account of the good work done by the Sisters in the hospitals. The Bon-Marché, later to become a centre of busy commerce, was, in Huysmans' youth, a tiny shop. The tramways had not been built, the traffic was negligible. The whole quarter was placid and almost de-serted. It might have been part of a great provincial town. A monastic air still brooded over it.

Only a few paces down the street was the Abbaye-aux-Bois. It became a prison under the Terror and was afterwards transformed into a *maison de retraite laïque*. It was here that Madame Récamier lived for thirty years and made it famous by her literary salon. In 1827 part of it became a convent again, which was not suppressed until 1905. When Huysmans was a child, it was intact, with its irregular silhouette, its win-dows barred like a prison, and its peeling walls. Every morn-ing at ten o'clock there gathered before the door a little crowd of cripples and beggars to claim the assistance of the nuns.

Its chapel was hideous, having been rebuilt in the early nineteenth century, but above the high altar was a Black Virgin saved from the sack of St. Étienne-du-Mont by a certain Comtesse de Carignan who, having shared a prison with the nuns during the Terror, bestowed on them, after their release, the famous image.

So near was the sanctuary to the Huysmans' home that Madame Og must often have heard mass there, and taken her young son with her. At least it seems so, from the effect it had upon him. His description of it is so intimate and moving that one could swear it was a reminiscence of childhood, if Huysmans had not always kept the sensibility of a child.

'On Sundays,' he says, 'at the nine o'clock mass, behind the grill of the cloister, the frail voice of a nun sings, unaccompanied, the *Kyrie Eleison*, and alternates, alone, with the great organ: and so violent is the contrast between this poor thin voice, sustained by nothing, imploring behind the grill, and this majestic tempest of the organ which takes up in its turn the same lament and amplifies it, rolls it round and carries it up to the roof, that one suffers from a kind of horror and cold. One feels very deeply then the nothing that one is.'

We do not know the exact date—perhaps it was after the birth of his second half-sister—when it was decided that young Huysmans should leave home. He was placed, as a boarder, in the Pension Hortus, No. 94 Rue du Bac. Here he received the first part of his education, and if we ignore all the differences between the French and the English systems, we can think of it as a kind of preparatory school. It had, however, none of the advantages of a healthy life for, instead of being situated in the country, like so many English preparatory schools, it was little more than a stone's-throw from his mother's door. It must have been inexplicable to his young mind why he was placed in the pension at all.

The Father of the Man

There can be little doubt that he hated it. In the novel *En Ménage* two of his characters who have been school friends in their youth discuss their life together in just such an establishment as the Pension Hortus. As both André and his friend Cyprien are merely two aspects of Huysmans himself, it hardly matters which we choose to speak for him.

'It wasn't yesterday that we became acquainted,' says Cyprien. 'I can still see you arriving at the pension. You were crying like a magdalen. But you weren't the most to be pitied. You had a family who were always coming to see you in the parlour; every Sunday you were free to go away . . .

'Don't imagine,' replies André, 'that such holidays were any gayer outside than in. My whole day was spoiled by the horror of having to go back in the evening. My family kept looking at the time. "We must be quick", said my mother, "it's getting late." I left the table after the second dish, with my dessert in my pocket, and then, after admonitions and kisses, I was taken back by Irma, the maid. The streets full of people clutched at my heart. I saw other children dawdling in front of the lighted shop-windows. They were *free!* I had to hurry to be back in time. Oh the streets, that evening! The noise of the cafés full of customers, the theatre posters promising unheard-of pleasures, all these things were like the death of the soul. I tried to walk more slowly but the maid was anxious to be rid of me so that she could join her young man. She lengthened her stride, and soon we were in front of the gloomy box where the concierge Piffard waited behind the windows of his cage. As soon as I stepped into it a chill fell on my shoulders as though I had entered a cellar; the maid's retreating back made me want to weep and fly. You remember, when one got back to the dormitory the usher threatened to deprive one of next Sunday's leave because of the noise of one's feet. One took one's shoes off and without slippers, in that dormitory lighted like a funerary chapel and sinister with its white row of beds, one slipped as quickly as possible between the sheets.

'To think that there are people who pretend to regret their school days. Not I, *par exemple*! However wretched I might be I would rather die than live over again that barrack life, the tyranny of fists bigger than mine, and the ushers' ignoble hate.'

The ushers, if we are to believe the author of *En Ménage*, were certainly not such as to inspire affection or respect in any boy: men who would not have endured their own life in the pension if they had been able to find anything better, dirty and ill-kept, thinking only of their next glass of absinthe, or suffering from the effects of their even more squalid vices, confiscating the boys' tobacco and smoking it themselves, allowing themselves to be bribed by the richer scholars to let them off punishments. Huysmans' life at the Pension Hortus according to his own account, bore very little resemblance to Tom Brown's schooldays.

He dwells, with characteristic exasperation, on the badness of the food, and the boredom of the inevitable sequence of dishes. He remembers the eternal hours of 'prep' in winter when the fumes of the stove and the gas-jets made it almost impossible to keep awake until the hour when the dictionaries were closed and the boys were herded back to their icy dormitory. There, keeping their socks on for warmth, and spreading their clothes over the bed, they finally slept, only to be awakened at half past five next morning by the servant banging a broomstick against the shelves of the boot-cupboard.

In summer it was even worse. The boys washed their feet in the refectory, once a fortnight, but this infrequent act of hygiene did not prevent the dormitory from being filled with a stale, sweetish odour enough to turn any sensitive stomach. André-Huysmans felt equally sick at the recollection of the classroom where he had sat, with its battered desks covered with the carved initials of his predecessors, the two gas-jets with their glass globes which cracked when you spat at them; and of one usher in particular who distributed slaps right and left and whose big signet-ring left a red mark on the boys' cheeks; and who tried to frighten them into morality by showing them pictures of syphilitics, their faces eaten away.

'And so it continued for months, for years; one left one class to enter another; new books had to be studied, one was expected to admire the solemn fiddle-faddle of Horace, the stupefying balderdash of Homer, recite passages of Racine and Virgil, Cicero and Boileau, to pass in review all the pompous boredom of the classical period, copy a hundred verses—or a thousand, learning meanwhile nothing of the slightest use. And the weeks followed one another, bringing the same bad food, diluted wine or pure cold water; the days passed, all equally melancholy, between the desolation of Monday morning, when one woke up horrified at the prospect of a week to be lived through, and the hope that began to dawn about Thursday, that Sunday would be reached at last.'

When Huysmans was about thirteen, he became an *externe* (or day-boy, as we should say) at the Lycée St. Louis, but it is quite plain from his narrative that he continued to board at the Pension Hortus. This arrangement, which it is difficult for the English reader to understand, was by no means unusual in nineteenth-century France, particularly among pious families, who feared the free-thinking atmosphere of the *lycées*. Huysmans recalls the terrible apprehension he felt when he left for the Lycée without knowing his lessons, and he remembers also, with a savage joy, the tricks he and his companions played en route, tormenting the tradesmen and shooting with their catapults at the bellies of the horses to make them bolt.

21

The Pension Hortus was situated in that portion of the Rue du Bac which lies between the Rue de Grenelle and the Rue de Varennes. If Huysmans in his progress from the Pension to the Lycée took the former he would find that he had to make a detour round the Abbaye-aux-Bois. He would presumably take the Rue de Grenelle, and indeed he mentions this street in the passage about the horses just quoted. He could then hardly avoid taking the little Rue du Vieux Colombier, and this would bring him into the Place St. Sulpice. Thence, by way of a maze of small streets—the portion of the Boulevard St. Germain between St. Germain-des-Prés and the Cluny being not yet opened up—he would arrive in the Boulevard St. Michel near to the Lycée St. Louis. It is interesting to note, therefore, that if he took the shortest way from the Pension Hortus to his classroom and back again he passed twice a day, in the most impressionable years of his life, beneath the shadow of the great church of St. Sulpice.

We know something about his academic career at the Lycée St. Louis. Although not the most brilliant pupil there, he was by no means a dunce. In 1862, when he was in the Fifth Class, he obtained the third 'accessit' for Latin, the fourth for History and Geography, and the second for Recitation. In the following year, when he was in the Fourth (the French system of counting the forms being the opposite of that usual in English public schools) he obtained the fifth 'accessit' for Latin.

In 1865, when he was in the Second Class and had reached the age of seventeen, he rebelled against both Pension and Lycée alike. In his own phrase he refused to return to any *boîte*, but he agreed to take lessons from a certain 'Professor' Delzons who coached private pupils for their examinations. The Professor found that he had already made himself a good latinist, in spite of his prejudice against classical literature, and he was able to obtain his diploma as *bachelier-ès-lettres* on May 7th, 1866. The family gave a little party to celebrate the event, and much discussion ensued concerning the young man's future. It was decided that he should study Law, and he seems, for a few months, to have attended lectures at the *École du Droit*.

In the first few pages of *Sac au Dos* he makes some thinly veiled allusions to this period of his life. He did not, apparently, take his law studies seriously, but wasted his allowance in the company of a 'blonde'. The identity of this woman—and indeed her identification with any friend of Huysmans—might have remained obscure for ever; but in the appendix to *Les Logis de Huysmans* we find a passage of the greatest interest setting forth details which seem to have been unknown to most of those who have written of Huysmans. The authors record that a certain 'Francis Baumal—and this is a souvenir both touching and precious—reminds us that J. K. Huysmans, before 1870, occupied as a student a certain modest room in the Rue du Dragon, and here took place one of those idylls which perfume, for almost all young men, the happy days when they are twenty.

'The war before the last (*Les Logis de Huysmans* appeared in 1920) separated the lovers, who met again, and lived together, round about 1878. When, later, the publisher Vanier asked the writer for some biographical notes for a fascicule of *Les Hommes d'Aujourd'hui*, Huysmans wrote the text himself . . . and signed it with the pseudonym A. Meunier, which was the very name of the Muse of the Rue du Dragon . . .

'Good old Rue du Dragon, which knew also Victor Hugo, young and poor! It has remained intact and its picturesqueness is doubled by the Cour du Dragon, which leads from it, so strange, so medieval, with an ancient Virgin behind a grill, where sometimes a pious hand drops a flower,' etc., etc.

The Father of the Man

The pious hands of our authors drop perhaps too many flowers, but we should certainly be grateful to them for so interesting and early a glimpse of Anna Meunier. We do not know if the family was aware of the liaison, but it soon became obvious that Huysmans was making no progress as a law student. Another family conference was held and his maternal grandfather, who was employed at the Ministry of the Interior as a cashier, suggested that a place might be found for him in the same establishment.

Huysmans was quite frank about this suggestion. 'Of two disgusts,' he says, 'I chose the less'; and he became a clerk in the employment of the Ministry on April 1st, 1868. He was then aged twenty, and he was to stay there, in all, for more than thirty years. There seemed no reason why his peaceful and humdrum existence should ever be interrupted. Fate, however, had other views, both for Huysmans and for France.

CHAPTER TWO

SAC AU DOS

———————— • ————————

Paris in the late eighteen-sixties had something of the frenzied gaiety of the years immediately before the French Revolution, but whereas the eighteenth-century aristocrats seem to have been conscious of a premonition of coming disaster, the financiers and adventurers who formed the top stratum of society in the Second Empire saw no reason why their paradise should not go on for ever. Paris had never been more gay. Whatever else Napoleon III had done or had not done, he had certainly cleaned up the capital, widened its streets, cleared away its medieval slums, opened up great boulevards and, with his innumerable gaslamps, had earned for the city its proud title of *la ville lumière*.

The Exhibition of 1868 was a triumphant success. Balls and banquets succeeded one another. In the Tuileries every night the lamps in the windows blazed till dawn. Paris swarmed with foreigners. The musical comedy queen Hortense Schneider entertained six kings in her dressing-room. On gala nights at the opera every box was filled with glittering uniforms, and if one of the uniforms clothed the grim, unsmiling figure of a certain Count von Bismarck, no one in Paris paused to notice it.

The world was gay and the half-world even more so. It was the epoch of the *grandes cocottes*, women whose names have become legendary: Cora Pearl and Blanche d'Antigny, Adèle

Courtois and Alice Labruyère, Léonide Leblanc and Marguerite Bellanger, the original *Dame aux Camellias*. The life
they lived has been depicted for all time in the pages of Zola's
Nana.

Huysmans, a junior clerk in the Ministry of the Interior,
saw, no doubt, little enough of this *grande vie*. The Rive
Gauche, except for a few survivors of the legitimate aristocracy, had ceased to be a fashionable quarter. It is true that
his Ministry was on the North Bank, in the Rue Cambacérès,
and as he crossed the Champs Elysées on his way home from
work, he must have glimpsed the carriages of the notables as
they swept westwards for their drive in the Bois; but he was
too humble an employee to penetrate even to an official reception. Not for him the glittering ball and the lavish banquet. He detested the crowd, with its loud voices and extravagant gestures. *Flâner*, the favourite verb of the *Siècle du
Boulevard*, meant for him the haunting of back streets, by
inclination as well as through lack of means. He never set
foot in a fashionable restaurant. We may well believe that he
hurried home as fast as he could to the room he had taken in
the Rue de Vaugirard.

He never throughout his life took the slightest interest in
politics. He had no enthusiasm for Napoleon III, and just as
little for his political opponents, now mostly silent or in exile.
He was conscious, no doubt, that the authoritarian rule of the
Emperor had been somewhat modified of late, that he had
been compelled to accept a quasi-Parliamentary control. The
spokesman of this control, one can hardly call it an opposition,
was Émile Ollivier, and this wordy but not far-sighted
politician had just announced that there was not a cloud on
the politicial horizon. The very next day was put forward the
candidature, for the throne of Spain, of a Prince of the House
of Hohenzollern.

The dynastic principle has been so completely forgotten in

the modern world that it is hard for us to realise the wave of excitement which passed over Europe. Queen Isabella had abdicated and the uneasy throne of Spain was vacant. There were various candidates and the government of France had tried to preserve at least an apparent neutrality with regard to their conflicting claims. But the candidature of the Hohenzollern prince was bound to be regarded as a provocative act. By the victory of Sadowa only four years before, when the Austrians had been decisively defeated, Prussia had established her hegemony in Germany. She was now, it would seem, endeavouring to extend her sway over the whole of Europe.

There is no need in a work like the present to pursue in their details the tortuous negotiations which followed. For a moment it looked as though peace might be saved. The Prussians even withdrew their candidate, and Europe might have been spared a second War of the Spanish Succession. Unfortunately, there were two people who were determined on war: the Empress Eugénie and Bismarck. The latter, who stopped at nothing, actually altered the final message of Napoleon III—the famous Ems telegram—in order to make it seem more provocative. The Empress saw in a possible war a chance to push back the rising tide of Liberalism. The ordinary people in either country had no chance of being consulted. Huysmans remarks acidly that his career was decided for him by the Emperor. 'He made me a soldier *de par les maladresses de sa politique.*'

War was declared on July 19th, 1870. A wave of enthusiasm swept over France; the Emperor was popular again and Eugénie was delighted with the success of what she regarded as her policy. All Paris was afoot. The crowds in the boulevards fought for the latest editions of the papers. People of all classes formed processions and marched along the boulevards singing the *Marseillaise.* A short time before, this would have been a criminal offence. Napoleon III did not care for the song and had done his best to suppress it, but now the police took no notice. A sailor raised a flag, and in a moment there were a thousand people round him, shouting and singing. A column of soldiers, on its way to the railway station, was greeted with cries of '*A Berlin!*'

It is true that this patriotic enthusiasm was not quite universal. From the poorer quarters of Paris there suddenly appeared on the *grands boulevards* a marching column of several thousand workers carrying white flags and shouting '*Vive la paix!*' And Authority, which had regarded the other manifestations with an indulgent eye, suddenly took action. The three-cornered hats of the police could be seen making their way through the crowd. In the twinkling of an eye the white flags were snatched away, the ranks of the column broken, the march of the pacifists was transformed into a battlefield. The watchers on the boulevards cheered and as the last cry of *Vive la paix* was extinguished, they raised again the shout of *Vive la guerre*.

What did Huysmans feel about all this? It is hard to believe that he, the son of the immigrant Dutchman, was animated by any very powerful patriotic fervour. When, some fifteen years later, he published in *Les Hommes d'Aujourd'hui* a precious fragment of autobiography, he spoke quite plainly on the subject. The interviewer is supposed to ask him what were his ideas on patriotism, and he makes a very curious reply, 'That,' he says, 'would lead us rather far. All that I can tell you is this. I hate above everything exuberant people. Now all southerners bawl, with an accent which gives me the creeps, and above everything they make gestures! No, between these people, with their curly black astrakhan hair, their ebony sidewhiskers, and the big, phlegmatic, silent Germans, my choice is in no doubt. I shall always feel more affinity with a man of Leipzig than with a man of Marseilles, with anyone, in fact, rather than a man of the Midi, for I know of no race which is to me more particularly odious.' It is perhaps as well that Huysmans waited fifteen years before expressing such sentiments. In the Paris of 1870 they would have been not only unpopular but dangerous. But patriotic or not, he had no choice. He was called up for the auxiliary troops as part of the *Garde Mobile de la Seine* and despatched immediately to the camp at Chalons.

The newspapers of the period give a highly coloured description of the departure of this *Garde Mobile*. The Baron de Felsheim, in a leader in *L'Illustration*, describes in the most eloquent terms the enthusiasm with which these improvised soldiers had buckled on their military trappings, abandoned their friends, their families, their positions, their whole agreeable civilian existence. 'Nothing,' he cries, 'is more moving than the departure of these brave children, who, soldiers of liberty and slaves of duty, are ready to eat their iron rations and sleep on the hard ground. The heart of France beats proudly in the bosoms of all these little soldiers who will become great soldiers, if God lends them life, and greater still if they find a glorious end on the road that leads to Berlin.'

He did not speak for Huysmans. In *Sac au Dos*, the *nouvelle* which he contributed some years later to the collection of stories known as *Les Soirées de Medan*, he describes his experiences and his sensations. It is not really a short story at all, but a fragment of autobiography written in the first person, and we can accept it as authentic. He did not share any of the exaltation of so many of his companions, although he admits that it existed.

'Crowded one against the other,' he writes, 'workers in blouses, working women in rags, soldiers belted and gaitered, without arms, drained their glasses, and sang the *Marseillaise* out of tune. In their incredibly high *képis*, with peaks like the eyeshades of blind men, and tricolor cockades, clad in navy blue tunics adorned with coloured braid, and light blue breeches with a red stripe, the *Mobile de la Seine* raised a cheer on their way to the conquest of Prussia. There was a deafening racket in all the drink shops round about, the noise of glasses mingled with cries and shouts and the creaking of windows in the wind. Suddenly a roll of drums was heard. A new column was arriving from the barracks, and a scene of wild revelry followed. The soldiers who were drinking in the shops rushed outside, followed by their relations and friends, who disputed the honour of carrying their knapsacks. Ranks were broken, there was a mêlée of soldiers and civilians. Mothers were crying, fathers breathed vinous fumes. The children jumped for joy and in their high-pitched voices trilled patriotic songs. There was a moment of silence broken by the sound of sobs, and once more a burst of the *Marseillaise*. Then they herded us into railway trucks like beasts. There were about fifty of us in one moving box; some cried freely, mocked by the others who, half-seas over, stuck lighted candles to their ration loaves and shouted their heads off. Others [among whom, perhaps, we may place Huysmans himself] withdrew into a corner and, in gloomy silence, watched the dust dancing on the vibrating planks which formed the floor of the truck.'

Anyone who, as a soldier in the First World War, or even in the Second, was condemned to make long journeys in horse trucks over the plains of northern France, can testify to the exactitude of Huysmans' observations and of his powers of description. The jolting of the train, the incomprehensible halts in the middle of the night while other convoys sped by, the darkness framed in the oblong of the door, the sense of utter loneliness in the middle of a crowd, the heartrending melancholy of the dawn: all are set down.

They arrived at last at Chalons less two of their number,

one of whom had fallen off the train into a river and another
who had broken his head against a tunnel. There was no more
order in their arrival than in their departure. Nothing was
ready, neither food, nor straw, nor coats, nor arms; nothing,
absolutely nothing, except rows of tents full of dirt and fleas,
which had just been evacuated by troops who had left for the
frontier. Whatever might be true of the regular troops the
auxiliaries did *not* find 'everything ready down to the last
gaiter button'. Gradually, however, the men sorted themselves out, workmen with workmen, and bourgeois with
bourgeois. The feet of two of Huysmans' companions smelled
so badly (a characteristic touch this) that he bribed them with
a couple of litres of wine to go elsewhere.

Eighteen battalions of the *Garde Mobile de la Seine*
occupied the camp. Huysmans was in the Sixth Battalion.
The camp itself was some eight kilometres from the station
and this did not commend it to those, like Huysmans, whose
idea of soldiering was to slip away as often as possible and
have a drink in a neighbouring café. He had no intention of
becoming a good soldier, or even of being a soldier at all, if he
could possibly help it. The authorities congratulated themselves that discipline was gradually being established, and
on the 15th August the Camp Commandant posted up the
following order of the day.

'*Gardes Mobiles!*

August 15th is generally a day of rejoicing in the whole of
France. But for you, and for all those who feel a heart beating
in their bosom, there can be no holiday so long as the foreigner
treads the soil of the Fatherland. You are about to be given
arms. Learn to use them quickly so that you can avenge your
brothers whose blood has flowed at Forbach and at Reichs-
hoffen. They have fallen as fall the brave before the enemy.
Let their last cry be also yours: '*Vive la France*, death to the
Prussians.'

'Avenge their brothers!' remarks a contemporary journalist. 'That is at present their one idea, and with that end in view they are preparing so as to be ready to meet the enemy. One and all they ask to advance. Be sure that, excited as they are, all these young heroes will perform wonders.'

Once more Huysmans writes in a somewhat less exalted strain. He describes one incident which finds no place in the official record. One day when he was on guard duty with some of his friends, a duty which did not prevent them from drinking quantities of *eau de vie*, in the neighbouring *estaminet*, an officer on horseback suddenly appeared in their midst. It was no less a person than Marshal Canrobert. It is true that history has not dealt very kindly with him; it has even been suggested that he owed his position not to what he knew about war but to what he knew about Louis Napoleon. He was particularly unpopular with the Parisians because of a recorded utterance of his shortly before the outbreak of war. The Left Wing politician Victor Noir had been shot under mysterious circumstances by Prince Napoleon. The Prince had been exonerated, but the funeral of his victim was made the occasion for an anti-government demonstration, and it was said that General Canrobert, Marshal of France, had asked permission to open fire on the immense column advancing along the Avénue de Neuilly, and had said that he was ready to shoot down a hundred thousand men in order to clear the street. At all events, when he appeared before the *Garde Mobile* at Chalons he could be in little doubt as to his reception. He was greeted with cries of '*Ran, plan, plan! cent mille hommes par terre, à Paris! à Paris!*'

The pale face of Canrobert assumed an even paler tint and, reining in his horse, he cried: 'Hats off to a Marshal of France!' This was answered by renewed shouts and whistles. Canrobert turned his horse and rode off, followed by his staff, and as he went he shook his fist at the refractory

THE WAR OF 1870

Departure of the Garde Mobile from Paris

THE BIÈVRE

From the etching by A. P. Martial

troops and cried, 'You'll pay dearly for this, *messieurs les Parisiens.*'

Two days later Huysmans went sick. His health was never robust and conditions in camp were very bad. Shaking with fever and hardly able to drag himself along, he was led to the hospital, but the hospital was already full of men in similar case. However, a bed happened to be vacant in one of the *ambulances*, and he was admitted to that.

He paints a vivid picture of himself in his hospital uniform. 'What a face and what a get-up, *bon dieu!* With my bunged-up eyes and yellow skin, with my close-cropped hair and shiny nose, with my great mouse-coloured robe and dirty red trousers, my immense heelless slippers and gigantic cotton nightcap, I was prodigiously ugly. I could not help laughing.' He turned his head and saw that the man in the neighbouring bed was in the act of drawing his portrait. A man who understood art! He and Huysmans became close friends at once, and this friendship did much in the next few days to mitigate the horrors of hospital life.

The occupants of the other beds were by no means so sympathetic. They came for the most part from the lowest quarters of Paris, and many of them made no secret of the fact that their profession in civil life was that of *souteneur*. They took an instant dislike to Huysmans and his friend as being more refined than themselves, and peace was only restored by giving them money to buy wine.

Treatment in the hospital was of the most elementary and arbitrary kind. Whatever might be wrong with his patients, from a broken leg to venereal disease, the major in charge prescribed for all the same purgative draught. But such a life was not destined to continue long. One day, at four o'clock in the morning, a doctor rushed into the room and ordered all to put on their clothes and get their packs ready. Ten minutes later they learned that the Prussians were marching on

33

Chalons. Stupor reigned; the men had been told of the French victory of Sarrebrück but not of the reverses which had followed in quick succession, and now the enemy was at the gates. The major hastily examined his patients; those who could walk were sent back to their units, and the rest were ordered to lie down fully dressed, and with their packs ready.

Huysmans and his friend were among the latter, and after a day and night of waiting they were hurried away. Hastily they were taken to Chalons and quickly piled into railway trucks, which moved off no one knew where. The authorities had forgotten to give them any rations, and when the train stopped at a station they raided the buffet and carried off everything that it contained, up to and including the toothpicks. After an endless journey they arrived in Paris at the Gare du Nord. Here those who were sufficiently active made off, and the rest were driven back into the train by the officials and soldiers, and it started again.

At Arras Huysmans and his friend were able to escape for a while and treat themselves to a good dinner in the town. Then they were sent on to Rouen and finally arrived at Evreux. This time Huysmans found himself in an efficient hospital run by nuns. He had a clean bed and was looked after properly. From his own account Huysmans seems to have taken no interest whatever in the course of events in the world outside, but these had not stood still. The Second Empire was approaching its final catastrophe and on the 1st September came the capitulation of Sedan. Three days later the Republic was proclaimed in Paris.

Life in hospital bored Huysmans extremely but there were consolations. From time to time, he managed with a friend to escape into the town, and even to sup in female company, to the great distress of the good nun who was looking after him. She did her best to shield him, merely remarking sadly, 'You are not serious, *monsieur le militaire.*'

Sac au Dos

This nun, Sister Angèle, seemed to the wretched boy, ill
and torn from his home, like a visitor from another sphere.
She was extremely pretty, with big eyes, long eyelashes, and
flashing teeth. 'I can see her still,' he writes, 'in the morning,
when the sun threw on to the tiles of the floor the shadows of
the window frames, advancing slowly down the corridor, the
great wings of her bonnet waving over her face. She would
come to my bed with a steaming plate, on the edge of which
shone her well-cut finger nails. She would say with a smile,
"The soup is a little thin this morning, so I have brought you
some chocolate. Drink it up while it is hot." ' There is no doubt
that she made an enormous impression on Huysmans and
even inspired in him a religious emotion which at this period
of his life he had almost completely forgotten. In the first
draft of *Sac au Dos* he includes some religious verses which
he was careful to expunge from the text when it was published in *Les Soirées de Médan*. The time for the frank
acceptance of all that Sister Angèle stood for was far in the
future.

Suddenly it occurred to Huysmans that a friend he had
known in Paris had a relation at Evreux, and the next time
he played truant he determined to seek him out. This gentleman, whom he calls Chevillage in the first version of *Sac au
Dos* and Fréchède in the second, bore in reality the somewhat
unlikely name of Chefdeville. He was a notary and a person
of some importance in the town, and he not only received the
young man kindly into his house but used his influence to
have him sent on convalescent leave. After what seemed endless delays, this was granted. He was given sixty days of freedom. Hastily he packed, and said goodbye to the kind notary,
who insisted on his accepting a scarf and sixty francs. One
thing remained: to take leave of Sister Angèle. He found her
in the garden of the hospital and, moved by a sudden impulse,
seized her hand and raised it to his lips. She blushed and,

shaking her finger at him, admonished him to be good and not to get into bad company on the journey. He promised her that he would not, rushed to the station and jumped into the train for Paris.

From the conversation of his fellow passengers, he gathered that it was more than doubtful that the train would ever arrive at the capital. The line, so rumour ran, was cut at Nantes. Actually, he just managed to get through. By the 19th September the advancing Prussians had cut off Paris from all communication with the rest of France.

In spite of this, Huysmans' first feeling was one of intense joy at having returned to civil life. His mother was still installed in the apartment in the Rue de Sèvres, his books and bibelots were about him. There was water to wash in and a clean, soft bed. It is characteristic of Huysmans that he enlarges upon the joy of having at last a lavatory to himself. Anyone who has ever passed through the military life, with its utter lack of privacy and its communal latrines, will sympathize and understand.

Meanwhile, the Prussian lines came closer and closer. Paris was besieged, and the news from outside grew worse and worse. On 27th October both Strasbourg and Metz capitulated. Could the capital itself hold out? On the following day there was a stiff fight at Le Bourget between the advancing Prussians and the *Garde Mobile de la Seine*.

Huysmans' leave terminated on the 8th November, but instead of returning to the Ministry of the Interior he was attached to the Ministry of War as Sous-Secrétaire de l'État Major. He was, in fact, a military clerk, but the post was not as peaceful a one as might have been expected, for one day he was sent out to the neighbourhood of the Fort d'Issy opposite Meudon, which was being heavily bombarded. In private conversation in later life, he described how he had smoked cigarettes under the bare and shattered trees, count-

ing the interval which elapsed between the distant flash of
the enemy gun and the explosion of the shell near at hand.
One shell exploded near enough for him to be able to pick up
the still hot fragments which he used as paper weights when
he got back to his office.

Used as we are in modern times to the bombardment of
open cities, it is hard to understand the shock to world
opinion caused by the bombardment of Paris in the war of
1870. Total war was only just beginning to be re-invented. The
dominant emotion of the Parisians seems to have been rather
of indignation than of terror. The shells by modern standards
were, of course, not very large, but there was a considerable
number of victims, including a whole schoolfull of children
in the Rue de Vaugirard, near Huysmans' home. The bombardment began on 27th December and lasted exactly a
month. Fortunately, the Praemonstratensian Monastery, in
which Huysmans' mother had her factory and her lodging,
had its vast and ample cellars, and in these the family was able
to take refuge. Similar shelters were contrived by the
authorities in the cellars of the Panthéon and other public
buildings, and many of the churches were converted into
hospitals.

Food became very scarce. Dogs and even rats were eaten,
and finally the animals in the Zoo, including the elephant
and the hippopotamus. Nothing disturbed Huysmans, except
that he was re-transferred from the Ministry of War to the
Ministry of the Interior, with its office in the Rue Cambacérès, north of the Champs Elysées, a little further from
home, but still within easy walking distance. The last shots
were fired in the suburbs on the 27th January. On the 28th,
Paris capitulated.

Except for the pillage by the mob of the goods in the central
market, there was little disorder, and it is pleasant to be able
to record that the first trains to arrive in Paris from the

outside world were full of provisions provided and paid for by English sympathisers. The Prussian conquerors made a symbolic entry into the capital. They marched through deserted streets, for no Parisian showed himself, and when they marched out again bonfires of purification were lit at the Étoile. A great calm seemed to have fallen on Paris, but it was the calm preceding the storm.

The French Government, which had been functioning at Bordeaux, had transferred itself to Versailles. It did not yet venture into the capital. Paris itself was full of armed men, some of whom were regular troops likely to obey their officers, and some *Gardes Nationaux*, whose temper was more uncertain. The latter, in defiance of government orders, refused to give up their artillery, and they occupied under their own commanders the heights of Montmartre, as well as the Place des Vosges and Belleville. On the 18th March some shots were exchanged at Montmartre, but in general the regular troops refused to fire on the rebels, and by mid-day it was claimed that the dissident *Gardes Nationaux* were the real masters of Paris.

Some of the government offices had already left for Versailles, and on the 20th March all were withdrawn from Paris. Huysmans, as an official of the Ministry of the Interior, went with them and was therefore not an eyewitness of the terrible events of the next two months. The Central Committee of the Commune took over the Hôtel de Ville, the Préfecture, and all official buildings. Those of their comrades who would not join their ranks were deprived of their arms. They took hostages, and shot out of hand two generals. The Government at Versailles realised that nothing but the most drastic measures would suffice to re-establish its authority, and on 2nd April, the second siege of Paris began.

The Communards, as they called themselves, also realised that this was to be a fight to the death. As an act of defiance they threw down the Colonne Vendôme, and they filled the cellars of all the public buildings they occupied with gunpowder and combustibles. There were stiff fights in the suburbs as the Government ring was drawn tighter. By erecting barricades in the streets the insurgents had hoped to make Paris impregnable, but they had forgotten that the town they defended was no longer the Paris of 1830 or 1848. At the back of Napoleon's mind when he ordered Baron Haussmann to drive his great boulevards through the city there had been two ideas; one was the embellishment of the capital, the other was that there should be no more barricades. It is easy to barricade a narrow street but very difficult to barricade a boulevard, and so the rebels, in their defence of Paris, were perpetually outflanked.

The barricade of the Chaussée d'Antin was taken by government troops on 23rd May. On the same evening, with superb effrontery, Jules Ferré, one of the most fanatical of the Communard leaders, held a great banquet in the Préfecture at which speeches of defiance were hurled at the reactionaries who were invading Paris. The same evening he set fire to the Tuileries. The following day, having set fire to the Préfecture itself, he went to the Prison de la Roquette and ordered the shooting of hostages. The victims included the Vicar of St. Sulpice and the Archbishop of Paris. On the same day a fearful struggle began in the Place de l'Hôtel de Ville. The defenders, seeing that they could not escape from its ruins, set fire to the building, and perished in it to a man.

By 26th May the insurgents had been driven from the centre of Paris and occupied the Buttes Chaumont and the Cemetery of Père Lachaise, two heights commanding the city. But their petrol-filled shells were answered by a cannonade from Montmartre now occupied by government troops. By 4 o'clock on 28th May, all organised resistance was over. Some of the insurgents escaped into the catacombs, and there, amid the bones of thousands of dead citizens, they were tracked down and shot like rats in a sewer.

Resistance over, the Government departments began to return to Paris. Huysmans' *laissez-passer* is dated 'Versailles, 2nd June 1871'. He had been absent for just over two months, but he found a very different Paris from the one he had left. The Hôtel-de-Ville was a smoking ruin, so was the Préfecture on the Ile de la Cité. It was possible to look through the burned out remains of the Tuileries into the great courtyard of the Louvre. The clocktower, whose clock had gone on bravely striking the hours when the galleries round it were tumbling in ruins, had now itself fallen. The remains of the captured barricades were still in the streets, and groups of their defenders were seen from time to time, their wrists tied together, being hurried along in batches to be summarily executed in the Caserne Lobau.

Apart from the destruction wrought by the incendiaries of the Commune, Paris had suffered almost as much from the bombardment of the civil war as from the Prussian siege. The Communards had fired a volley of petrol-filled shells into Husymans' own beloved *Quartier Latin*. There had been a desperate battle at La Croix-Rouge, within a stone's throw of the house in the Rue de Sèvres, and many buildings had been damaged. Fortunately, General de Cissey, who was in charge of the Government troops on the Left Bank, had attacked so rapidly and with such complete success that the incendiaries had not had time to finish their work. The Institut and the École des Beaux-Arts had escaped owing to the intelligence and courage of the concierge, who had himself made a breach in the wall facing the *quai*, and so had allowed in a company of French sailors who were able to fall upon the insurgents in the rear.

Some of the Government offices, in particular the Ministry of Finances, had suffered severely. Huysmans' own Ministry of the Interior, situated as it was towards the west of Paris, had fallen into Government hands very early in the conflict and so had escaped destruction. Huysmans has left us no record of his feelings on entering his office once more in the peaceful Rue de Cambacérès. No major upheaval was to trouble him for the rest of his official life. He probably shrugged his shoulders, opened the next official file, and, with a sigh, dipped his pen in the ink. He never pretended to take the slightest interest in the work he was called upon to do.

WITH THE STREAM

———————————— • ————————————

The lives of literary men present a problem of peculiar difficulty to the biographer, especially if their works are essentially autobiographical, like those of Huysmans. He hardly troubles to distinguish himself from his characters. In his later works he frankly identifies himself with Durtal, the character who appears in all of them. But he is also Cyprien (and, to some extent, Ludo) in *Les Sœurs Vâtard*, he is André in *En Ménage*, he is Folantin in *A Vau l'Eau*; he is even, in spite of the difference in their social status, des Esseintes in *A Rebours*. When a writer does this, although it supplies the biographer with the facts he needs, it does not simplify his task. For the life-cycle does not correspond with the art-cycle, not only because there is always a time-lag between the events experienced and the events described, but because even the sequence is not the same. In *A Vau l'Eau*, for example, which did not appear until 1882, Huysmans drew upon his experiences in the very early years of his service at the Ministry of the Interior; in *En Ménage*, published in 1880, his hero, André, is already a literary man, and represents a later stage in Huysmans' own development.

We shall therefore begin with Folantin, who is a self-portrait—almost a self-caricature—of Huysmans in the days when he was merely a minor civil servant, before he had realised that authorship could open the door to a larger world. Folantin indeed has no literary pretensions at all, and from his wretched, poverty-stricken life he sees no possibility of escape. We are given a picture of a day in the life of a poor clerk, without ambition and without hope.

The day—a typical day, we are led to believe—begins badly with a reprimand from his chief for arriving at the office at 11.20 a.m., instead of 11 o'clock. He copies interminable and boring letters, irritated and distracted by the chattering of one of his colleagues who loves to hear himself speak. The theme of his discourse was, as usual, the incompetence of editors and journalists and his own state of health. Unable to concentrate on his work, Folantin makes many mistakes and is compelled to do it all over again.

He sees himself condemned for ever to the same routine. Hope of promotion there is none. If only he had been born in the Provinces, he reflects bitterly, the local Deputy might have been induced to do something for him, to use his influence to advance him in the Service. But who was likely to take any thought for a Parisian-born? He goes on copying his letters, doing as little work as possible and watching the clock. At last he is free, free to wander through the muddy streets, his feet wet and frozen, in search of what he knows will be an execrable dinner.

Once he had tried to set up an establishment of his own, with a *bonne*, but his miserable rate of pay—two hundred and thirty seven francs forty centimes a month—had soon brought this experiment to a close. Since then he had started a voyage of exploration throughout the whole of the *Quartier Latin*, in the hope of finding a tolerable place in which to eat. A considerable part of *A Vau l'Eau* is concerned with this search.

To most Englishmen, it would seem that there is something almost incredible in Folantin's pilgrimage. Surely there are a thousand little restaurants in Paris, where every kind of delicacy is to be had for the asking, where even the simplest dishes are prepared with loving care, and where, if the surroundings are simple, the service is all that could be desired. Do we not remember between the two wars, when it is true the exchange was somewhat in our favour, wandering through what we imagined to be the back streets of Paris in search of a dinner and with very different results? We forget the question of price, we forget that when we did these things we were on holiday with at least some money to burn. We do not realise that we never penetrated to the real back streets at all. The difference between the price of a tolerable meal and an execrable one may be no more than a few pence, but if one does not possess the few pence. . . .

We cannot, however, entirely accept Folantin's adventures as a picture of Huysmans' own life, even in his earliest days at the Ministry of the Interior. He was never really poor, as Zola had been at a similar stage in his career, and there were, indeed, in Paris, plenty of cheap restaurants which most men would have found good enough. Gustave Coquiot has related that he was often in a restaurant with Huysmans in later life when the latter never ceased complaining about the dishes which Coquiot thought delicious and well-served. Huysmans was equally difficult in his rare visits to private houses. One of his hostesses remarked: 'I would invite him with pleasure, but if I thought of him at the moment of serving, my sauces would curdle.'

In the book, Folantin's search merely results in the progressive deterioration of his health. His digestion grows worse and worse and is not improved by the bad wine, of which he is sometimes tempted to drink too much, or by the occasional *absinthe* which, in the Paris of the 'seventies, was dangerously cheap.

Seated in a restaurant, if restaurant be not altogether too

grand a term, at a table with a wine-stained cloth encumbered
with dirty plates, he is overcome with disgust. Having tried,
and rejected, the main dish, he asks for cheese. The waiter
recommends a Roquefort but, as he expects, it is deplorable
Roquefort, with the appearance and taste of a piece of
Marseilles cheese. In Huysmans' view nothing good could
come out of Marseilles. The mere thought of the place
doubled him up with horror. He had an intense dislike,
amounting to an obsession, of *les gens du Midi*, with their
loud voices and their extravagant gestures, their aggressive
personalities and their reek of garlic. The idea of human contact with such people gave him gooseflesh, and even Paris
seemed full of them. Huysmans' sensibility was almost
pathological. He had, as they say, a skin too few. To be
hustled on the pavement or to be crowded into an omnibus
was enough to bring on a nervous crisis. The French, even
the northern French, seemed intolerably noisy to the trans-
planted Hollander who, if he had never known the quiet
streets of Breda, longed for them with all the fervour of a
dispatriot.

Folantin nibbles a crumb or two of his execrable cheese,
pays his bill and departs. Outside it is raining, an icy drizzle,
and under his feet is a mush of melting snow. He opens his
umbrella and hurries back to his lodging, wondering if he will
find the stove still alight. Of course it is not and, while he is
struggling with it, his lamp goes out for lack of oil. His feet
frozen, his head hot from the proximity of the single hissing
gas-jet, he presents as complete a picture of misery as could
be desired. Even his tobacco is wet and will not draw. Un-
utterably discouraged, he throws himself in an armchair and
gives way to gloomy thoughts.

He has no relations and no friends. The few who had been
his intimates in his student days—Huysmans, as we have
seen, had been a law student for a short time—had married

or merely disappeared. Once, poor as they were, they had had good times together, or what appeared in the eyes of youth to be good times. The theatres and the cafés had seemed to him places of enchantment, and the Bullier—famous *bal* of the Latin Quarter—a vision of Paradise, with its music, its dancing feet, and its troupes of girls, with their slender waists and their laughing lips, and the intoxication of their imagined caresses. Imagined, because they were not for him. He was timid, physically unattractive—Huysmans confessed in later life that there was nothing about him which could possibly attract a woman—and he had no money. Still, in those days he was content with so little; a word in passing, a smile thrown over the shoulder, something he could take away with him as a stimulus to his dreams.

It was not that Folantin was particular. *Faute de mieux* he had accepted the squalid room and the ageing harlot. Sometimes he could not afford even such pleasure as these might give him, and some evenings, without hope of satisfying his appetite, he still wandered in the Rue de Buci, in the Rue de l'Égout, in the Rue du Dragon, simply to touch these women, to talk with them for a moment, then to say a hurried good-night for fear of spoiling their trade.

Looking back on these days, Folantin almost envied his own youth, for now that he had a little more money he suddenly found that the appetite had left him. Once he had thought himself happy. He had made the acquaintance of a working girl, attractive enough, and kind, who seemed to like him, and then one evening she had disappeared and left him for no apparent motive. A few days later, he had discovered that he had a venereal disease. Huysmans several times refers to this adventure, and there can be little doubt that it was his own.

There was, however, one tremendous difference between Folantin and his creator. Folantin had no intellectual curiosity, and no talent. Huysmans was bursting with both. He might suffer as much as the creature of his imagination from the minor miseries of life, he might be as easily rubbed the wrong way in an almost literal sense, he might have an even more prickly horror of the people he saw about him, but he observed them, if without indulgence, yet with a passionate interest. The man who does this can never fall into the bored desperation of a Folantin.

The true literary man, indeed, has an unfair advantage over the rest of mankind. There is hardly anything that can happen to him, hardly any circumstance in which he may find himself, that he cannot turn to account. Like the painter, he finds 'subjects' everywhere; his eye is ever open, his creative imagination ever busy. So we must not waste too much sympathy on the poor Civil Servant condemned to spend his days in the company of unsympathetic persons, and to wander about the streets of a great city alone. In spite of his complaints, everyone he met added to his stock, and he adored Paris.

There are many people who say, and think, that they adore Paris, but by Paris they mean the bright lights, the smart cafés, the theatres and the boulevards. What they love is the city of pleasure, the cosmopolitan rendezvous. The true lover of Paris is very different. On him the unfashionable quarters, the back streets exercise a perpetual fascination. For there are other boulevards beside the Boulevard des Italiens, other squares beside the Place de la Madeleine; by-streets and for- gotten corners, alleys and culs-de-sac, dilapidated doorways and peeling façades, houses in abandoned *quartiers* where once the famous lived. What mere tourist explores the Rue d'Alésia, enters the backyard of the Rue du Paradis, or is brought to a halt, pensive, in the Impasse Floriment?

There is a poetry of cities which has nothing to do with the things that receive three stars in the guide books: a person-

47

ality behind the public personality displayed in the palaces of government or even in the churches it is fashionable to visit. All this is too obvious, too much *à portée de tout le monde*. Paris reveals its secret only to pedestrians, with time on their hands. Huysmans was an indefatigable pedestrian and in his early days, apart from the hours when he was imprisoned in his Ministry, he had infinite leisure.

His duties merely stole from him the hours when he would have loved Paris least. He loved it most in the very early morning or late at night when the streets were almost deserted. It is then that the solitary wanderer, resting for a few moments his elbows on the stone balustrade and gazing at the gently moving waters of the Seine, or sitting on a seat in one of the little squares behind St. Sulpice, can listen to the beating of a heart; and hardly knows whether it is the heart of Paris or his own.

The muffled bell of some near-by church sounds in his ears —St. Séverin perhaps, or St. Julien-le-Pauvre—footsteps crunch on the gravel, the rumble of distant traffic begins in the Boul' Mich', the leaves stir. Anyone who has ever savoured the solitariness of great cities, refining his nostalgia to the razor-edge of ecstasy, knows that Paris is the most rewarding of all. For it is both old and modern. It does not overwhelm you with the past, like Rome, nor bully you, like Chicago, with the insistent present; nor does it, Cairo-fashion, offer you two worlds at once, old and new, but unassimilated, divided by a chasm. Paris is one; it has to be accepted as a single experience. It has the unity of a work of art.

The infinite melancholy of the *quais*, the blind, imploring menace of the tall yet huddled houses, the sudden vista of grey belfry or soaring spire, the strange poetry of the suburbs. All these add up to something real yet indefinable, something as mysterious as the mind of a woman, something as elusive as the meaning of a poem. The true poem cannot be explained in any other words than those it uses; we cannot explain Paris except in terms of itself.

Huysmans complains of Paris as he complained of everything, as one might complain of a difficult mistress, or of a wife who did not minister very carefully to one's creature comforts. But she was the only mistress from whom he was never estranged and one might call her the only wife he ever had. He, the son of the immigrant, was a Parisian of the Parisians, not, of course, in the sense of the boulevardier who would claim the title, but in a manner more subtle, more intimate and more profound. And of all Paris, he knew best and loved most deeply his own *quartier*, the little square of earth enclosed by the Rue St. Jacques, the Boulevard St. Germain, the Rue du Bac and the river.

The Paris he knew was half way between our Paris and the Paris depicted in the etchings of Méryon. That great artist etched the city when the improvements, and the depredations, of Baron Haussmann had only just begun; we see the process completed. But the *Quartier Latin* has suffered comparatively little, and Huysmans, if he were to return to his familiar haunts, could still find his way. He could still explore the book-stalls along the *quais*.

These indeed were his passion, and the only University he ever attended. From them he gained his erudition, 'enormous, but chaotic', as he himself described it. Guided by his natural dislike of the pompous and official, or merely of the academic, he made himself familiar with all the books the professors despised. Perhaps he could have made no better preparation for the work it was in his power to do. He loved the decadent in literature, long before the word, and the idea, had become fashionable, and it was the same impulse which led him to see, even in the suburbs of Paris, a beauty no-one had seen before.

If it be the hallmark of the great writer and the original

painter to extend the borders of human sensibility, to feel anew, to explore what Sainte-Beuve, speaking of Baudelaire, called the Kamchatka of the spirit, such a writer, such a painter was Huysmans. Nature only interested him when she was ailing. He did not deny her prestige and her glory when (the phrase is his own, and very characteristic) her great laugh cracked her corsage of sombre rocks, and brandished in the sun her bosom with its green nipples, but it was not in such moods that she moved him to a tender pity, such as was awakened in his heart by some desolate corner of a town, some small and now polluted stream.

Such a corner he found in the district of Paris which lies between the *Quartier Latin* and what was once the village of Ivry; such a stream he found in the Bièvre, now a sewer. A generation earlier, in the time of Louis-Philippe, the region had still retained a certain rural charm; in our day it has all been cleaned up, and is dull rather than squalid. In Huysmans' time the Bièvre was still an open stream but its waters were used by a whole population of tanners, and along its banks stretched a world of slums, with occasional patches of surviving vegetation.

Huysmans liked it like that; his indignation was reserved for those who were trying to modernise and 'improve' it. 'At bottom,' he says, 'the beauty of a landscape resides in its melancholy.' And thus the Bièvre, with its air of desperation and the thoughtful look of those who have suffered, charmed and fascinated him, and he deplored its threatened destruction as an outrage. 'Nothing', he complained, 'will be left us of this dolorous landscape, this river in rags, this plain in tatters, which is going to be cut up into lots. They are going to hang up on hooks each parcel of land, sell by auction each fragment of water, drain the marshes, level the roads, tear up the dandelions and the reeds.'

This melancholy suburb, this strange, derelict land that

lay between the city and the country, moved Huysmans almost to tears and its disappearance to indignation. 'Ah!' he cried, 'they who have decided on the pillage and sack of these banks have never been touched by the desolate passivity of the poor, the mingled groans and smiles of the sick. Do they only admire Nature when she is proud and adorned with jewels? Have they never, in their own days of spleen, stood upon the little hills which dominate the Bièvre, have they never looked upon this strange river of the colour of slate and molten lead, bubbling here and there into green eddies starred with murky expectorations, which ripples over a grid and is lost, sobbing, through a hole in the wall. . . . Here are green huts and blind sheds with walls of the colour of saltpetre and tartar-stained bricks, a whole collection of sombre tints on which the window of a room with its curtain of red serge throws, like an awakening, its brilliant note of colour. Here are fleeces shaken by the wind, drying skins, crudely white, standing out against the rotting green. On the ground enormous vats full of a liquid of the mingled colour of dead leaves and dirty blue. . . . Farther off, poplar trees stuck into the muddy earth and a heap of roofs climbing in rows one above the other, sordid hovels where a whole population of children is in fermentation at windows hung with dirty linen.

'Yes! the Bièvre is nothing but a moving dunghill, but it waters the last poplar trees of the town; yes! it gives out the fetid odour of rubbish heaps and factories, but hear at the foot of one of its trees an accordion spitting out one of the melodies of which its belly is full; hear in this vale of sorrow the voice of a poor woman singing lamentably one of those melancholy songs picked up by chance at some concert, celebrating the little birds and asking for love, and tell me if this groan does not wring your entrails, and if this sobbing voice does not seem the poor suburb's desolate cry.'

From *Les Sœurs Vâtard* we can obtain a valuable picture

of Huysmans at a period of his life when he was just ceasing to be Folantin and was beginning to discover that the escape from the miseries of a routine existence was to be found through Art. But his hero, Cyprien Tibaille, is not a writer; he is a painter, a painter who has been trained in the academic traditions of Cabanel and Gérôme. Naturally, he is in revolt against them, and the character that emerges, while unmistakably Huysmans, bears also a singular resemblance to Toulouse-Lautrec. There are, it is true, no external likenesses—Cyprien is neither an aristocrat nor a cripple—but his preoccupation, his choice of subject matter are the same. He chooses his models among prostitutes or among the work girls of Paris who are so miserably paid that they are always on the edge of prostitution. He finds in the unconscious grace of their movements, in their pale little faces touched with cheap paint, in their pathetic finery, in their nervosity and fragility a charm which healthier and less complicated painters have found in rosy flesh or aristocratic elegance. In all this Huysmans was certainly speaking for himself.

In the picture of a street-walker which appears in his *Croquis Parisiens* he declares that 'for her, as for the others, vice has done its work'. Then comes the surprising statement: 'It has refined and made desirable the cheeky ugliness of her face. Without losing anything of her suburban grace, the harlot, with her showy clothes and her daringly made-up face, tempts the blasé appetite of those whose exhausted senses can only be provoked by the vehemence of cosmetics and the tumult of striking clothes. She has attained that *distinction dans la canaille* so delicious in working girls once they are washed.'

Like his creator, Cyprien was not a robust type, and his love-affairs were a curious mixture of refinement and squalor. The perversity of his love-making was even more exciting when practised on girls of the lowest class, and we seem to find here an echo of Baudelaire's own attitude—Baudelaire being one of Huysmans' gods. It should not escape our notice, even at this point, that Baudelaire's opinion, adopted by Huysmans, that there is no spice in love without a feeling of deliberate self-degradation, a *goût du péché*, is essentially Christian. It is the exact opposite of the pagan acceptance of sex as a natural good, and provides a valuable pointer towards Huysmans' later development.

One wonders if he even wished the girls to be washed. When, under the influence of *Naturalisme*, he described his sensations, he admitted, as most writers would have been afraid to do, how large a part in seduction is played by the sense of smell. He speaks, in *Croquis Parisiens*, of the exquisite and divine odour given out by the women of our towns whenever they are together and grow warm, at the ball in winter, or in summer in the street.

Less filtered by the cambric or the linen which vapourizes it, as does also the scented handkerchief, the perfume of feminine arms is less clarified, less delicate and less pure in the *décolleté* gown of a ball. There, the aroma of *valerianate of ammonia* and of urine is sometimes brutally accentuated, and often even a slight flavour of prussic acid, as of an over-ripe peach, mingles with the perfume and powders.

But the moment when the Parisienne is most charming is when, under a leaden sky, and the suffocating menace of the coming storm, sweating like a drain-pipe, her eye glazed with the heat, and her whole air languid and washed out, her odour escapes, filtered by her underclothes, at once deliciously bold and timidly delicate. Then the appeal of the 'balm of their arms' is less insolent, less cynical than at a ball where women are more naked, but it rouses all the more easily the beast in man. The reader who wishes to follow Huysmans in his detailed distinction between the odours of brunettes, redheads, and blondes may be referred to the original text.[1] The passage ends with a hymn of praise to Nature who 'has given us these "spice-boxes" to season the amorous stew that habitude makes so indigestible and so dull'.

Beside these confessions, as one may very well call them, it is interesting to place Paul Valéry's portrait of Huysmans, drawn, it is true, somewhat later in life; but the essential Huysmans remained the same. 'He was', says Valéry, 'a great creator of disgusts, welcoming the worst, and thirsting for the excessive, credulous to an incredible degree, easily accepting all the horrors that can be imagined in human life. . . . There emanated from him the reflection of an erudition vowed to the extraordinary . . . His strange nostrils quivered as they sniffed everything in the world that had a bad smell. The sickening smell of cook-shops, the pungent adulterated incense, the unsavoury or tainted odours of low drinking shops and night-shelters: everything that revolted his senses excited his genius.'[2]

This preoccupation with the repulsive, or at least with the sordid, was, of course, not only Huysmans' personal predilection. It was one of the trade marks of the new school of *Naturalisme* then rising into prominence, and of which the apostles were Zola and the Goncourts. Already in 1866 we find Zola writing: 'My taste, if you like, is depraved. I like literary stews to be highly spiced, decadent works in which a sort of aching sensibility replaces the rude health of the classical epochs.' As M. Bachelin[3] remarks very justly: 'This declaration is infinitely precious. It might serve as a motto for the entire output of Huysmans. He was born to fulfil what remained, for Zola, a mere tendency.'

If Huysmans had something in common with Zola, his

[1] *Croquis Parisiens*, 1905 edition, p. 127.

[2] Paul Valéry, *Variété*, II série, Paris, 1930, p. 235 *et seq.*

[3] Henri Bachelin, *J.-K. Huysmans*, Paris, 1926, p. 72.

early work bore an even closer resemblance to that of the Goncourts. He lacked, as they did, Zola's large sweep, his air of making each of his works a document of sociology. One thinks of Zola as a reformer, a man who wanted things altered. Huysmans never dropped any hint that he wanted anything altered, indeed as we have seen in the passage about the Bièvre, he detested 'improvements'. He preferred his suburbs to be 'ailing' and his women consumptive.

We must, however, distinguish. A man may be capable of feeling these emotions and yet be unable to express them. Once more we must make allowance for the time-lag between the feelings of the man we are describing and the works in which he was later to express those feelings himself. In the middle seventies Huysmans had not yet mastered the Goncourt language. He was still feeling his way. Like so many young men with literary aspirations, his first ambitious work was a tragedy in Alexandrine verse, no trace of which now survives. Having realised that this was not his *métier* he next turned, as so many young men have done, whose sensibility and powers of evocation exceed their capacity for constructing a story, to the prose poem. Having written a number of such pieces, he collected them in a slender volume which he called *Le Drageoir à Epices,* and looked about for a publisher.

It is a sign of Huysmans' lack of literary connections at this period of his life that it was his mother who took the manuscript to the well-known publisher Hetzel and asked him to read it. Hetzel did so and was horrified, not so much by the subject matter, similar to that of the new school of *Naturalisme,* or by the sentiments, with their echoes of Baudelaire, but by the style, the coloured, daring, decadent style which was to remain with Huysmans throughout his life. '*Il recommence la Commune de Paris dans la langue française,*' he cried; and to understand the force of such a phrase it is necessary to remember that the Commune was only just over.

It was hardly three years since the Tuileries and the Hôtel de Ville had gone up in flames. The revolutionary excesses of the *Communards* were still an open wound in the memory. And here was a young man who wished to begin them all over again in the realm of language. As a critical comment Hetzel's remark could hardly be bettered. But it shattered Huysmans' hopes of publishing his book.

His few friends did not belong to the literary world, but rather to the world he had abandoned when he ceased to be a law-student. Among them was a certain Polish law-tutor named Chodsko, and it was at this man's house that he fell in with Ludovic de Vente de Francmésnil. The two men took to one another at once; they found they had much in common in their attitude to life, and they began to go about together, to explore the back streets and to frequent cafés and less reputable resorts, observing and talking, talking.

Such a friend can be invaluable to a young author. In Ludo's company Huysmans found his sensibility sharpened and his powers of expression enormously enhanced. And Ludo was useful in other ways for he introduced him to Henri Céard, a young literary man with an immense enthusiasm for the writings of Zola; and Céard came to Huysmans' lodgings at 114 Rue de Vaugirard and heard him read *Le Drageoir*. Ludo also, through his brother-in-law who was a wholesale paper merchant (an ironical touch) got him an introduction to the influential Arsène Houssaye, proprietor and editor of *La Revue du XIXᵉ Siècle*. Houssaye had published Zola's *Thérèse Raquin* in 1868 and he now consented to print extracts from *Le Drageoir*. Then Huysmans did what so many young authors do who cannot bear their first brain-child to be disregarded. He brought out *Le Drageoir* in book form at his own expense. It sold very few copies but received some quite favourable reviews.

It was in Ludo's company that he began to collect materials

for a more ambitious project. The original notion was to write a book entitled *La Faim*, and it is to be regretted that only a few notes for this survive. The first draft gave a picture of Paris during the Siege, and this would have been invaluable to the biographer of Huysmans. However, the project was abandoned and Huysmans resolved to write a study of life among the work-girls of Paris. He knew something of them from his mother's work-shops, and was to use this material later for *Les Sœurs Vâtard*. With Ludo, he attempted to document himself concerning the girls working in the factories for making imitation pearls. Such girls were so badly paid that they were always on the edge of prostitution. Huysmans decided to write a study of a working-girl-prostitute and to do so in the new manner of *Naturalisme*, the school which the Goncourts and Zola had brought into fashion with young writers. This was the book which was finally called *Marthe*.

Soon afterwards he moved to a flat on the third floor of 73 Rue du Cherche-Midi, and it is interesting that he not only makes Ludo a character in *Marthe*, but gives his address as 73 Rue du Cherche-Midi. This was indeed to push the doctrine of *Naturalisme* to its extreme, and serves to show that if the character of Ludo was founded on the real Ludovic, he was also beginning to be identified with the author himself. But *Marthe* was not yet finished when, on May 4th, 1876, Huysmans' mother died.

Her husband, M. Og, was already dead, so that Huysmans found himself the part owner with his two half-sisters of the *atelier* at 11 Rue de Sèvres.[1] He moved back to what had been the home of his childhood and was to be his lodging for

[1] He never seems to have taken any active part in the business, but he remained a sleeping partner until 1892 when he sold out to his associate Léon Jules Leroux. The *Bottin* of 1914 still lists 'Leroux, Atelier de brochage', at 11 Rue de Sèvres.

the greater part of his working life. His share of the profits of the business made his situation a little easier, and as he was advancing, if slowly, in his profession (in 1873 he had been promoted *'employé 3ᵉ classe'* at the Ministry of the Interior), he thought he could allow himself a holiday. He went to Tilburg in Holland to visit his uncle and while there, or shortly afterwards, he changed his French Christian names Charles Georges to their Dutch form, Karl Joris, and reversed them for greater euphony. Henceforward it was as J.-K. Huysmans that he was to fight his way to fame as an author.

CHAPTER FOUR

ZOLA THE MASTER

———————————— ● ————————————

I t is an exciting moment when the aspiring young author first begins to make contact with the World of Letters. One acquaintance leads to another, and doors which he had imagined to be closed against him begin to open of their own accord. According to the account given by Huysmans to his faithful disciple Gustave Coquiot, one of his first important connections was with Léon Cladel. This was a strange character who lived in a suburb of Paris, surrounded by a troop of dogs who followed him everywhere. He was a large and hairy man with the manners and enthusiasms of a Romantic of the previous generation. His friends and the editors who exploited him thought him a little mad, but he had a real passion for literature, and welcomed young writers both to his house and to his office at *La République des Lettres*. He was sufficiently taken with Huysmans to make him a *rédacteur* of the paper, and it was here that he met a writer named Hennique and a young man whose real name was Guy de Valmont, but who is known to literary history as Guy de Maupassant.

The founder of *La République des Lettres* was Catulle Mendès, or, to give him his full name, Abraham Catulle Mendès. Born at Bordeaux in 1841 he had come to Paris while still very young and at the age of eighteen started *La Revue Fantaisiste*. His literary situation was strengthened in 1866 by his marriage to Judith, daughter of Théophile Gautier, but he soon broke with her and with the generation of Romanticists represented by his father-in-law. He was a brilliant and facile writer whose poems are generally considered to be better than his prose. His novels are marked in general by a curious perversity, a preference for themes of incest and other sexual aberrations. He was an indefatigable editor of literary journals and for this reason occupied, during the seventies and eighties, a situation in the world of letters more important than his own works might be thought to justify.

Through Mendès Huysmans renewed contact with Henri Céard, a scholar rather than a writer, who later became librarian at the Musée Carnavalet; and soon a little group had come into existence, a group of young literary men inspired by a common enthusiasm and as yet unaware of the divergent paths into which their talents would eventually lead them. The group consisted of Céard, Huysmans, Paul Alexis, Léon Hennique and Guy de Maupassant, and they met once a week for dinner at a restaurant at the corner of the Rue Coustan and the Rue Puget, in Montmartre. It was, according to the account of one of the *convives*, a frightful den where one devoured raw flesh and drank horrible wine. 'It was execrable, and it was perilous, but I do not know if any of us have ever dined so joyously.' Even Huysmans, with his finicky palate and fragile digestion, seems to have enjoyed it. The friends then went on to finish the evening at a 'house' in the Rue Clauzel, a kind of 'Maison Tellier', in fact one might call it *the* Maison Tellier for Guy de Maupassant actually lived there.

It was a case of blending theory and practice, All these young men were (naturally) in rebellion against the authors beloved of the middle-class reading public. All of them were ready to enroll themselves under the banner of revolt, and there could be no doubt, at that period, who the leaders of revolt were: the brothers Goncourt and Émile Zola. In that very year, 1876, Zola had proclaimed the doctrine of *Naturalisme*, which meant, or seemed to mean, a process of exact description of preferably sordid scenes. It was necessary to escape from the cloud-cuckoo-land of the Romantics and to depict life as it was really lived in contemporary France. We may be sure that Huysmans and his friends drank a final cup to the honour of Zola and the Goncourts before hurrying off to satisfy their artistic consciences by an exact documentation of the neighbouring *maison tolérée*.

Huysmans in particular must have regarded this part of the programme with professional interest. He had just finished his *Histoire d'une fille*, later to be entitled *Marthe*. As we have already noted it was a study of the career of a Paris prostitute, but not one of the gorgeous *grandes cocottes* who had flourished so exceedingly under the Second Empire. This was no Cora Pearl or Marguerite Bellanger, but a simple *fille du peuple*, a girl whose history exhibited vice at its most squalid and unattractive. He was most anxious to get the work published, for he knew that the brothers Goncourt were engaged on a similar project and he was determined to anticipate them by bringing his book out first.

He found, however, some difficulty in having it published in Paris. Publishers were, understandably, shy, for Zola's recent work had provoked a public scandal, and Jean Richepin had actually been fined and imprisoned for his writings. Huysmans, accordingly, decided to seek publication in Belgium and, having obtained leave of absence from his Ministry, on 6th August, 1876, he left for Brussels, taking his manuscript with him.

The response was favourable. A printer named Callewaert undertook the task, and the work was pushed forward with such rapidity that by the early autumn Huysmans was able to send a copy of the book—with a deferential inscription no doubt, but also with a smile of triumph—to the man he had forestalled. On October 3rd, Edmond de Goncourt notes in his *Journal:* 'Yesterday I received a book from a young man named Huysmans: *L'Histoire d'une Fille*, with a letter telling me that the book has been stopped by the censor.'[1]

Marthe: l'Histoire d'une Fille, to give it its proper title, is not usually placed very high by the critics in their estimate of Huysmans' *œuvre*. He himself, nearly ten years later, in the pseudo-interview which he published under the name of A. Meunier, remarks: 'This book contains, here and there, some exact observations and reveals already some qualities of style, but the language is too reminiscent of the Goncourts. It is a beginner's book, curious and vibrant, but cut short, and insufficiently personal.' There is also insufficient motivation of the actions of the three principal characters. They are too plainly puppets. Still it was a remarkable achievement for a young man of twenty-eight, and if it had no great success with the general public it marked him out in literary circles as a young man who not only had some talent as a writer, but was daring enough to concern himself with the life-history of a prostitute. By getting in ahead of *La Fille Elisa* he had snatched from the Goncourts the credit, if credit it be, of being the first to do so.

Huysmans had produced a work in the style of *Naturalisme*, but he had not yet met Zola. It was Henri Céard who brought them together. One Sunday in 1876, finding he had time on his hands, he decided to go to the Rue St.-Georges and introduce himself personally to his favourite author. Zola thought he was a commercial traveller trying to sell wine, and was not at all anxious to admit him, but Céard said: 'I have read

[1] This turned out not to be true. Huysmans was not troubled by the authorities, nor even by his own chief, M. de Marcère, Minister of the Interior.

all your books, and, as I admire them very much, I have come
to see you.'

Zola was unaccustomed to this kind of visit and was more
than a little embarrassed. He got rid of his visitor as soon as
he could and went to see Flaubert, Sunday being Flaubert's
reception-day. He told him of the visit and Flaubert was
touched. 'That', he said, 'was very nice; it is the sort of thing
that always gives one great pleasure.'

Huysmans shared Céard's enthusiasm for *Le Ventre de
Paris*, Zola's most recent novel, and some Sundays after his
first encounter with Zola, Céard returned to the Rue St.-
Georges, taking Huysmans with him. Huysmans brought his
book *Marthe* and presented it to Zola.

The above details are related by Paul Alexis, the author of
La Fin de Lucie Pellegrin. 'I, on my side,' he continues, 'had
made the acquaintance of Léon Hennique; I used to meet
him in the afternoons at the office of the *République des
Lettres*, a review edited by Catulle Mendès. After he had
given a lecture at the lecture-hall in the Boulevard des
Capucines on Zola and his work, I took him to the Rue St.
Georges and introduced him. I had made Huysmans'
acquaintance through Mendès also, and after an exchange of
volumes—he sending me his book *Marthe*, and I my *Fin de
Lucie Pellegrin*—I was invited to dine at his house. Hennique
was there, and so was Henri Céard, whom I had not yet met.
It was I also who introduced Guy de Maupassant to my three
new friends, having made Maupassant's acquaintance at
Flaubert's house. Then we were five. . . . One fine Thursday
afternoon we set out in a solid phalanx for Zola's house.
Since then we have gone there every Thursday evening.[1]

---

[1] A somewhat different account is given by Léon Deffoux and Émile
Zavie in *Le Groupe de Médan*, Paris 1920, pp. 7–9. Here it is stated that
Céard and Huysmans first visited Zola when he was living at No. 23
Rue de Boulogne, later Rue Ballu.

This is an invaluable passage, giving, as it does, an almost complete list of Huysmans' friends at the moment when he was beginning to find his way into the world of letters. It also throws considerable light on the position of leadership which Zola had already attained. It is true that Paul Alexis denies this, at least by implication. 'And now,' he says, 'I ought to say a word about our real attitude towards Zola. I am forced to do this in order to do away with the absurd stories that are current. I have before my eyes some of the amiable articles which certain of our confrères of the Paris press have been good enough to consecrate to us. . . . According to these kind friends we are needy beggars, and are kept by Zola. The truth is that our relations with Zola, far from being those of pupils with a master, differ in no respect, in point of intimacy and of affectionate comradeship, from those existing amongst us five. On the contrary, each of us, I think, is more at his ease with Zola than with any of the others. We are simply Zola's friends, and no more.' This is all very well, but we hear of no 'solid phalanx' setting out to visit Hennique, or Céard, or Alexis himself.

It is true that with the general public Zola had not yet attained the enormous *réclame* which was soon to be his. It is true that his last book, *Son Excellence Eugène Rougon*, published in 1875, had been violently attacked, particularly by Barbey d'Aurevilly, the avowed enemy of Zola and all his works. But he had already a solid achievement behind him, and his vigour as a journalist was feared even by those who did not admire his novels. By those who had any awareness of literary developments he was already recognized as a *'chef d'école'*.

Certainly there was much, both in his life and in his writings, to excite the youthful admiration of Huysmans. He too, like Zola, was an anti-Romantic. He had a shrinking horror of the grandiloquent phrase and the excessive gesture.

He had, like Zola, great powers of vivid and minute description, even if they were, as yet, undeveloped. He had even a marked preference for the seamy side of life. He shared Zola's contempt for the smugness of the bourgeoisie, and pushed it to even more extravagant lengths. There was much also in Zola's career for which he must have felt an instinctive sympathy.

Here was a man who had not even had the advantages of Huysmans himself. Zola had *really* starved in a garret, had subsisted for months on a daily ration of a pennyworth of bread or a pound of potatoes. Huysmans, for all his complaints, through the mouth of Folantin, had never been as poor as that. Zola had struggled on with heroic persistence, doing just enough hack-work to keep himself alive while he produced his creative work. He had won through by sheer indomitable persistence, and to Huysmans he must have seemed not only an example but a kind of elder brother showing him the path he must tread.

The final destinies of the two men were so different that we are apt to forget the striking similarities which united them when they first met. The parallelism is indeed astonishing even to such minor details as the monk's cell which Zola inhabited in what had once been a cloister in the Impasse St. Dominique. Huysmans spent most of his life in rooms which had once been monks' cells. Even the passion for exploring the dilapidated regions to the east of the *Quartier Latin* and taking long walks on the banks of the Bièvre was shared by the two men. Zola's methods of work, his zeal in documentation, his indifference to plot: all these were in accord with Huysmans' instincts. Huysmans was a natural *Naturaliste*, and he remained so to the end of his days, in spite of the very different ends to which he was to devote his talents.

At the time of their first meeting, Zola had already begun to bring out *L'Assommoir*, which was to make his fame and fortune. He had conceived the book the previous year while staying at the seaside, and he intended that it should be a simple story of a woman of the people who has two children by a lover and then marries another man. At first the marriage is happy; she is industrious and well-behaved, but the husband takes to drink, and she is gradually dragged down with him until she is on the streets.

For a long time Zola struggled with this theme, feeling that something was missing, until he hit upon the idea of bringing the lover back into the family circle. This was a situation he knew he could handle and with his systematic methods of work the manuscript was soon in the hands of the publishers. He had arranged for it to be printed first as a serial in a paper called *Le Bien Public*, and the first instalment appeared on 27th June, 1876.

The title, which means a low drinking shop, is taken from Delvau's *Dictionnaire de la Langue Verte*, which Zola had carefully studied. Indeed the whole work is written in the slang of the suburbs, even when the author speaks in his own person, and this constitutes one of the striking novelties of the work. Zola, as always, had taken immense pains with his documentation. The horrors of being on the verge of starvation in Paris he had experienced in his own person, but he had also visited workshops, had sat, busy with his notebook in, the corner of drinking-dens, had attended a workman's wedding and a workman's funeral; had, in a word, done everything that a good *Naturaliste* should do to make his report authentic.

Le Bien Public was an ultra-democratic journal to which Zola had already contributed dramatic criticism. The editor paid him £400 for the serial rights of this novel about working class life hoping, no doubt, that his readers, who largely belonged to that class themselves, would be pleased. He was soon undeceived. The People, or the political leaders who lived by flattering them, were outraged by Zola's realism. *L'ouvrier* had been insulted; the sacred cause of Republicanism was threatened. Letters of abuse began to pour in to the editor's office. Zola himself was threatened with violence if he ever dared to show himself in the *quartiers* of which he had painted so unflattering a picture. The circulation of *Le Bien Public* began to fall in a most alarming way.

The editor bowed to the storm and told Zola that he could no longer continue the publication of *L'Assommoir*. Very honourably he paid the sum agreed upon in full. Catulle Mendès offered Zola the hospitality of his journal, *La République des Lettres*, and although all he could pay was fifty pounds, the novelist accepted. By this time public interest had been aroused, and *La République des Lettres* gained as much circulation by publishing the second half of *L'Assommoir* as *Le Bien Public* had lost by publishing the first. When the novel came out in book form its success was immediate and immense. Four years later it had run through more than eighty editions. Zola was always an author who thrived on controversy. Quiet and peaceful in private life, in the world of letters he was always finding himself in the middle of a battle.

Huysmans plunged into the fight with all the enthusiasm of an avowed disciple. At the famous *Bœuf nature* dinner at the Café Procope he sat at table with Cézanne, Bourget, Bouchor and Coppée, and raised his glass to Zola in the chair. And, not content with such public appearances, he contributed to *L'Actualité*, a periodical edited in Brussels by Camille Lemonnier, a remarkable essay, a piece of constructive criticism which has been called his first important work. It was certainly a whole-hearted defence of Zola.

The general public inevitably finds it difficult to distinguish between a writer and his work. Zola had shown the effects of alcoholism: therefore he must himself be an alcoholic. He had depicted characters whose morals were deplorable: therefore he must be himself a debauchee. Such was the simple argument and it was never less *à propos* than when applied to Zola. For Zola himself, whatever may be thought of his novels, lived a life of exemplary bourgeois virtue. He was industrious, sober, honest, economical and faithful to his wife. He was almost pedantically well behaved.

It was the early nineteenth century Romantics who had made 'bourgeois' a term of abuse in artistic circles and who had convinced the bourgeoisie that artists were inevitably as immoral as Byron, as drunken as Musset and as unlikely to pay their debts as any of the characters in *La Vie de Bohême*. Huysmans began his essay by ridiculing this notion as hopelessly outmoded, and painted, as it were, in parenthesis, a vivid picture of the Zola ménage, the master seated industriously at his desk or surrounded by his disciples, Alexis, Céard and Hennique.

He passes on to expound and defend the doctrine of *Naturalisme*, which consisted, in his view, of an attempt to live in one's own time, and to paint the world as it really is. Dead and buried are the cape and sword rigmaroles of the Romantics, the Greek and Hindu fantasies of writers like Théophile Gautier, the 'boiled veal' of the sentimental fashionable writers such as Octave Feuillet. The business of the novelists is analysis, not fancy, and if in their analysis they are constrained to uncover the sores of society, they are doing no more than their duty. 'Art,' proclaims Huysmans, 'has nothing to do with modesty or immodesty', but if a book is true and alive it cannot help promoting morality. *L'Assommoir* is such a book, in particular in the splendid pages describing the death of Lélie and Gervaise's descent into the gutter.

It was a magnificent defence. Zola wrote him a modest and

appreciative letter of thanks, and his place in the circle was now assured. Huysmans' *Sac au Dos*, upon which we have already drawn for his adventures during the war of 1870, was first published in a Belgian review in 1878 and two years later found its natural place in the *Soirées de Médan*.

This publication consisted of a collection of short stories by Zola and the friends who came to visit him in his country retreat near Poissy. Huysmans' contribution is still of interest for the light it throws upon Huysmans; the tales by Céard, Hennique, Paul Alexis and even Zola himself have been forgotten. The book is now treasured because it contains one of the supreme masterpieces of the short story: Maupassant's *Boule de Suif*.

For *Sac au Dos* Huysmans had drawn upon his personal reminiscences; for the wider canvas of his next book he turned to the factory formerly run by his mother. We have seen him at work on his documentation while he was still too uncertain of his talent to make use of his material. Now he has found his method, the idiom of *Naturalisme* which he was to retain all his life, and he thinks he has found his subject matter, *Naturaliste* also, under the shadow of Zola. *Les Sœurs Vâtard*, published in 1879, tells the story of two working girls, Céline and Désirée, who live, like all their kind, on the borderline of prostitution. The elder, Céline, is already over the line; Désirée has higher ideals or more sensibility, but neither suffices to save her from the degradation to which she is doomed from birth.

Some of the descriptions are veritable *tours de force* but the general effect of the book is depressing in the extreme. Zola, even in *L'Assommoir*, never induces in the reader the feeling of utter despair which is the almost inevitable reaction to *Les Sœurs Vâtard*. This puddle reflects no gleam of heaven, no ray of hope.

Flaubert did not care very much for the book. Writing to

Maupassant on 27th February, 1879[1] he remarks: 'With regard to the *Naturalistes*, what should I do about your friend Huysmans? Is he a man to whom one can speak frankly? His *Sœurs Vâtard* arouses in me very moderate enthusiasm. But as he seems a good fellow, I don't want to offend him.'

Even Zola, to whom the book was dedicated by 'his fervent admirer and devoted friend,' found much to criticize in it. 'As to Huysmans,' he remarked, 'of whom I am very fond, when he brought me his book, *Les Sœurs Vâtard*, I did not disguise from him my opinion that the excessive colour of his style displeased me. I went so far as to add, that the work girls about whom he wrote had nothing whatever to do with the people, and were only connected with the people by an imperceptible thread. As a matter of fact, I admit that they constitute the bookbinding workshop that M. Huysmans directs, and nothing more. It is true that M. Huysmans would be the first to admit that all that he wanted to do in *Les Sœurs Vâtard* was to paint but a small corner in the life of the people. In the same way, the de Goncourts never paint *tableaux d'ensemble*. And repeating that I have no disciples, I will point out to you that Huysmans by no means proceeds from me. If he proceeds from anybody, it is from the Goncourts.'[2] Zola reproached Huysmans with using rare words which took away the verisimilitude of the 'slice of life'.

Even Edmond de Goncourt was not satisfied, but for the opposite reason. It seemed to him that the 'slice of life' theory had served its turn, and in a letter to Huysmans[3] he says: 'Will you take an older man's advice? Very well! I believe that *Germinie Lacerteux*, *L'Assommoir*, *Les Sœurs Vâtard*, have, at this moment, exhausted the *canaille* in literature;

---

[1] Gustave Flaubert, *Correspondance*, 4ᵉ série (1869–1880), p. 322. The letter is dated February 27th, 1879.

[2] R. M. Sherard, *Emile Zola*, London, 1893, p. 125.

[3] Dated 24th March, 1879.

and I urge you to choose, for your next book, another sphere, a superior sphere.'

Coming from the author of *Germinie Lacerteux* himself such an appeal must have made an impression on Huysmans. But if he was no longer to seek his subject matter in the lower depths of society, where was he to find it? Of the *haut monde* he knew nothing whatever; for the sensibilities and the polite adulteries of the upper bourgeoisie he had nothing but contempt. The only thing that redeemed his own life from ennui and squalor was his passion for Art. He would cease to write about people; he would write about things; not necessarily beautiful things in any obvious sense, but about works of art which had about them some quality of novelty or strangeness.

Here again Zola had shown him the way, Villemessant, the editor of *Le Figaro*, encouraged by the success of Zola's literary gossip column, 'Books of Today and Tomorrow', asked him in 1866 to do art criticisms as well. Zola agreed and his first 'Salon' appeared in that year. As might have been expected he attacked the works of the academic painters, and praised those of Manet and those other painters who, with him, were beginning to be called Impressionists. Zola's pugnacious journalism helped to launch the new school but his attacks on the fashionable painters of the time gave great offence to the readers of *Le Figaro* and Villemessant decided to discontinue Zola's articles.

Huysmans had already declared himself a champion of Zola by his defence of *L'Assommoir*, and therefore, when he began his own art criticism in *Le Voltaire*, people expected that he would take very much the same line. And to a large extent he did so. From 1879 to 1882 he 'covered', as journalists say, the official Salon and the Salon des Indépendants. He praised Manet for having opened a new route in painting, but declared that he had advanced no further in it himself.

This is sound criticism for Manet was never an Impressionist in the later sense of that word. He was a supreme colour harmonist, never a noter of evanescent effects of light.

He praised Degas and Mary Cassatt, he admired Raffaëlli for having interpreted 'the poignant note of spleen in land-scape, the plaintive delights of the suburbs'. Here indeed was something after his own heart, and we find the authentic Huysmans' accent when he declares that this art was 'the elixir of the crapulous, extract of urinal'. Of Degas he said that no painter since Delacroix had so completely understood *'le mariage et l'adultère des couleurs'*. Even the painters who were being praised must sometimes have raised their eye-brows a little at Huysmans' phrases.

Rather oddly, he admired, in the Salon of 1881, the works of Walter Crane, Kate Greenaway and Rudolph Caldecott, although, fortunately, he did not celebrate them in terms likely to offend their English prudery. He did not like the more famous paintings of Millet, preferring, quite soundly, his drawings. He did not care at all for the work of Puvis de Chavannes. But generally one can say that Huysmans' art criticism has stood up to the test of time better than most. He had a more acute sensibility than Zola, and he lacked altogether the sheer wrong-headedness which makes some of Ruskin's contemporary judgments read so strangely today.

The personal note, however, soon makes itself heard. As Zola's disciple and successor his obvious line was to be the swashbuckling champion of 'the Moderns'. But there were two painters who fascinated him, painters altogether outside the Impressionist movement. Huysmans admired them enormously, and in his admiration for them we can already catch a hint of his own future development. Their names were Odilon Redon and Gustave Moreau.

He admired them precisely because they were *not* modern. In the article on Gustave Moreau which finds its final form in *Certains*,[1] he wrote: 'The theory of environment adapted to art by M. Taine is true—but true in reverse, so far as great artists are concerned, for the environment acts upon them by revolt, by the hatred it inspires in them; instead of modelling and fashioning the soul in its image, it creates in immense Bostons, solitary Edgar Poes; it acts backwards, and creates in the shameful contemporary France of each, Baudelaire, Flaubert, Goncourt, Villiers de l'Isle-Adam, Gustave Moreau, Redon and Rops, creatures of exception who retrace the steps of the centuries, in disgust at the promiscuities they have to suffer, into the abyss of past ages, the stormy spaces of nightmares and of dreams.'

Taine's theory of environment is true in reverse! Huysmans' phrase is *juste à rebours*, and it gives us a flash of insight into the way his mind was working at this period of his life. It was true that he had accepted the tutelage of Zola and had enrolled himself under the banner of *Naturalisme*. But when he looked into his heart he knew perfectly well that the reforming zeal of his master was entirely foreign to his nature. He detested the 'moderns', he hated the age in which he lived. He saw no hope for the future. It was only the past that excited his sensibility. When he speaks of 'disgust at the promiscuities' of modern life, and of retracing the steps of the centuries, he is speaking for himself. He too was a creature of exception on whom the environment acted 'in reverse'. He had arrived, in his studies of art, at a kind of mystique of beauty, a strange and terrible beauty 'of nightmares and of dreams'. But art criticism is a frustrated form of expression at best. It is only in fiction that one can tell the truth! What if out of his disgusts, his passions, his secret dreams, he could create a work of fiction which would show him his own face as in a mirror—in reverse—*à rebours?*

[1] When Huysmans was asked, towards the end of his life, which of his books he himself preferred, he replied without hesitation, *Certains*.

CHAPTER FIVE

A REBOURS

———————————— • ————————————

By this time Huysmans had begun to realise that objectivity was not his forte. Not for him the creation of a 'gallery of characters'; there is in his whole *œuvre* no Pickwick, no Mr. Micawber, not even a Becky Sharp. His characters, in his most successful and typical works, are simply aspects of his own personality; his hero is himself. Before *A Rebours*, however, his heroes had been diminutions of himself. What if he were now to attempt an enlargement? Folantin had been a Huysmans without talent and with even less money than his creator. What if his next hero should inhabit a larger instead of a smaller world and should enjoy an income a hundred times as much as Huysmans was receiving from the Ministry of the Interior? What would he do with such an income? Huysmans began to dream, and the result of his dreaming was one of the most remarkable books of the nineteenth century.

It was also one of the most influential. '*A Rebours*', says Mario Praz, in that remarkable work of literary and psychological penetration which he called *The Romantic Agony*, 'is the pivot upon which the whole psychology of the Decadent Movement turns; in it all the phenomena of this state of mind are illustrated down to the minutest detail, in the instance of its chief character, des Esseintes. "*Tous les romans que j'ai écrits depuis 'A Rebours' sont contenus en germe dans ce livre*",

74

Huysmans remarked. Not only his own novels but all the prose works of the Decadence, from Lorrain to Gourmont, Wilde and D'Annunzio, are contained in embryo in *A Rebours*.'[1]

We have said that des Esseintes is simply Huysmans himself transported into a larger world; but with such a world Huysmans was entirely unacquainted. His treatment of his hero is therefore merely perfunctory until des Esseintes abandons *le monde* and becomes a hermit of aesthetic mysticism. Yet although des Esseintes *is* Huysmans, an excuse for his opinions, a peg for his dreams, he was modelled upon a real person: Count Robert de Montesquiou. Anatole France, in his essay on Robert de Montesquiou,[2] denies that he was ever the 'Parisian Heliogabalus' described by Huysmans. 'If one could penetrate', he says 'the secret of his discreet and hidden life consecrated to a charming but prolonged and heavy labour, one would find nothing of the legendary and mythical Montesquiou, except a delicate lover of beautiful things, surrounding himself with those forms of art which responded best to his dreams, living in the chosen sumptuosities of Empire furniture and Japanese decoration. He was, first and foremost, a poet'.

France agrees, however, that he was credited with having rubies and emeralds set in the carapace of a tortoise and that people attributed to him a marvellous refinement, an unheard of search for the exquisite, 'the delicious malady of the rare and the precious'. That was his legend and it was, after all, the legend that set Huysmans dreaming. We can be almost certain that Huysmans, *dans son coin*, never met the real Comte Robert de Montesquiou-Fezensac at all. But perhaps France protests too much, for if Montesquiou, in his

[1] Mario Praz, *The Romantic Agony*. Translated from the Italian by Angus Davidson, London, 1933, p. 308.

[2] Reprinted in *La Vie Littéraire*, Ve Série, Paris (1949) but originally published in *Le Temps*, 13th Nov. 1892.

youth, was not the model for des Esseintes, he is generally supposed to have been, in his age, the model for Proust's Charlus, and Proust, unlike Huysmans, did move in the world of the cultivated *haute noblesse*, and presumably knew his man.

Montesquiou was certainly not quite the blameless æsthete that France, rather surprisingly, tries to make out. Mario Praz, basing himself on the Goncourt *Journals*, calls him 'an amateur of gems and of handsome gymnasts of the *éphèbe* type'. In 1890 he spent a month in London, partly in order to be painted by Whistler, and, in a recent life of Whistler,[1] we learn of the elaborate precautions he took to conceal his identity, precautions which remind one of the 'blaze of secrecy' in which the late Montagu Norman used to set out on his financial missions to the United States. After sitting sixteen times for Whistler, Montesquiou was almost dropping with fatigue and revived himself with what he called *vin de coca*, i.e. cocaine.

The same author records that he (Montesquiou) 'lived at the top of his father's house on the Quai d'Orsay, and it was a weird experience to go from the austere rooms of the old Comte into the oriental atmosphere of his son's apartments where the walls of the sitting room were of different shades of red, where another room was entirely grey, and where the main feature of the bedroom was a black bulbous-eyed dragon which on inspection resolved itself into a bed. "It was all queer, disturbing, baroque," decided one visitor. Portraits of himself in different attitudes and outlandish costumes filled the walls and strange scents filled the air. He was known among his acquaintances as "Chief of Fragrant Odours"; at one time he was frequently seen in society carrying a gilt tortoise; and it was generally believed that he was a connoisseur in various forms of vice.'[2]

[1] *The Man Whistler*, by Hesketh Pearson, London, 1952, p. 152.
[2] Pearson, *op. cit.*, p. 15.

A Rebours

Sir William Rothenstein, who probably met Montesquiou while he was sitting for Whistler, also mentions that he 'had a tortoise whose shell was inlaid with jewels; the tortoise's retort on this outrage was direct and emphatic—it died. . . . I met him one day on his way to hear Weber's music, when he told me that one should always listen to Weber in mauve.[1]

Such stories must long have been current in Paris, and we can be certain that some of them at least reached Huysmans' ears, and that he used them—especially the jewelled tortoise —in order to build up the character of des Esseintes. But this of course was only the starting point and we can still consider *A Rebours* as its author's personal confession; not of what he did but of what he would like to have done if he had had the means, even what he would like to have been if fortune had made him, instead of the son of a poor Dutch immigrant, the descendant of a long line of French seigneurs.

Des Esseintes was an aristocrat, the last scion of a family that had once possessed nearly the whole territory of the Ile-de-France and the Brie: 'a young man anaemic and nervous, with hollow cheeks, steel blue eyes, a thin yet aquiline nose, and dry tapering hands . . . he had a pointed beard of an extraordinarily pale blonde and an ambiguous expression, at once weary and subtle.'

He was thirty years old (that is, almost exactly the age of Huysmans). His parents had both died when he was about eighteen. He had been educated by the Jesuits, and under their care had become a good latinist. But he could not be persuaded to pursue any regular course of study. He detested science and modern languages but showed, from an early age, a curious interest in theology.

When he attained his majority he found himself in posses-sion of a considerable fortune; but the amusements of society soon palled upon him, partly by reason of his excessive

[1] W. Rothenstein, *Men and Memories*, London, 1931. Vol. 1, p. 15.

sensibility and partly (one cannot help thinking) because Huysmans felt himself quite incapable of describing anything so foreign to his own experience.

He began to dream of 'a refined Thebaid, a comfortable solitude, a warm and static Ark where he could take refuge from the incessant deluge of human folly'. He therefore sold his ancestral chateau, and all his other possessions, in exchange for an annual income, keeping back just enough to purchase and furnish a small house where he could be quiet and alone. After some search he found one to his liking at Fontenay, not far from Paris, and set about installing himself according to his particular taste.

The furnishing of the house at Fontenay occupies a considerable portion of *A Rebours*. For des Esseintes was not a man who was easily satisfied. Before leaving the world he had made himself conspicuous by his extravagances, his baroque sense of the *mise-en-scène*. On one occasion in order to celebrate 'the most futile of misadventures' (presumably the end of a love-affair) he had organised a 'mourning banquet'. Perhaps the description of it is worth transcribing as an example of the strange fancies that flickered in the brain of the little clerk at the Ministry of the Interior.

In a dining room hung entirely with black and opening on a garden which had been transformed by putting down paths of coaldust, changing the basin of the fountain into black basalt and filling it with ink, the dinner had been served on a black table-cloth, decorated with baskets of violets and scabious, and lit by candles which burned with a green light. . . . While a hidden orchestra played funeral airs, the guests had been served by naked negresses, with slippers and stockings of silver tissue, sewn with pearls like tears. The plates were black-bordered and the food also had been black: caviar, black puddings and truffles. Even the drinks were as black as possible, a list of dark wines—and stout!

78

All this was childish enough as Huysmans—and des Esseintes—now realised. He had put such follies behind him and proposed to decorate his apartment not to astonish others but merely to please himself. But it was to be, nonetheless, *paré d'une façon rare*.

Having had the house at Fontenay practically rebuilt he was much exercised over the choice of colours for the rooms. The chief requirement was that the colours should look best by artificial light, for des Esseintes did not propose to keep normal hours, and some of the rooms were built to exclude the daylight altogether. He decided that orange was his favourite colour, as being most in harmony with 'the sensual nature of a true artist', for his were no 'bourgeois eyes, insensible to the pomp and victory of strong, vibrating tones', nor yet the eyes of *'solides mâles'*, who would naturally prefer red and yellow. The woodwork was painted deep indigo. The greater part of the walls was covered with bookshelves of ebony, the floor with blue fox skins, and the furniture included high-backed arm-chairs and an old church lectern supporting a massive folio. The window spaces were filled with bulls-eyes of glass the main function of which was to filter the harshness of the light, and also to prevent any view of the outside world.

On the chimney piece, which was draped with a sumptuous piece of stuff cut from a Florentine dalmatic, stood, between two monstrances, a kind of triptych in the Byzantine style, its three compartments containing three sheets of 'authentic vellum' on which were written in letters like those of a missal and with illuminated initials, three pieces by Baudelaire: the two sonnets entitled respectively, *La Mort des Amants* and *L'Ennemi* and (in the middle) the poem in prose entitled 'Anywhere out of the world'.

All this is very revealing. It is nearly always possible to deduce a man's taste and character from the decoration and arrangement of his room; how much more so when the room is an imaginary room, decorated regardless of expense, and even without consideration for convenience and practicality. In the dream apartment of des Esseintes is the whole of Huysmans: his love of the extraordinary and the factitious, his naïvety, his passion for ecclesiastical properties and the hint of blasphemy in the use of them, his devotion to Baudelaire. The man who could devise such a scheme of decoration was plainly a much more complicated being than any mere disciple of Zola had any right to be.

Having decorated the salon des Esseintes next turned his attention to the dining room. This was to be arranged like the cabin of a ship, and it was to be inserted (the word is Huysmans' own) in a larger room, the real dining room built by the architect. And between the real window and the porthole of the inner room was a large aquarium, through which the light of the outside day was filtered. Not content with this, des Esseintes, on the rare occasions when he was awake in the afternoon (for his usual practice was only to get up when the sun was setting) would change the water in the aquarium by means of a system of pipes, and tint it with coloured essences, thus being able to enjoy 'the green or salmon-pink, the opalescent or silvery tones of a real river' reflecting the changing sky.

The reader should not imagine that the injection of coloured essences in the water of the aquarium was bad for the fish. The fish (perhaps it is hardly necessary to say) were not real fish but mechanical contrivances moving by clockwork among artificial marine plants. When he entered this room, which had been perfumed with tar, he was able to imagine himself at sea; and a slightly comic touch is added by the provision of advertisements of voyages hung on the walls, together with framed time-tables of the Royal Mail Steam Packet Company and other shipping lines. This nautical nostalgia seems all the

THE APPARITION

From the painting by Gustave Moreau in the Louvre

COUNT ROBERT DE MONTESQUIOU
From the caricature by Sem

more remarkable when we reflect that Huysmans was never on shipboard in his life. But perhaps when he remarks that, after all, the pleasures of travel are almost entirely imaginary, and reside in the anticipation and remembrance of a voyage rather than in its actual experience, he is uncomfortably near the truth! It is when he declares that no real moonlight can equal stage moonlight, that no real flower is better than an artificial flower, and that no woman can compete in 'plastic beauty' with a locomotive of the *Chemin de Fer du Nord*, that the normal man begins to rub his eyes.

Chapter three gives an account of the literary tastes of Huysmans' strange hero. One whole section of his library was devoted to works in Latin and it goes without saying that they were all in what the professors of the Sorbonne would call 'Latin of the decadence'. According to des Esseintes these were the only authors worthy of notice. Not for him the writings of Virgil, who was not only a pedant of the deepest dye, but one of the most sinister *raseurs* that Antiquity had produced. His admiration for Ovid was extremely moderate and he detested Horace and all his works. As for Cicero, Caesar, Livy, Suetonius, Tacitus, he rejected them all. The only 'classical' author with whom he had the least sympathy was Petronius.

Things began to improve, in his opinion, in the second century A.D. with Apuleius. Then follows a list of authors which to the classical scholar are mere names, and of which the ordinary cultivated man has never heard; and it is interesting to note that although Huysmans, speaking for des Esseintes, makes several disobliging remarks about Christianity, he is plainly already fascinated by those authors of the Dark Ages who 'spiced the corpse of latinity with the aromatics of the Church'. He even professes a liking for the acrostic verses of St. Boniface.

It is in the following chapter that, as if afraid of having

exhausted the patience of the reader, Huysmans introduces the famous jewelled tortoise. The first idea had been, he tells us, merely to gild its shell, but the effect was too glaring, so he chose a Japanese design (the passion for japonaiserie, owing to the influence of the Goncourts, being then in full blast) and had it reproduced in jewels set in the carapace. There is a long discussion of the jewels used, and when the work is at last completed des Esseintes feels 'perfectly happy'. The sight of the tortoise, thus bedizened, even gives him an appetite which he satisfies with a cup of tea—no ordinary tea, of course, but a subtle blend of three rare varieties, brought all the way from China by caravan.

Des Esseintes, however, did not confine himself entirely to tea. When in need of stronger stimulus he repaired to the dining room where, in one of the panels, there was concealed a cupboard housing a miniature bar. Small sandalwood barrels with silver stopcocks contained a large assortment of liqueurs, and by an ingenious arrangement of push-buttons these could be blended drop by drop. He called this apparatus, with a typical touch of Huysmans' humour, his *mouth-organ*.

In a celebrated passage, suggested no doubt by Zola's famous 'symphony in cheese' in *Le Ventre de Paris*[1] he elaborates this idea of the relationship between taste and sound. 'The taste of each liqueur corresponded, according to him, to the sound of an instrument. Dry curaçao, for example, to the note, at once sharp and smooth, of the clarinet; kummel to the sonorous yet nasal oboe; crême-de-menthe and anisette to the flute, at the same time sweet and pepper-sharp, soft and yet wailing; while to complete the orchestra, kirsch is like a trumpet, gin and whisky assault the palate like the strident sounds of pistons and trombones,

[1] See the present author's 'Symphony in Cheese, or Zola goes to market', in *Wine and Food*, No. 37, 1943, p. 17.

marc resembles a tuba, while the thunder claps of drums and cymbals are represented in the mouth by the *raki* of Chios. . . '

He imagined also that it might even be possible to play string quartets on the palate, with the violin represented by old brandy, the viola by the more robust rum, the violoncello by *vespétro*, and the bass-violin by fine old bitters. If one wished to add a fifth instrument and make the performance a quintet, one could figure a gustatory harp by adding 'the vibrant savour, the silver note, detached and fragile of *cumin sec*'.

Once the principle was admitted, he had found it possible to transfer to the inside of his jaw (the phrase is Huysmans' own) whole passages of music, following the composer step by step, expressing his thought, and echoing every nuance of his effects by means of the contrast and learned blending of liqueurs. He even composed melodies himself, executing pastorals with the benign *cassis* which produces, in the throat, the pearly notes of nightingales, or the tender crême-de-cacao which hums syrupy old-fashioned airs. Huysmans concludes, amusingly enough, that 'this evening des Esseintes felt no inclination for music and contented himself with a glass of real Irish whiskey!'

From these exquisite refinements of the pleasures of tasting, he passes to the visual arts, and it is interesting to note that he rejects, by implication, almost the entire *œuvre* of those modern painters for whom, following Zola, he had fought so many battles in his printed art criticism. What he desires, he says quite frankly, for the joy of his eyes and the delectation of his mind, is something quite different: works suggesting the world of the unknown, giving rise to new speculations, attacking the nervous system by means of 'learned hysterias, complicated nightmares, nonchalant and yet atrocious visions'. What he wants, in a word, are the pictures of Gustave Moreau.

A Rebours

Huysmans has been called the 'discoverer' of Gustave Moreau, but Moreau was far from being an unknown painter at the date of the publication of *A Rebours*. In the Salon of 1876 he had exhibited two paintings: *Salomé* (now in the Mantes Collection) and *L'Apparition* which was afterwards purchased for the Luxembourg. The first was an oil-painting and the second a watercolour, and it is interesting that Huysmans was so much excited by them that he includes them both by name in the imaginary collection of des Esseintes. In other words, he would have purchased them himself if he had had the money, for what des Esseintes does represents his own wish fulfilment.

Huysmans evokes the figure of Salomé in one of the most famous of his purple patches. 'With a face withdrawn, solemn, almost august, she began the lascivious dance which was to awaken the exhausted senses of the aged Herod; her breasts quivered and, at the touch of her whirling necklaces of jewels, the nipples rose; diamonds, attached to the dampness of her flesh, scintillated; her bracelets, her girdles, her rings gave out sparks on her triumphal robe sewn with pearls, patterned with silver, spangled with gold, the cuirass of jewels, of which each scale was a stone, seemed to be on fire, little snakes of flame swarming over the pale flesh, over the tea-rose skin, like splendid insects, with dazzling shards, marbled with carmine, shot with pale yellow, diapered with steel-blue, striped with peacock green.'

Mario Praz has shown[1] that even the details of Moreau's picture were inspired by Flaubert's evocations of oriental *luxe* and *luxure* in his *Tentation de Saint Antoine*, so that Huysmans in his descriptions is following Flaubert at one remove. And he concludes: 'There is in these despairing and learned works a singular enchantment, an incantation profoundly moving like that of certain poems of Baudelaire.'

[1] Mario Praz, *The Romantic Agony*, p. 292.

Baudelaire indeed has much to say in the matter. It might even be contended that Flaubert, and Moreau and Huysmans are, in their different works, merely expanding and elaborating the famous line:

> *La très-chère était nue, et, connaissant mon cœur,*
> *Elle n'avait gardé que ses bijoux sonores . . .*

But the attitude is common to the whole Decadent Movement and Salomé is a favourite, almost an obsessional, figure, reaching its final expression (and the culminating touch of making Salomé in love with, or in lust for, John the Baptist) in Wilde's famous play.

Mallarmé also made a formal treatment of the theme. It is true that his *Hérôdiade* was not published until 1898, but it had long circulated in manuscript among the poet's friends, and it was certainly known to Huysmans, for he pictures his des Esseintes reading a fragment of it while gazing at Moreau's watercolour. It 'subjugates him like a sortilege, at certain hours'. But it would perhaps be better to finish with the paintings on the walls of des Esscintes before we turn our attention to his literary enthusiasms.

In addition, therefore, to the two paintings by Moreau, he hung, in ebony frames, a series of prints by Jan Luyken, 'an old Dutch engraver, almost unknown in France'. The choice may seem surprising, for Luyken was an ardent, indeed a fanatical Calvinist, who lived a life of great austerity and went about preaching the Gospel. He was, however, an engraver of some ability and what fascinated des Esseintes was his choice of subjects. His 'Religious Persecutions' display every variety of torture that the mad ingenuity of mankind has ever invented. There was more than a hint of sadism in the Salomé pictures; here it was more openly expressed, albeit with a very different conscious intention. The worthy Calvinist would no doubt have been extremely scandalised if he could have foreseen how his crude Protestant propaganda would appeal to ultra-refined decadents some three centuries later, decadents who, whatever else they might have been, were certainly not Protestants.

Huysmans indeed, in the Preface which he wrote for *A Rebours*, after his conversion, calls sadism the 'bastard of Catholicism'. It 'presupposes a religion to be violated. It consists above all in a sacreligious practice, in a moral rebellion, in a spiritual debauch, in an aberration which is completely ideal, entirely Christian. . . . The power of sadism, the attraction which it offers, resides entirely in the prohibited pleasure of transferring to Satan the homage and the prayers which are due to God; it resides therefore in the non-observance of the Catholic precepts, or even in observing them in reverse (the key word *à rebours*), by committing, in order the more to spurn Christ, the sins He has expressly cursed: the pollution of the cult and the carnal orgy.'

This is surely to claim too much. Sadism and sacrilege are not necessarily the same thing, although they are closely allied; but the passage is interesting as showing that the germ of *Là-bas* was already present in *A Rebours*.

In addition to the engravings of Luyken, des Esseintes exhibited on his walls the lithograph by Bresdin called *La Comédie de la Mort*. Rodolphe Bresdin is not a name that is very well-known today,[1] but there was a certain vogue for his work, at the time of the publication of *A Rebours*, in the circles with which Huysmans was in contact. He was an extraordinary character who was employed for a time as a railway-man and road-mender. When he was in Paris he lived in a dilapidated shack in the suburbs 'surrounded by a collection of incongruous objects amongst which cats lay

---

[1] But see an excellent article on his work: 'Rodolphe Bresdin called Chien-Caillou,' by Claude Roger-Marx, *Print Collectors' Quarterly*, XIV, 1927, p. 251.

feeding their young and spiders spun their webs'. He had considerable skill as an etcher, 'pulled his proofs by means of a shoe brush and some blacking and sold them for a few francs to second-hand dealers who passed them off as Rembrandts.' He taught etching to Odilon Redon, one of whose early etchings is signed 'pupil of Bresdin'. Huysmans may even have met him through Redon, or through Catulle Mendès, for whose *Revue Fantaisiste*, Bresdin made a series of etchings. Later he produced lithographs of which *La Comédie de la Mort* is the most ambitious.

It is easy to see why it appealed to des Esseintes with its fantastic foliage, its lowering clouds, its gesticulating skeletons. In detail it is fantastically minute, but there was no question of drawing from the model. 'The artist,' said Bresdin, 'should not even glance at Nature. He has everything within himself.' This might have stood as a motto for des Esseintes; it shows how completely Huysmans had broken with Zolaism and the doctrine of the Impressionists, when he could prefer to Manet and his followers the works of men like Bresdin and Odilon Redon.

For des Esseintes hung Odilon Redon too, in the vestibule leading to his bedroom, and Redon, who was a considerable artist, paid no attention to the outside world at all but drew his strange forms, his evocative images, his monstrous flowers terminating in human faces, entirely from the world of dream. He takes his place today as a precursor of the Surrealists.

In the bedroom itself was a drawing by Théotocopuli, 'a Christ of singular hue, exaggerated design and ferocious colour. It was a sinister picture, in tones of wax-yellow and cadaverous green.' Huysmans' reference to it is half-apologetic, but it is interesting to see him anticipating, if he did not foresee, the now universal passion for El Greco. What he was seeking, of course, in all these pictures was an excitation of his sensibility, one might almost say a sharpening of his neurosis.

It is impossible to follow des Esseintes in all his researches. There is a chapter on flowers, there is a discussion of the effects of perfumes. He is tempted to start on a journey to England, but after a single visit to an English tavern in the Rue de Rivoli, decides not to risk losing by actually visiting the country, the 'imperishable sensations' procured by a meal of ox-tail soup, haddock, beefsteak, Stilton, and rhubarb tart. Then, as if exhausted by this unwonted effort, he returns to his books.

It is his choice of these, perhaps, which throws most light on Huysmans at the moment when he was writing *A Rebours*. Pride of place, it is perhaps unnecessary to say, is given to Baudelaire. He has had his works specially printed 'in a large format like that of missals'. There follows a veritable pæan of praise for this writer for whom 'his admiration was boundless'. Beside him the older French classics seemed pretentious and empty. Rabelais and Molière did not amuse him; he cared little for Voltaire, Rousseau or Diderot. He was touched, however, by the melancholy *ballades* of Villon, and had quite a liking for Christian orators like Bourdaloue and Bossuet. He respected Pascal for the austerity of his pessimism.

Of contemporary authors he admired Barbey d'Aurevilly, finding particular pleasure in *Les Diaboliques*. He praises Barbey for his violent oscillations between mysticism and sadism, and declares that this book alone among the works of 'contemporary apostolic literature (the phrase is Huysmans' own), is the perfect witness of that state of mind, at once devout and impious, towards which his memories of Catholicism, stimulated by his neurosis, had often driven des Esseintes'.[1]

[1] *A Rebours*, p. 213.

He had an almost equal admiration for the writings of Villiers de l'Isle-Adam, and he embarks on a long discussion of his short stories which recall, on the one hand, the 'mystifications' of Edgar Allan Poe and, on the other, the cold and ferocious irony of Swift. In this there was much to chime with Huysmans' own predilection, but perhaps he did not realise completely at the time what it was in Villiers which attracted him so much.

Villiers de l'Isle-Adam, says Anatole France,[1] 'was of that family of literary neo-Catholics whose common father was Chateaubriand, and which has produced Barbey d'Aurevilly, Baudelaire, and more recently M. Josephin Péladan. These men savoured above all in religion the charms of sin, the grandeur of sacrilege; and their sensuality caressed dogmas which added to voluptuousness *la suprême volupté de se perdre.*' He might have added to his list, says Praz,[2] the names of Huysmans, Verlaine, Barrès and Henri de Montherlant.

As may well be imagined, *A Rebours* was a literary sensation of the first magnitude. Nothing quite like it had ever appeared before, and the public hardly knew what to make of it. Huysmans wrote to Zola: 'I have trodden on everybody's corns. The Catholics are exasperated: the others accuse me of being a clerical in disguise, the Romantics are offended by the attacks on Hugo, on Gautier, on Leconte de Lisle; the *Naturalistes* by the book's hatred of the moderns.'

Zola himself was not very pleased. He saw that his young disciple was no longer of his company; he had gone off in another direction altogether. The story of the reproachful telegram: '*Naturalisme pas mort, lettre suit*' is probably apocryphal, but it almost certainly illustrates Zola's state of mind.[3] The well-known critic Sarcey, during a lecture in

---

[1] *La Vie Littéraire*, IIIe série, p. 121.   [2] *Op. cit*, p. 301.
[3] The telegram was actually sent by Paul Alexis, Zola's disciple. See Pierre Mille, *Le Roman Français*. Paris, 1930.

the Salle des Capucines, complained that he was unable to understand the book at all. Brunetière, writing in the influential *Revue des Deux Mondes*, compared *A Rebours* to a vaudeville.

With considerable acumen Jules Lemaître wrote of Huysmans,[1] soon after the publication of *A Rebours:* 'Penetrate to his inmost heart and you will find, first, a Fleming, much concerned with detail and with a lively feeling for the grotesque; then the most disgusted and bored and contemptuous of pessimists, an artist, in fact, who is very incomplete, but very determined, very conscious, and refined to the point of malady, the *détraqué* representative of the extreme tendencies of a literature nearing its end.'

The most penetrating criticism came from the pen of no less a person than Barbey d'Aurevilly himself, reviewing *A Rebours* in *Le Constitutionel*.[2] He began by ridiculing the toys that des Esseintes had played with: the battery of flavours, the paper flowers, the jewelled tortoise, and he continued: 'Des Esseintes is no longer a being organised in the same way as Obermann, René, Adolphe, those heroes of novels who are human, passionate, guilty. He is a piece of mechanism out of order. Nothing more . . . In writing the autobiography of his hero (Huysmans) makes the particular confession of a depraved and solitary personality, but at the same time he charts the symptoms of a society putrefied by materialism . . . Certainly, in order that a decadent of such power should be produced and that a book like that of M. Huysmans should germinate in a human head it was necessary that we should have become what in fact we are—a race which has reached its final hour.'

Barbey, of course, did not blame Huysmans for reflecting what he believed to be the universal decadence, or at least

[1] *Les Contemporains*, 1ʳᵉ série, 1886, pp. 312–317.
[2] 18th July, 1884. Reprinted in *Le Roman Contemporain*, Paris, 1902.

the *finis Latinorum*. Huysmans was, he believed, a great writer, and a Catholic writer, even if he was unaware of the fact. And he quotes the closing passage of *A Rebours*:

'Ah! courage fails me; I feel sick. Lord, have pity on the Christian who doubts, on the sceptic who would believe, on the prisoner of life who sets out alone, into the night, under a sky no longer lighted by the consoling lamps of the ancient hope.'

'Is this not', wrote Barbey, 'humble enough and submissive enough? It is more so even than the prayer of Baudelaire:

> "*Ah! Seigneur! donnez-moi la force et le courage*
> *De contempler mon cœur et mon corps sans dégoût!*"

Baudelaire, the satanic Baudelaire, who died a Christian, must have been one of M. Huysmans' admirations. One feels his presence, behind the most beautiful of the pages that M. Huysmans has written. Well, one day, I defied all Baudelaire's originality to recommence *Les Fleurs du Mal*, and to take one step further in the direction of blasphemy. Today, I am quite capable of offering the same challenge to the author of *A Rebours*. After *Les Fleurs du Mal*, I said to Baudelaire, "nothing logically remains for you but to choose between the muzzle of a revolver or the foot of the Cross"; but will the author of *A Rebours* make this choice?"

CHAPTER SIX

THE HAUNTED MAN

———————— • ————————

Huysmans, on the morrow of *A Rebours*, was very far from sharing Barbey d'Aurevilly's opinion. In the preface to a new edition published after his conversion, he says: 'I was not educated in clerical schools but in a lycée; I was never pious in my youth, and memories of childhood and of the first Communion which frequently play so large a part in a conversion, played no part in mine. And what complicates the difficulty still further and upsets all analysis, is that when I was writing *A Rebours* I never set foot in a church. I did not know any practising Catholic, or any priest; I felt no Divine hand guiding me towards the Church. I lived at my ease in my sty; it seemed to me quite natural to satisfy the impulses of my senses, and the thought that such adventures were forbidden never even entered my head.

'Between 1884, when *A Rebours* appeared, and 1892 when I left for La Trappe in order to be converted, nearly eight years elapsed before the seeds of this book sprouted; if we allow two years, or even three, for the work of Grace, muted, persistent, at times perceptible, there still remain not less than five years during which I do not remember having felt any Catholic impulse, any regret for the life I was leading, any desire to amend it.'

This is a precious testimony. Certain it is that in the years immediately following the publication of this, his first successful novel, Huysmans was far from happy. It was as if he were pursued by a demon, as if he were, in an almost literal sense, a haunted man.

Nor was he happy, in the other sense of the word, in his literary work. He does not seem to have realised that with *A Rebours* he had opened a new vein. He reverted to an earlier manner, the manner of straightforward Naturalism. It might be objected that he had never left it: that *A Rebours* is, after all, written in the same idiom; but the piquancy of that book lay precisely in the contrast between the detailed naturalistic descriptions and the fantastic nature of the hero. In *Un Dilemme* and *En Rade* he reverts to characters who have no interest in themselves.

The heroes, if the word be not an absurdity, of *Un Dilemme* are two frightful provincial bourgeois, one a lawyer and the other a politician, father and son. They are joint heirs of the son of the younger man who possessed a personal fortune from his mother. He has just died of typhoid fever, and has been nursed in his last hours by his mistress. They are determined that none of the money shall be hers, in spite of the fact that she is about to bear the dead man's child, and the novel, or rather *conte*, is concerned with their manœuvres to keep the fortune for themselves. Finally they present the unfortunate girl with a dilemma: either she was the servant of the deceased, in which case she will receive fifty francs as outstanding wages, or else she was his mistress, in which case she will receive nothing. She has no remedy, falls into despair and dies in child-bed. Such is the gloomy theme. It is the kind of thing that Maupassant did better, and it is one of the few really objective works by Huysmans in which it is impossible to identify the author with any of his characters.

En Rade has a more personal interest. A young Parisian has married, against the wishes of his family, a girl of a lower social stratum. The early years of their married life have been passed in Paris, fairly happily, for the wife is submissive and devoted and the husband is an intellectual who finds plenty to occupy his mind. He has, however, no powers of continuous concentration and passes from history to the classics, from theology to alchemy, losing interest in any subject as soon as he has skimmed the surface. He acquires in this way *une science énorme et chaotique*, rather similar in fact to Huysmans' own. But the neglect of his affairs soon brings him into financial difficulties, and to escape his creditors he takes refuge with his wife in an old ruined chateau in Normandy, the caretaker of which is the wife's uncle, an unimaginative and avaricious peasant.

As a piece of descriptive writing the evocation of the old chateau is a tour-de-force. The young couple find it in an almost unbelievable state of decay, the walls damp, the plaster crumbling, some of the rafters fallen in. There is only one habitable room, and here they make for themselves what comfort they can. Unfortunately the health of the young wife is very precarious. She suffers from the most terrible migraines. Both she and her husband are in a state of exasperated nervous tension, and what is worse, the husband begins to detect in her all the peasant characteristics which he both despises and detests.

All this has more than a little resemblance to Huysmans' own life at this time. In 1885 he spent some time at the Château de Lourps, which is, however, in the Brie district (*Seine et Marne*) and not in Normandy. He had with him a woman he has known for some time. She had two daughters and Huysmans acted as tutor to the elder. The name of the woman was Anna Meunier.

Now the authors of *Les Logis de Huysmans*[1] state categorically that A. Meunier was 'the very name of the muse of the

[1] M. C. Poinsot and G. V. Lange, *Les Logis de Huysmans*, Paris, 1920.

Rue du Dragon,' that is of the girl who had lived with Huysmans there when he was a student, before the War of 1870. He seems to have lost sight of her for some years, but they had certainly met again by 1879, in which year he dedicated *Les Sœurs Vâtard* to her as '*ma vieille amie*'. She was probably the only woman in his life for whom he felt more than a passing attraction.

She was three years younger than he, having been born at Metz in 1851. She was therefore no more than nineteen when she became Huysmans' mistress. She earned her living as a seamstress, a poor living as can well be imagined. It is not known who was the father of her two daughters. The elder, while still under age, married a medical practitioner and Huysmans is entered on the marriage certificate, as her guardian. The younger, who became a *danseuse* at the Opera, was still alive in 1927,[1] and remembered the holidays spent at the Château de Lourps in 1885 and 1886.

Anna Meunier was still with Huysmans in 1888, when Gustave Guiches found her presiding over the Sunday dinners at No. 11, Rue de Sèvres, and he draws a vivid portrait of her in the volume of his literary souvenirs which he entitled *Le Banquet*.

'From the depth of the dining room an imploring voice called out: "Georges! He hasn't come and the joint will be overdone, as usual!"'

'The soft and plaintive voice preceded the apparition of a young woman at the door of the study. She was, at most, thirty-five years old.[2] Neither her appearance nor her silhouette revealed her social class: she was not a workgirl and yet not quite a *bourgeoise*. She was dressed with simple taste not without a certain *coquetterie* which her instinct would

[1] J. K. Huysmans, *En Marge, Etudes et Préfaces réunies et annotées par Lucien Descaves*. Paris (1927), p. 61.
[2] Actually, thirty-seven.

have turned into elegance, if a visible lassitude had not discouraged it. An interior malady had attacked her youth, which no longer fought back. She was tall and good-looking, under a mass of blonde hair. But her eyes were of so pale a blue, her lips so discoloured, her complexion so dead that with its languishing white and faded gold, her face had the faltering grace of a broken and dying lily.

'Huysmans introduced me. She held out her hand saying, "Bonjour, monsieur." But when I pressed it to my lips, she drew it back so quickly that her friend, smiling with embarrassment said, "She is not used to it." She pulled herself together and said to him, plaintively: "I have the migraine—for a change."

'As usual!—for a change! What an involuntary and tragic refrain! . . .

'After the coffee, we tasted, amid the cigarette smoke, that Dutch "Schiedam" which reminds one of dust and oriental raki, and the taste of which gives to the tongue, said Huysmans, the sensation of licking a newly-painted panel.

'I watched her getting up so slowly, coming and going with so much indolence, sitting down again with so much languor, that white and gold silhouette which seemed like the sweet phantom of a dead joy. I saw that she was suffering, and I watched Huysmans who, out of the corner of his eye, saw it too. I heard, at intervals, the name so faintly spoken, that it seemed to come from very far away: "Georges!" She called him Georges instead of Joris . . .'

This itself would have been enough to show that she had known him before his literary success. It had been Georges in the Rue du Dragon, and it was Georges still. Shortly after the meeting described by Gustave Guiches her mind became clouded. She seems to have ceased to share Huysmans' apartment, for she was living in the Rue Monge when, in 1893, she was removed to a mental asylum. Huysmans visited her there from time to time and, when he was unable to go, sent his housekeeper *la mère Giraud*. Anna Meunier died in the asylum in February 1895.

Perhaps it was the state of her health which prevented him from marrying her and setting up a permanent establishment. Certainly in 1885 he thought enough of her to put her name to the article which he wrote about himself and published in *Les Hommes d'Aujourd'hui*.[1] This takes the form of an alleged interview of Huysmans by 'A. Meunier', and the imaginary interviewer proves himself (as why should he not?) a penetrating as well as a kindly critic.

Asked if he, who had been considered one of the most fanatical sectaries of *Naturalisme*, still thought of himself as fighting under the same banner, he replied: 'I describe what I see, and live through, and feel, as well as I can. If that is to be a *Naturaliste*, so much the better. At bottom, there are writers who have talent and writers who haven't, whether you call them *Naturalistes, Romantics* or *Decadents*.' As for himself he was a curious mixture of a refined Parisian and a Dutch genre-painter. If one added a touch of grim humour *et de comique rêche anglais*,[2] that was the recipe of his works. As for his style, some of his pages were 'of a magnificence without equal' (there are certain advantages in interviewing oneself), and in particular the chapter on Gustave Moreau in *A Rebours* was justly celebrated.

He had also great powers of psychological analysis. He had explored remote corners of the soul with a learned lucidity never attempted before. His claim to have taken over from Baudelaire the 'prose poem' and in *Croquis Parisiens* to have renovated and rejuvenated it will be less easily accepted. As

---

[1] *Les Hommes d'Aujourdhui*, Paris, 1885.

[2] Huysmans always claimed to be a humorist *in the English manner*. He was presumably thinking of Hogarth and Gillray. He admired Dickens, but Dickensian humour was scarcely his forte.

for his art criticism he had accorded his rightful place to Degas, made Raffaëlli known, and had explained and launched Odilon Redon. Quite rightly he did not claim, as some of his admirers have done, that he had 'launched' Moreau.

But however high one might place Huysmans among the real writers of a century which can boast so few (!) one must consider him, says the interviewer, as a creature of exception, a writer at once bizarre and ailing, capricious and daring, an artist to the tips of his fingers, 'dragging the image (in the words of Léon Bloy) by the hair or by the feet down the worm-eaten staircase of terrified syntax'.

Huysmans takes the opportunity of describing his own physical appearance. 'He had the effect on me of a well-behaved cat, very polite, almost amiable, but nervous, ready to unsheath his claws at the least word. Dry, thin, going grey, the face expressive, the manner worried, that was my first impression.' He was himself the sharp misanthropist, the nervous anaemic of his own books, and their great fault was to display always the same character, whether he was called Cyprien, André, Folantin or des Esseintes. And, quite evidently, that character was Huysmans. His sardonic, *crispé* face appeared as one turned each page. 'And the constant intrusion of a personality, however interesting, diminishes the greatness of a work and wearies in the end by the invariability.' As a piece of penetrating self-criticism the whole article is a tour-de-force.

'You do not see much of men of letters, I believe?' says the interviewer.

'The least possible,' replies Huysmans. 'I got tired of their perpetual complaints against their publishers and their chatter about royalties. I am very well pleased not to have to listen to the same thing over and over again.'

Once he had broken with, or rather drifted from, the Zola circle, Huysmans had few literary friends. There were, however, a few who did not fall into his general detestation of the scribbling tribe and chief among these were Mallarmé and Villiers de l'Isle-Adam.

The two men were very different in circumstances and temperament and appealed to Huysmans for different reasons. Stéphane Mallarmé was a man rather like himself. He lived very quietly on a small regular income as professor of English in a French college. He never expected his writings to reach a large public, he was content with self-expression, not in the Huysmans sense of expounding his personal crises, but in the search for a new æsthetics, a new use of language. His famous '*L'Après-midi d'un faune* had appeared in 1876, and his Tuesday evening receptions formed a rallying point for some of the most interesting of young French writers. Huysmans had a high regard for his intellectual integrity and, different as their methods were, found something common in their modes of thought. It is curious that Arthur Symons should remark that there are pieces of Mallarmé's, both prose and verse, 'which have the haunting quality of Gustave Moreau's pictures, with the same jewelled magnificence, mysterious and yet definite.' Huysmans, as we have seen, was, at this period of his life, obsessed by Moreau.

Huysmans' other friend, Villiers de l'Isle-Adam, is one of the most enigmatic figures in French literature. In his lifetime he had no success at all, if success is to be measured by any standard of monetary reward. His work was appreciated by an *élite* for its force and originality, but the general public and most of the critics regarded him as a *farceur*, if not a madman. His revenge was to cultivate the legend of his own eccentricity, and to wrap himself in the cloak of a 'proud and disdainful poverty'. He became famous for his mordant wit and his shafts were justly dreaded, for he did not suffer fools gladly. Few but his intimate friends knew of the sorrows, and the heroisms, of his private life.

The Haunted Man

Philippe Auguste Mathias, Comte de Villiers de l'Isle-Adam, was born at St. Brieux in Brittany, in 1840. His *noblesse* was authentic; his family could trace its descent back to the eleventh century, and had intermarried with all the great French houses. One of its members had been the actual founder of the Knights of Malta, another had been a Marshal of France.

The family was ruined by the French Revolution and when the poet's grandfather returned to his native land early in the nineteenth century, he found himself a poor man. The poet's father refused to accept any government employment after the fall of Charles X. He spent his life in a series of the most extravagant projects in the hope of redeeming the family fortunes. It is perhaps no accident that his son was haunted all his life by the idea of buried treasure, but, being a poet, he did not even try to make his dreams come true.

He worked for a bewildering variety of journals and to them contributed the *Contes Cruels* on which his fame chiefly rests. He wrote plays and had one or two of them produced, but they were received by the critics with hilarious contempt. The public preferred the worldly wisdom of Dumas *fils* to Villiers' idealism *à l'outrance*. Worldly wisdom indeed was not his climate. He preferred what he himself called 'the light of dreams' to the 'darkness of common sense'.

His early poems were written under the influence of Chateaubriand, although to say so is perhaps to state the obvious and the inevitable. Indeed there is not much exaggeration in claiming, as Rémy de Gourmont does in his essay on Huysmans,[1] that 'all modern poetry, and by poetry I mean all works of imagination, derive from Chateaubriand. . . . He formed Victor Hugo as well as Flaubert; Taine as well as Michelet; George Sand acted the part of René all her life, and one of our last great writers, Villiers de l'Isle-

[1] Rémy de Gourmont, *Promenades Littéraires I*, Paris, 1919, p. 25.

Adam, born of the same earth as the author of *Mémoires d'Outre-tombe*, felt his literary domination profoundly. One thinks of one of the most recent best-sellers, *Quo Vadis?* What is this novel but a modern transposition of *Les Martyrs* adroitly made accessible to the vast ignorant public? What is *L'Oblat*, what is *La Cathédrale* but the amplification of a few chapters of *Le Génie du Christianisme?* Between the eighteenth and the nineteenth century stands Chateaubriand; to pass from one to the other, it is necessary to cross his garden.'

Rémy de Gourmont links Huysmans and Villiers de l'Isle-Adam as common children of Chateaubriand, but this must have been far from obvious to either of them when the two men first met in 1876. Their first reactions to one another were not favourable when they were brought together by chance in the *bureau* of *La République des Lettres*, the literary review conducted by Catulle Mendès. In the words of Villiers' biographer,[1] 'they mutually scared one another by their outward semblance, not realising what they had in common in the psychic and intellectual sphere.' Until 1884 they were acquaintances and no more, for Villiers was a true Bohemian, living from hand to mouth, and Huysmans was a punctual if reluctant Government official.

Then appeared *A Rebours*, in which Villiers, desperate in his poverty and lack of recognition, saw with gratitude that Huysmans had devoted to him a long passage of appreciation, the more remarkable in that Villiers' two major works *L'Éve Future* and *Axel* were yet unpublished. Des Esseintes (that is, Huysmans himself) expresses the greatest admiration for Villiers' *Contes*, for their hallucinatory power as well as their bitter irony, and when he has an anthology of his favourite pieces privately printed, he includes in it the story called

[1] R. du Pontavice de Heussey, *Villiers de l'Isle-Adam*, Paris, 1893, p. 270.

Vox Populi, a piece stamped like a golden medal with the effigy of Leconte de Lisle and Flaubert.

Even the proud, shy Villiers could hardly fail to respond to such a tribute; the two men became friends, and nothing reflects more credit on Huysmans than the trouble he took to save Villiers from himself, and to help him in every way. Unfortunately their friendship came too late; Villiers was already a dying man, worn out by his vagabond life, his late hours, his lack of proper food, and also by the grandiose visions of his own imagination, his perpetual state of cerebral excitement.

In 1885 another burden fell upon him. His father, the Marquis Joseph de Villiers de l'Isle-Adam died, fortified by the rites of the Church and leaving to his son, as he fondly imagined, a fortune 'equal to that of the most princely houses of the world'. In reality Villiers had spent almost his last penny in comforts for the dying man, and when he was dead, made over to the Society of Dramatic Authors his own royalties in order to pay his father's debts.

Until then he had lived in furnished lodgings; now, for economy, he rented a small unfurnished apartment where he installed a few pieces of family furniture. These included a piano, for he was an excellent musician, and passionately devoted to Wagner. He saw only a few friends: Madame Méry Laurent, Nina de Villars, Mallarmé and Huysmans. Madame Méry Laurent was his good angel, doing him many kindnesses. Nina de Villars was a literary hostess who liked to receive authors and provided for them, according to the rather malicious account of Gustave Guiches,[1] 'an unheard of profusion of tins of sardines and mediocre *hors-d'œuvre* destined to distract the attention of their stomachs from the absence of roast meat.'

[1] Gustave Guiches, *Villiers de l'Isle-Adam*, '*Le Figaro*', *supplement littéraire*. 31st August, 1889.

Here, or elsewhere (anywhere, in fact, even at a café table), Villiers would declaim his works and those of others, occasionally with ironic intention. Sometimes it seemed as if he were composing aloud, and as if, unaware of his audience, he spoke from the depths of the unconscious, pursuing an idea and a vision, clothing the most extraordinary images in words which seemed inspired. He wrote voluminously but what he wrote is only a fragment of what he thought and spoke. Huysmans must often have heard him improvising in this fashion, and the very contrast with his own manner of going to work (as of a civil servant compiling a dossier) must have increased the prestige of Villiers in his eyes.

He was attracted also by his complete disinterestedness, his hatred of modernity and all its works, his savage irony against the complacency of the mediocre, his macabre humour. Huysmans was never Villiers' disciple (he had already advanced too far on the road of his own development) but he was certainly his friend.

Early in 1889 Villiers, who was working furiously to complete his drama *Axel*, felt the first symptoms of the malady which was to destroy him. He left Paris and lived for a while at Fontenay-sous-Bois (Fontenay, the imaginary refuge of des Esseintes! Was it Huysmans who suggested it?) but soon left it for Nogent-sur-Marne. His condition grew worse and the doctors diagnosed cancer of the stomach. Huysmans managed to have him taken in by the *Religieux Hospitaliers de Saint-Jean de Dieu*, at their Hospice in the Rue Oudinot in Paris, and spared no pains to notify Villiers' friends of his condition. He wrote to distant relatives in Brittany to try to collect some money for the treatment. He invoked the aid of Mallarmé and François Coppée, he interested the editor of *Le Figaro* and the *Société des Auteurs Dramatiques*. And he busied himself with tact and efficiency to arrange what was both a delicate and pressing affair.

This was nothing less than Villiers' marriage to the woman with whom he had been living and by whom he had had a son; and in his efforts to bring it about Huysmans showed a side of his character which would scarcely be suspected from his writings. It was not that, at this period, he cared two straws about the institution of marriage; it was for the simple and human reason that the mother of Villiers' child could not, as his mistress, enter the hospice; as his wife she could. By the kind complicity of one of the Franciscan Fathers she was married to him at his bedside and was with him when he died.

During the night of 19th August, 1889, he passed peacefully away. Mallarmé and Huysmans arranged the funeral which was not without its simple grandeur. It is true that the hearse was of the kind that the Parisian undertakers designate 'sixth class', but it bore on its side an escutcheon of the dead man's arms, the same as those borne by the long-dead ancestor who had been Grand Prior of the Order of Malta. In the procession walked a long file of the notabilities of letters and the arts: Mallarmé, Coquelin Cadet, Leconte de Lisle, Paul Alexis, Paul Hervieu, Henri Lavedan, Fleury, Huysmans. 'No one', said the orator at the grave-side, 'had believed more firmly than he in the creative magic of words, written or spoken, in their mysterious harmony, in the omnipotence of human speech; the joy of embodying in some noble phrase a profound or subtle idea, a poignant or rare sensation, was sufficient to make him forget the daily, sterile cruelty of his hard life.'

Villiers left an immense mass of manuscripts behind him, with the proviso that those which could be recovered and pieced together should be published under the direction of Huysmans and Mallarmé. The most important of the unpublished writings was *Axel*, unfinished or, at least, unrevised. It is, as the world now knows, an extraordinary work. Villiers had died a good Catholic; Catholicism indeed was part of his tradition, of his *fierté de gentilhomme*, and he would have indignantly denied any suggestion that he had ever departed from it, in his faith, whatever he had done in his life. Yet *Axel* is very far from being a Catholic work.

It is true that Villiers hoped to revise it, to change the end. In the text, as it stands, the two lovers, Axel and the mysterious Sara, find the world at their feet and kill themselves rather than risk the realisation of their dreams. The Christian solution would have been renunciation, not suicide, but it is hard to see how Villiers could have adopted it without making nonsense of the whole work. There was never written a more proudly Satanic line than the famous:

'Live? Our servants can do that for us!'

The whole work is the supreme cry of romantic idealism pushed to its last excess. To think of it as, in any way, a picture of 'real life' is to mistake its meaning altogether. Villiers meant something much more recondite and profound. He had rediscovered, by intuition, the secret that was known to the troubadours, that 'romantic love' is a concealed death wish. The great lovers (how the phrase has been cheapened!) do not even desire their consummation on this earth. For Tristan and Isolde (and Villiers' characters are equally symbolic and remote) there can be no 'happy ending'.

Axel is heretical in its bones, in its very structure, and its heresy is the heresy of the Cathars, those same Albigensians that the Church, in the thirteenth century, exterminated with fire and sword. 'Most troubadours were heretics,' says Otto Rahn, and 'every Cathar was a troubadour'![1] And though the Provençal civilisation was ruined, its seed was scattered abroad, and from it sprang the whole mighty harvest that we call Romanticism.

[1] Denis de Rougemont, *Passion and Society*, trans. by Montgomery Belgion, London, 1940. The original French title is *L'Amour et l'Occident*.

Axel is a profoundly disturbing work for any reader capable of understanding its implications. Huysmans, as one of Villiers' literary executors, could hardly have avoided studying it closely and it must have contributed, at this time, to the turbulence of his thoughts. It is in vain that the biographer of Villiers[1] protests that *Axel* was written by a Catholic immersed—oh! quite theoretically!—in the secret sciences. *Axel* is an occultist work; certain passages in it could only have been written by 'an initiate, deeply versed', and it must have helped to push Huysmans into the path he was shortly to follow, although it is true that his occultism was of a different and much lower kind. There is a nobility about Villiers de l'Isle-Adam, even at his most extravagant, which Huysmans never attained, perhaps never even wished to attain. Nevertheless, *Axel* opened vistas; it suggested new trains of thought, and if some of them led downwards into the abysses of the human soul, that made them, at this period of Huysmans' life, only the more attractive.

He was, as we noted at the beginning of the chapter, a haunted man. Sex had become for him not an occasional impulse but a constant obsession. The *crise juponnière*, the skirt-fever, which he had so well described in *En Ménage*, had been replaced by a veritable *hantise de la femme*. He suffered from the most frightful nightmares, one of which is described, under the title *Cauchemar*, in *Croquis Parisiens*. The pictures of Moreau and Odilon Redon coalesced in his imagination and presented themselves in his dreams. Amid scenes of oriental splendour, strange, venomous flowers floated in the air and transformed themselves into human faces, faces of creatures without hope. The dreamer wandered through underground caverns, through vaulted reservoirs containing a vast expanse of standing water, a subterranean Dead Sea. Strange suns emerged from the

[1] E. de Rougemont, *Villiers de l'Isle-Adam*, Paris, 1910, p. 346.

darkness, eyes peered at him; the landscape was a landscape of the moon. And once again the flower, springing from the white soil of the desolate planet and in the middle of the flower, a human face, smiling a fearful and ironic smile. *Cauchemar* is one of Huysmans' most extraordinary and evocative pieces of writing. There is nothing like it in literature except the opium dream of De Quincy.

He tried to rationalize his obsession by writing a critical account of the work of the Belgian artist Félicien Rops. In later days he was to maintain that what he sought in Rops was chiefly a 'mine of phrases'. That he certainly found, but what drove him to Rops was a desperate need to bring some order into his ideas, to justify his neurosis, if only to himself.

The sight of an erotic work, he declares, by an artist of real talent, leads to obscure descents into the depths of souls. Far from an interest in the nudities which he once found a melancholy pleasure in contemplating, now he thinks of their creators and asks himself what impulses, what feelings they obey, when they execute such works. Debauchery cannot be the end, for debauchery is an end in itself and makes the creation of works of art impossible; and after a glance at English hypocrisy (an article of faith with every Frenchman) which conceals who knows what infantile passion for violation (!), he concludes that it is only the chaste who can be really obscene.

He is certainly speaking for himself when he declares that it is the artists, impure or not, whose nerves are stretched to breaking point, who have to submit to the continual and unsupportable attacks of Lust. He is not talking of the mere act of fornication which he characteristically calls *malpropre*, but of the Spirit of Lust, isolated erotic ideas, without any material issue, without any need of a physical consequence which would satisfy them. Almost always, he says, the scene dreamed of is the same; images arise, nudities offer

themselves;—and, suddenly, the natural act is put aside, as
having no interest, as too short, as providing no more than an
anticipated commotion, a banal cry—and suddenly there is a
bound towards the extranatural of lubricity, a leap beyond
the orgasm. The soul's infamy is increased, if you like, but it
is ennobled by the thought of superhuman faults, sins which
one would have entirely new.

This is special pleading indeed; but however 'ennobling'
such practices might be, Huysmans was not unaware of their
danger. This spiritualising of filthiness, he says, involves a
real loss of phosphorus from the brain and makes for physical
impotence. Science calls it cerebral erethism, and if the condition persists and grows worse to the point of deranging the
organism, she pronounces the word 'mental hysteria'. Was
this what Baudelaire was thinking of when he said: '*J'ai
cultivé mon hystérie avec jouissance et terreur*'?

Reason as he would, and find what excuses he might,
Huysmans was now in the grip of this disorder of the mind,
this malady of the soul. He had thought to escape from the
sordidness of life, from the down-to-earth preoccupations of
Naturalisme, by a kind of mystique of beauty. He was almost
the inventor of the doctrine of Art for Art's sake. But Art for
Art's sake inevitably becomes Sensation for Sensation's sake,
and the penalty of aesthetic mysticism is that it must always
be pushing the search for sensation further. It seeks always
the more acute, the more *pimenté*. It must go on adding
condiments until the tongue is scorched.

And if such condiments cannot be found, then the sensibility must be heightened, and its area extended. Drugs are
known to promote the former, at least for a time; and there
are certain practices of which Huysmans must have heard
which claim to effect the latter. They are grouped under the
generic name of Magic.

Huysmans had said goodbye to materialism when he broke

with Zola. His unconscious mind was open to every invasion. Already he complained of *attouchements*, touches by unseen hands, cold fingers laid upon his forehead.[1] He had been attacked, he believed, by a succubus, the female demon of the erotic dream. The road was plain before him and he could not but follow it, even if it led, through the mire of occultism, to Sadism and Sacrilege.

[1] *The Goncourt Journal*, VIII, 1889–91, pp. 219, 220.

CHAPTER SEVEN

LÀ-BAS

———————————————●———————————————

The opening chapter of *Là-bas* is the reflection of a debate which had been going on for some time in Huysmans' mind. For the purposes of the argument he divides himself into two characters. One he calls Durtal, a name he had found in the railway time-table and which was to remain that of his central personage for the rest of his literary career. The other character he calls des Hermies. Ultimately, they coalesce and des Hermies vanishes *as a character*, because Durtal re-absorbs him. Perhaps it would be truer to say that des Hermies re-absorbs Durtal, for it is des Hermies' point of view that prevails.

Durtal is a novelist who is growing increasingly tired of the narrow range of subjects offered to him by Naturalism in literature. Leaving the worn-out subjects of adultery, love and ambition, he is thinking of writing a book about Blue-beard, the extraordinary character who is known to history as Gilles de Rais. Des Hermies approves this decision, and then launches a frontal attack on the whole doctrine of Naturalism. He does not blame it for its language, its vocabulary of the latrine and the hospital. He admits that it has produced powerful works like Zola's *L'Assommoir*. His reproach is based not on the clumsiness of its style but on the baseness of its ideas. Materialism in literature! Democracy in art! 'Say what you will,' he cries. 'What a miserable cerebral theory, what a wretched and narrow system! To try to confine oneself to the impulses of the flesh, to reject the suprasensible, to deny the dream, not even to understand that the curiosity of art begins at the point where the senses cease to serve!'

Its psychology is elementary. It has no light to throw on the motives of human actions except to attribute them to appetites or instincts. It diagnoses 'sex' or 'madness' and thinks it has explained the human heart. And not only is it inexpert and obtuse but its subject matter is the atrocious life of modern times. It has exalted the new 'Americanism' of manners, and ended in the praise of brute force and the apotheosis of the strong-box. By a prodigy of humility it has accepted the taste of the crowd, repudiated style, rejected all high thought, and every impulse towards the supernatural and the beyond.

Durtal, or that part of Huysmans which was still not completely convinced, replies that the great service which Naturalism had rendered to literature was to sweep away all the absurd marionettes of Romanticism, to create real people, visible and palpable and properly placed in their surroundings. Also it had helped in the development of language.

When des Hermies cries that the Naturalists had loved the century they lived in and that was enough to condemn them, Durtal replies that neither Flaubert nor the Goncourts had done so. Des Hermies admits that these men were honest, seditious (the word is curious and revealing) and high-minded artists. He has even a good word to say for Zola as a grand landscape painter and a handler of masses. Fortunately his books were better than his theories.

So the debate continues and when des Hermies takes his leave, Durtal is visibly shaken. But if he is to abandon Naturalism, which has been his doctrine ever since he began to write, what remains? Is he to return to the nonsense of the

Romantics or to join the ranks of the sentimental best-sellers, like Cherbuliez and Octave Feuillet?

What he must do, he decides, is to keep the documentary veracity, the detailed precision, the living language of Naturalism and at the same time to escape from the narrowness of its ideas; not to be content to explain everything in physiological terms; in a word, to produce a spiritualist Naturalism. He must recognise the need of the supernatural and, if he could not find it in more elevated ideas, he must look for it in spiritism[1] and the occult.

Durtal, or rather Huysmans, was already making experiments in this direction. It so happened that there was in the Ministry of War, of which Huysmans himself had once been a member, a certain *chef de bureau* named François. He was, according to some accounts, a professional magnetizer and according to others, a medium of extraordinary powers. He was also, with Papus, of whom we shall have much to say later, one of the founders of the Martinist Lodge in the rue de Trévise. Huysmans invited him to his house and there took part in several séances, which convinced him of the existence of the spirit world. Huysmans, speaking through the mouth of Durtal, declares that he had been present at spiritualistic experiences where no trickery was possible. Raps on the table expressed messages in English, a language known to no one present, and spoke to Huysmans of secrets of his own life, of which no one else could have had any knowledge.

Perhaps such remarks indicate a certain naïvety in Huysmans' approach to the problem, but he also claims that he saw apparitions, materialisations formed by the fluid of the medium combined with the fluid of the persons present. He was ready to admit the existence of elementals, or spirits of the dead. It was perhaps characteristic of Huysmans that he

[1] It is a pity that the English word for '*spiritisme*' is spiritualism; it leads to an unfortunate confusion.

came to the conclusion that all spirits who made themselves manifest at spiritualistic séances were necessarily evil. They had the power not only to cause raps on tables but to move objects and produce other phenomena, and also to enter into possession of human souls. It seemed to Huysmans quite obvious that they did so, and from such a belief it is but a step to Satanism.

In the novel Durtal is the enquirer, des Hermies the source of information. They meet from time to time in the Salon of a certain Catholic historian named Chantelouve who, ambitious for both literary fame and ecclesiastical patronage, likes to invite to his house both priests and men of letters. He has a wife, bizarre rather than beautiful, who fulfils her duties as a hostess like a self-possessed woman of the world, although from time to time there is a look in her eyes which seems to suggest that behind her placid façade is something more mysterious and even sinister.

Durtal and des Hermies take a fancy to one another (which was natural enough seeing that they were really the same person) and des Hermies carries Durtal off to see some other friends of his named Carhaix. Carhaix is the bell-ringer at St. Sulpice, and he and his wife have an apartment high up in one of the great towers. Here, in spite of his poverty, he loves to entertain a few chosen friends. He is a man of some erudition, having once studied for the priesthood, and both Durtal and des Hermies find in him a kindred spirit.[1]

While Madame Carhaix is producing an excellent repast, the conversation of the three men turns to Satanism, the historical existence of which is, of course, not denied. Durtal could certainly not deny that it had been practised by Gilles de Rais in the fifteenth century. In the sixteenth century Catherine de' Medici was deeply engaged; the writings of

---

[1] Carhaix was not a real person. The actual bell-ringer at St. Sulpice was a man of a very different calibre who detested Huysmans.

Sprenger and Lancre are filled with details of the diabolism of their time. In the seventeenth the Black Mass was common; the famous Abbé Guibourg made quite a speciality of celebrating it, using as his altar the naked body of a woman. No less a person than Madame de Montespan is said to have played this part in such rites, rites in which the blood of a murdered child and the sperm of the officiating priest were mingled with the Elements.

But, objects Durtal, all this is in the past. No one nowadays murders children in order to use their blood for such a purpose. Perhaps not, admits the bell-ringer, but this is not absolutely necessary. The essential part of a Black Mass is to use a real Host for infamous purposes, and if no real priest can be found to operate the miracle of transubstantiation on the spot, the host can be stolen. There existed in Paris, in 1855, a number of women who made a practice of communicating every day, or even several times a day in different churches. They did not swallow the wafer which was placed in their mouth, but spat it out as soon as they could safely do so, and sold it to the Satanists.

This was not the only method of procedure. In the preface which he was later to write for Jules Bois' *Le Satanisme et la Magie*, Huysmans gives a whole list of recent thefts from churches in Paris and in the French Provinces, the object of which was plainly not the value of the vessel in which the Host was contained—such vessels being for the most part of little value—but the Host itself. No less than fifty consecrated Hosts had been stolen from Notre Dame itself. Thirteen churches in the diocese of Orleans had been robbed in the same manner, and at Lyons the theft of the consecrated Host had become so frequent that special precautions had to be taken to protect the Tabernacle; and not in France only were such depredations committed. They occurred even in the Monastery of Our Lady of the Seven Sorrows in Rome. What could be the object of all these thefts? There was only one answer—the wafers were destined for use in a Black Mass.

Once Huysmans was convinced of the existence of such Masses, his natural curiosity and his probity as a writer of the documentary school—for such he remained even after he had broken with Zola—led him to make every effort to be present at one himself. He had not far to look. In the very street in which he himself lived, the rue de Sèvres, there was a chapel in which the Black Mass was celebrated, and the report which he gave of the ceremony ensured the success of *Là-bas*. How did he succeed in obtaining admission?

In the book Durtal is still wondering how to pursue his researches when he receives a mysterious letter. He is in his study working on his projected book about Gilles de Rais when the concierge knocks at his door and hands him a missive 'smelling discreetly of heliotrope'. He opens it and reads:

'Monsieur,

I am neither an adventuress nor a woman of intelligence who can make herself drunk with conversation as others do with liquor. Neither am I one who is on the look out for adventures, still less a vulgarian curious to know if an author resembles his work. Nothing in fact that you might suppose. The truth is that I have just read your last novel, painful as the struggles of an imprisoned soul. And now, Monsieur, although I think it is infallibly foolish to try to realise a desire, would you allow one of your sisters in weariness to meet you, one evening, at any place you suggest. After which we shall each of us return to our homes . . . Adieur, Monsieur; rest assured that I hold you for someone of importance in this century of worn ha'pence. Not knowing if this letter will receive a reply, I abstain from making myself known. This evening my maid will call on your concierge to ask if there is a reply for Madame Maubel.'

Durtal is much intrigued by this letter and without meeting the mysterious lady allows himself to be drawn into a correspondence. He learns that she is married to some man he knows, that her Christian name begins with an M, and the unknown begins to excite his imagination to such a degree that he feels obliged to visit a prostitute in order to be rid of his obsession. In this, however, he fails and suddenly a chance remark of des Hermies makes him realise that the writer of the letters is none other than Madame Chantelouve.

At first he is rather put out by this, for Hyacinthe Chantelouve, as he has already remarked, was 'rather bizarre than beautiful'. But soon she possesses his imagination completely, so that 'both brain and senses are at white heat'. Her image follows him everywhere, even when he is immersed in the documentation for his book. A description of a fifteenth-century dress, and lo! Madame Chantelouve is suddenly inside it. He tries to push the vision away, to think of other things. There is a ring at the door. He opens it. Madame Chantelouve stands before him.

For the brilliantly observed scene which follows the reader is referred to the novel itself. It is enough for our purposes to note that the lady, after lamenting that a man and a woman could not be 'just friends', promises to return to Durtal's lodging at nine o'clock 'on the day after tomorrow'.

Huysmans certainly knew how to keep his readers' curiosity awake. He purposely puts off the assignation to the day after tomorrow, and Durtal employs the intervening day not only in thinking about his prospective conquest, but in dining once more with Carhaix and des Hermies. This gives the author the chance to introduce yet another character: the astrologer Gévingey.

Now Gévingey was a real person, according to Jules Bois,[1] although the account he gives of him is tantalisingly vague.

[1] Jules Bois, *Le Monde Invisible*, Paris (1902), p. 281.

'Certain indiscretions,' he says, 'permitted me to believe that Gévingey existed in flesh and blood. Thus I came to discover the last confidant of the stars in the Place de l'Odéon, above (oh, irony!) the Café Voltaire. Nothing eccentric about him. An elderly Faust. No black dog, no owl, no pentagram. Following Baudelaire's precept that astrologers should live in the top storey, his chamber was on the fourth floor . . . an austere room with some books, casts, a few skulls, perhaps a skeleton. His eyes were of an unexpected clairvoyance.'

Real or not, his purpose in the book is to give variety to the discussions between Durtal and des Hermies and to provide yet further information about occultism in all its branches. After dealing learnedly with astrology Gévingey turns to the evocation of spirits and makes the excellent remark that modern Spiritism has inaugurated as great a revolution as that effected in material things by the events of 1789. It has 'democratised evocation'.

Then follows a long discussion on the incubus, and its feminine counterpart the succubus, with some anatomical details which reveal Huysmans' determination to carry the methods of Naturalism into the world of spirits. And suddenly we hear for the first time of Dr. Johannès, 'the most powerful exorcist of our time' who, it seems, had been able to succour several nuns who were troubled day and night by the attacks of demon-lovers. He had also saved Gévingey himself:

' "I slept one night in the room which had been lived in by the most redoubtable master that Satanism possesses . . ."'

' "Canon Docre," interrupted des Hermies.

' "Yes, and I could not sleep, it was daylight, and I swear to you that the succubus came, exciting, palpable, tenacious. Luckily I remembered the formulae of deliverance. At all events, I ran, the same day, to Dr. Johannès who delivered me, once for all, I hope, from the enchantment." '

Durtal feels constrained to ask what the demon was like.

'Like any naked woman,' replies Gévingey. Durtal then
wants to know more about Canon Docre, and he is told that
he lives near Nîmes, that he evokes the Devil, that he feeds
white mice with the consecrated Host, and that his appetite
for sacrilege is such that he has had the image of the Cross
tattooed on the soles of his feet so that he can always tread
the Saviour underfoot. But if Durtal wanted to know more
about him he had only to ask Chantelouve for he and his wife
had at one time seen much of him.

So we are brought back to Madame Chantelouve and the
reader is left to wonder at the skill with which the practised
novelist has managed the transition and at the same time
insinuated that there is something satanic about the lady,
that she is indeed a kind of succubus herself.

Succubus or no, it is not until the fourth rendez-vous that
she becomes Durtal's mistress, and hardly has she done so
before Durtal, the incurable *littérateur*, is trying to pump her
about Canon Docre. Madame Chantelouve agrees that she
had known him and even that he had once been her confessor. She refuses, however, to put Durtal in touch with him.
'You will have to procure your information about Satanism
in some other way.'

That other way she herself suggests. After some contemptuous remarks about the beginners in Satanism who call
themselves the Society of the Rose-Cross, she promises to
take him to see a Black Mass. When the day comes he finds
himself with her in a cab travelling along the Rue de
Vaugirard. It turns off into a side street, a cul-de-sac. They
get out in front of a small door in a blank wall. Madame
Chantelouve rings, the door opens, and after crossing a
garden and a courtyard they enter an old house in which is a
chapel. There are some men there and more women. A
choirboy clad in red lights the candles, and by their light
Durtal sees a crucifix. But the figure on the cross has a satanic

leer. It is completely naked and *en rut*. Soon the ceremony begins, the officiant being Docre himself.

His chasuble bears the image of a black goat, and, underneath it, he is naked. He intones a kind of litany, but a litany of insults and blasphemies. What else he does had better perhaps be left in the original French:

'*Il titubait entre les deux enfants de chœur qui, relevant le chasuble, montrèrent son ventre nu, le tinrent, tandis que l'hostie, qu'il ramenait devant lui, sautait, atteinte et souillée, sur les planches.*'

Then a wild hysteria seizes on all present, and an orgy begins. Durtal drags Madame Chantelouve from the accursed place. Exhausted, they take refuge in a café near at hand, but the *patron* refuses to let them refresh themselves in the ordinary public room. They are too conspicuously elegant. He offers them a room upstairs. Durtal is horrified. The last thing he wants at that moment is to go to bed with Hyacinthe Chantelouve. But she throws off her clothes and draws him to her. Suddenly he sees that the bed is sprinkled with fragments of the Host!

Is this all 'literature'? Did Huysmans himself have a similar adventure? Had he really been present at such a Mass? The question has never been completely cleared up. When asked after his conversion he replied, 'Durtal confesses as much in *En Route*.' Rémy de Gourmont was sceptical and declared that Huysmans' description was based on accounts of the Black Mass of the Abbé Guibourg in the seventeenth century. However, there is some evidence that Black Masses were said at this period. An account of one appeared in *Le Matin* in May 1899. It was said to have taken place in the Saint-Sulpice Quarter. The journalist, according to his own account, having written an article in which he had declared his scepticism as to the existence of Black Masses, had received an invitation to attend one. His eyes blindfolded, he had been conducted to the place, found a dark room with erotic paintings on the walls, and some fifty people, men and women, assembled. On an altar, surrounded by six black candles, was a goat trampling a Crucifix. A priest appeared in red robes; the congregation chanted hymns. A woman stretched her body on the altar, and after the Consecration, fragments of black Hosts had been distributed to those present. The ceremony had ended in an erotic orgy, from which the journalist had fled in horror. *Le Matin*, which was not usually considered a sensational journal, affirmed that its reporter had really been present at the scene he described, but the editor refused to answer any more questions. It seems safe to assume that Huysmans had also really been present at a Black Mass, even if the description he gave of it is somewhat coloured for literary effect.

This is made more probable by the fact that the character of Madame Chantelouve was based, at least in part, on an actual person whose name in real life was Berthe Courière, or, as she preferred to call herself, Berthe de Courière. She was the daughter of a financier named Charles André Louis who lived at Lille, and it was in this city that she was born on June 1st, 1852. She was more than a little mad, and indeed was twice an inmate of lunatic asylums, once at Bruges where she was so violent that she had to be put into a straitjacket, and once at Uccles near Brussels. She died during the First World War.

When Huysmans knew her her conduct was already rather peculiar. According to Rachilde, the wife of Alfred Valette, director of the *Mercure de France*, from the carpet bag which she always carried with her, she was continually producing a number of consecrated wafers (at least she claimed that they were consecrated) which she then proceeded to give to her dogs. She was thought to be the mistress of Rémy de Gourmont which may, perhaps, shed some light on that author's attempt to play down Huysmans' account of the Black Mass by saying that it was imitated from the history of the Abbé Guibourg. It might have been thought that it was through Rémy de Gourmont that she met Huysmans but the latter tells us plainly[1] that he received a letter from 'Chantelouve', then unknown to him, after the publication of one of his books. The introduction, in fact, happened exactly as he related it in *Là-bas*.

Or was it really otherwise? Was Huysmans, usually so frank, concealing the truth on this occasion? Or had he simply forgotten? Certainly at this period of his life he was well acquainted with Rémy de Gourmont, a writer who, even yet, has not been accorded his full stature and who had many qualities likely to appeal to Huysmans.

Rémy de Gourmont was ten years younger than he, having been born in 1858. He came from Normandy and sprang from a long line of minor gentry, some of whom had distinguished themselves as soldiers, artists and clerics. One of his forebears, Gilles de Gourmont, had been responsible for the first book published in France in Greek letters. On his mother's side he was connected with the family of the famous Malherbe.

He came to Paris in 1883 and was, for a time, employed at the Bibliothèque Nationale but, having written an article urging Franco-German co-operation, he was dismissed from his official post and adopted a semi-monastic life as a literary recluse. From his apartment on the third floor of No. 71 Rue des Saints-Pères, he seldom ventured out except to his favourite restaurant the Café de Flore, to the office of the *Mercure de France*, the influential review of which he was one of the founders, or for a short stroll along the *quais*, turning over the contents of the book-stalls. A life, in short,

[1] In a letter to the Abbé Mugnier, quoted by Lucien Descaves in *Deux Amis*, Paris (1946), p. 54.

even more regular than Huysmans' own and confined within even narrower geographical limits.

He had a passion for fine old books—another point of contact—an absorbed interest in the liturgy of the Church, an 'almost sensual love of words'. a hatred of all excessive gestures and a 'cerebral perversity' in love. The learned criticism of the language of medieval religious texts which he called *Le Latin Mystique* appealed to Huysmans so strongly that he wrote a preface for it, although this preface was suppressed by Gourmont in later editions.

Even the binding of this book must have delighted Huysmans, for some of the copies were bound in '*violet archevêque*' and some in '*pourpre cardinalice*'. And when his 'poem in prose', *Théodat*, was produced in 1892 at the *Théâtre de l'Art* it was preceded by a piece accompanied by an '*orchestration musicale, lumineuse et odorante*', and the programme explained the concordance between the voices, the notes, the colours and the perfumes. It all sounds like a page out of *A Rebours*.

Rémy de Gourmont's first important work had appeared in 1890. It was called *Sixtine, Roman de la vie cérébrale*. It was dedicated to Villiers de l'Isle-Adam, and its heroine (there can be no doubt about it) was Berthe Courière, although this was not apparent, even to some of Gourmont's friends, until long afterwards. Indeed it was not until after his death that the publication by his brother Jean of his early *Lettres à Sixtine* made it clear that 'Sixtine was a real being of flesh and blood whom Gourmont had once adored and who was devoted to him, early recognising his genius. The novel was the cerebral transposition of real love.'[1]

'The identity of "Sixtine" is veiled,' says Havelock Ellis,[2] 'at first by Gourmont's reserve in personal matters, and still

[1] Havelock Ellis, *From Rousseau to Proust*, London (1936), p. 324.
[2] *ibid*. p. 324, Footnote.

in the published *Lettres*. It is only by vague indications in Voivenel's book[1] that I have realised that 'Sixtine' was the Madame Berthe Courière (sometimes called de Courière) whom I knew in Paris in 1890, sometimes in her tiny salon, sometimes with Huysmans, but never with Gourmont. The love-letters all belong to 1887 and end with coolness on Sixtine's part and continued devotion on Gourmont's, friendly relations not absolutely ceasing. I never heard of this love-affair, but I did hear of some unexplained estrangement between Gourmont and Huysmans. At some later period Sixtine's affection for Gourmont revived. She was his devoted nurse at the end and died shortly after him,[2] first placing the letters for publication in the hands of his brother Jean, who speaks with tender regard for her "inspiration" of Rémy and her "Olympian heart and face".'

Havelock Ellis was in Paris in 1890 with Arthur Symons, and the two young men, as they then were, tried to meet as many French writers as possible. Ellis gives a valuable account[3] of a visit to Mallarmé on one of his 'Tuesdays' in the little apartment in the Rue de Rome, when the company sat at the long dining table passing round the bowl of tobacco which was all the hospitality Mallarmé could afford. Henri de Régnier was there and Gabriel Mourey, the translator of Swinburne. Huysmans was introduced by Gourmont. It was therefore, if Ellis is correct, Gourmont who brought Huysmans and Mallarmé together.

The young Englishman was more impressed by Huysmans than by Mallarmé, and, while in Paris, saw much of him. With Arthur Symons he visited him in his government office, accompanied him to a café to drink vermouth, and even, in Ellis's own words 'spent an evening with him in the

---

[1] Dr. Paul Voivenel, *Rémy de Gourmont vu par son Médecin*, Paris (1924).

[2] They both died in 1915.   [3] *Op. cit.* p. 10.

apartment of his friend and Gourmont's, Madame Courière, a tall and gracious person, in earlier years, it is said, the favourite model of a famous sculptor; she was Gourmont's 'Sixtine' and also perhaps the original of Madame Chantelouve in *Là-bas*, which had just then been published. It was a tiny room and the walls at every possible and impossible spot were covered by knick-knacks and bric-a-brac.'[1]

All this makes one wonder whether the 'estrangement' between Gourmont and Huysmans was not due to the action of the latter in depicting Madame de Courière as Madame Chantelouve in *Là-bas*, and also to some extent to his drawing for the character of Chantelouve on Gourmont himself. But this is speculation. Certain it is that Berthe Courière was an even more complicated character than her relations with Huysmans might have led one to suppose. To Gourmont she was an angel of light and gave to him almost a lifetime of devotion. To Huysmans she was something between a maenad and a succubus, and his initiator into the lower depths of occultism.

If Madame Chantelouve was a real person so also was 'Dr. Johannès', and it was almost certainly through her that Huysmans was put in touch with him. His real name was Boullan, and, like Dr. Johannès, he lived at Lyons and practised exorcism. They exchanged letters. Boullan seemed to Huysmans a man who could open up a new world and, on 7th February, 1890, we find him writing to his new friend, 'I am tired of the theories of my friend Zola, whose absolute positivism disgusts me, and not less tired of the systems of Charcot, who has tried to prove to me that demoniality is a kind of hysteria. I am even more tired, if possible, of occultists and spiritualists, whose phenomena, although real, are always the same. I wish to confound all these people, to create a work of art of a supernatural realism

[1] *Op. cit.* p. 12.

and of a spiritualist naturalism. I wish to prove to Zola, to Charcot, to the spiritualists and others, that nothing is explained in the mysteries which surround us.'

Boullan replied three days later, 'Your judgments and appreciations on Zola and the others, on Charcot and company, are perfect. With regard to the occultists, Péladan, de Guaita and others of the same sort, I have only one desire, that you should know them thoroughly. There remain the clergy and other schools of magic. There I could tell you many things. As for your aim, to prove that Satanism, which is thought to have vanished, is still in existence—ah of that question, no one could put you in a better position to speak with conviction, supported by established facts.'

There is no doubt that much of the material for *Là-bas* was obtained from Boullan, and this explains Huysmans' prejudice against 'the occultists, Péladan, de Guaita and others', for Boullan, having been the intimate of these men, had now become their sworn enemy. Yet they were at the very centre of the occultist movement in France at the end of the nineteenth century.

Stanislas de Guaita was a marquis—a real one, as Jules Bois rather pompously informs us—descended from an old Hungarian family possessing a château at Alteville in Lorraine. He was a man of considerable culture and talent who had already published three volumes of verse—*Oiseux de Passage*, *La Muse Noire* and *Rosa Mystica*—when, in 1885, came *le coup de foudre occultist*, the thunder-clap which revealed to him the course of his destiny. Catulle Mendès, himself deeply interested in such matters, advised him to read the works of Éliphas Lévi.

He could have given no better advice for this strange figure is indeed the fountain-head of the revival of occultism in modern times. His real name was Alphonse Louis Constant. He was born in Paris in 1810 and, being destined for the priesthood, studied at the seminary of St. Sulpice. But when he had taken only deacon's orders he found his ideas becoming less and less orthodox. His book *La Mère de Dieu*, published in 1844, was condemned by the ecclesiastical authorities. Four years later he 'quitted the soutane' and married, but his marriage was not a success and was shortly afterwards annulled. He was a man of immense learning and was engaged, at this time, on a *Dictionnaire de littérature chrétienne*. This, in 1851, he turned over to the Abbé Migne in order to devote himself to the study of magic. Taking up the system of Martinez de Pasqualis and the 'Unknown Philosopher', Claude de Saint-Martin, he set himself to systematise and expand it and, having changed his name to Éliphas Lévi, as a sign of his devotion to the Kabbala, he brought out, between 1860 and 1865, a whole series of volumes of which the most famous were his *Histoire de la Magie* and his *Dogme et Rituel de la Haute Magie*. Before his death in 1875 he was reconciled to the Church, but his influence as an occultist remained, and indeed continues to this day.

Guaita at least, having studied his writing, felt that he had found his master and was launched upon the studies which were to occupy him for the rest of his short life. Henceforward he ceased to frequent the purely literary circles, where his tall and elegant figure, his distinguished manners and his pale aristocratic face had given him a certain prestige. He retired from the world and in his ground-floor flat in the Avénue Trudaine, hung entirely in red, gave himself up to the practice of magic. Clad in his cardinal's robe, as Jules Bois tells us, surrounded by precious and curious books, he passed his time between his study and his laboratory, sleeping in the daytime, working all night, stimulating his imagination with caffeine, morphine and hashish, also with the contents of an excellent cellar. It was as if des Esseintes had become a real person, although his occupations were a little more sinister than those of Huysmans' hero. It is just possible that a rumour of his occupations and of the kind of life he led had had something to do with Huysmans' conception.

Certainly Stanislas de Guaita became rapidly known in the world of occultists and congenial spirits were not slow in making their appearance. According to his own account, in a letter to Jules Bois, he made the acquaintance, in quick succession, of Péladan, Barlet and Papus. Little is known of Barlet except that he was a priest. Papus was a practising physician whose real name was Gerard Encausse. He was a serious student of occultism and his published works are not without value. He is now chiefly remembered for his ingenious book on the Tarot, that fascinating series of divinatory images from which our own pack of playing cards is derived. Péladan, or as he liked to call himself, Sar Péladan, merits a chapter or even a book to himself.

Joseph Aimé Péladan was born at Lyons in 1859. He liked to pretend that he came of a long line of good Catholics, some of whom had been *Chevaliers de Saint-Louis*. In actual fact his ancestors had been Protestants until the Revocation of the Edict of Nantes when they became, perforce, Catholics. They seem to have been simple peasants and small traders.[1] Joseph's father was, however, an extraordinary character with some pretensions as a writer. In 1871 he published, at his own expense, his '*Nouveau Liber Mirabilis*', a work dealing with 'all authentic prophecies concerning the present time', with 'notes, explanations and concordances'. In his mind Legitimism, Catholicism and Mysticism combined to produce a permanent state of cerebral intoxication. He was also an enthusiastic homœopathist. His eldest son was a homœopathist physician but unfortunately died poisoned, at an early stage of his career, by an overdose of strychnine, his

[1] Joséphin Péladan, *La Nouvelle Revue du Midi*, No. 10 (Special), Decembre 1924. Nîmes.

homœopathic pharmacist having made a mistake in the prescription. He had just completed his great work on 'Homœopathy for Families and Physicians', in which he developed the theme of the triple symmetry of the human organism, therapeutic polarity, and the *'pharmacotaxie des polychrestes'*, whatever that may be. In such an atmosphere it would have been strange if Joséph, or as he was soon to call himself Joséphin Péladan, had grown up without developing some touch of eccentricity.

The young man was immersed in occult studies from his earliest years; but he was also a staunch Catholic and even got himself into trouble in 1880 with the authorities at Nîmes (to which town the family had now removed) by too noisy a manifestation against the recent anti-monastic laws. In 1882 he came to Paris and through the influence of Arsène Houssaye, the influential editor of *L'Artiste*, began his long literary career by writing about art.

Falling in with Barbey d'Aurevilly he acknowledged him as his master both in literature and life. Incidentally, it was Péladan who hailed him as *'Connêtable des lettres françaises'* a title by which Barbey is still remembered. He made friends with Villiers de l'Isle-Adam, and in 1884 he published his first novel, *Le Vice Suprême*.

It had considerable success and it might have seemed that he was launched as a writer. But Péladan could never be merely a literary man. Too many conflicting ambitions were bubbling in his mind. He wished to be a dandy and he wished to be a Magus. It would perhaps be difficult to find two desires more completely incompatible. 'Péladan', says Henry Colomb,[1] 'paraded through life clad in tawdry rags, bizarrely draped—morally even more than physically—in divergent idealisms, heterodox religiosities, occultism, disquieting eroticism, transcendental æsthetics and inexplicable costumes.'

[1] *La Nouvelle Revue du Midi*, p. 180.

Brummel would certainly had disapproved of a dress which excited so much public attention. It was Péladan's habit to stride through the cafés dressed in a kind of medieval doublet, hiding beneath a cloak, which he might well have stolen from the wardrobe of the Opera, his walking stick, which he carried as if it had been a sword. Even apart from such eccentricities of dress his appearance was striking enough, for he had a mop of curly black hair and a black beard like that of an ancient Assyrian monarch. Such indeed he imagined himself to be, either by descent or re-incarnation. He accordingly baptised himself Mérodach (a name derived no doubt from Marduk) and crowned himself with the title of Sar, or King. Henceforward, until almost the end of his life, he was known as Sar Mérodach Péladan, or more shortly as Sar Péladan.

Beneath all this nonsense there was, however, a real fund of sincerity and idealism. Anatole France, who might have been thought the last person in the world to appreciate such a character, wrote of him: 'M. Joséphin Péladan is an artist. He is absurd if you like, and as mad as you please. Nonetheless he has plenty of talent.'[1] And the destructive German critic Max Nordau in the chapter of 'Degeneration' which he called 'Parodies of Mysticism' said: 'There is only one of these master-sorcerers who is certainly sincere, and as he is at the same time much the most considerable of them from the intellectual point of view, I want to deal with him thoroughly. I mean M. Joséphin Péladan.'

Such opinions are not lightly to be disregarded, but, at the time of which we are speaking, Péladan seems to have disgusted the public with his affectations and, after the success of his first book, there was something like a conspiracy of silence on the part of the press about all his subsequent writings. When he fell in with Stanislas de Guaita he was

---

[1] Anatole France, *La Vie Littéraire*, IIIe Serie.

almost penniless, and had to live on plates of vegetables which he bought from the wine-merchant at the street corner. Like Villiers de l'Isle-Adam he had no settled abode. However, he had good friends, including Stanislas de Guaita, with whom he entered into a close alliance.

These two, and another man called Albert Jounet, formed a triumvirate sworn to deliver the soul of the world from materialism. Péladan was called Mérodoch, Jounet was called Nergal, and Guaita Nebo, these being the names of Assyrian planets. Like Péladan, Jounet was from the Midi, and like Guaita he was a poet. 'In his occultist days, with his great moustache and his hair in ringlets and his splendid figure, he looked,' says Jules Bois, 'like the reincarnation of Apollonius of Tyana, although it is a little difficult for us to envisage that ancient sage with a moustache.' In the end his mysticism took a Catholic turn, and he was reconciled to the Church.

The most extraordinary of the group was undoubtedly Guaita himself. Like Baudelaire he 'cultivated his hysteria with delight and terror'. He practised what the occultists call the 'dissociation of the astral body', a dangerous practice, since the tenuous thread which connects the astral body with the physical body may snap, in which case the catalepsy of the latter turns into real death.

Nearly all occultists believe in the possibility of this dissociation and some who are not occultists have had the power to bring it about with or without conscious intention. St. Joseph of Copertino is the most famous case in Christian hagiography, and the great St. Dominic himself is said to have had the faculty of being in 'two places at the same time.'[1]

Certainly very strange meetings were held in the ground-floor flat of the Avénue Trudaine. They were attended by such well-known initiates as Paul Adam, author of the

[1] See Herbert Thurston, S.J. *The Physical Phenomena of Mysticism*, London, 1952.

fatalist novel *Être*, by Gary de Lacroaze, and by the anarchist poet Laurent Tailhade. Another poet of the circle was Edouard Dupus, the husband of the well-known actress Suzanne Gay. Dupus died in a urinal in the act of giving himself a final injection of morphine. His wife too became a morphino-maniac and died miserably. The practice of occultism goes hand in hand far too often with the use and abuse of dangerous drugs, and perhaps it has always done so. The unguents with which the witches anointed themselves were probably of the same nature, and the fact that so many of the Guaita circle were what we should call drug-fiends makes one wonder where the dividing line can be drawn between hallucination and 'real' phenomena—if the phrase has any meaning.

All this, however, was what might be called private occultism, or at least occultism within a very restricted circle. The decision to attempt the founding of an Order was probably inspired by Péladan who was, indeed, according to his own account already Grand Master of the '*Rose + Croix*'. Henry Colomb[1] calls this a straying branch of Freemasonry.

It would be out of place in a work like the present study to attempt to trace the history of Freemasonry or to try to solve the complicated problem of its relations with the Rosicrucian movement. Somehow, and some time, in the seventeenth century the old Masonic Guilds, both in France and England, ceased to be purely operative; now masonry was interpreted in a mystical sense, and the members of the new Lodges included alchemists, Rosicrucians, Kabbalists, neo-Platonists and astrologers.

In France in the eighteenth century the Lodges inclined towards a Christian mysticism, possibly under the influence of the Jesuits who are thought to have infiltrated into them and made a determined attempt to capture the movement.

[1] *Op. cit.*, p. 224.

But they were never completely orthodox, although it was still possible in the late eighteenth century for a pious Catholic, and even for a priest, to be a Mason.

The atmosphere of the Lodges varied from place to place. Some of them progressed towards 'free thought'. Some elaborated new degrees, some served as a mask for revolutionary activity. One of the most important centres was Toulouse, a town where the old heretical tradition of the Albigensians was not quite forgotten, and although the Rite of the *Rose + Croix* officially came to an end there in 1767, some seeds must have remained, for in the early years of the nineteenth century we hear of a certain Firmin Boissin receiving the Rosicrucian accolade from the members of 'the last branch of the Order, that of Toulouse'. In 1858, by which time he was himself 'Doyen of Toulouse' and 'Doyen of the Council of Fourteen', Boissin received into the Order Adrien Péladan. On the death of Adrien by an overdose of strychnine (as we have already related) his place was taken by his younger brother Joséphin. This happened in 1885.

Unless this was all moonshine, Sar Joséphin Mérodoch Péladan was already the head of the Rosicrucian Order. However when, three years later, the new foundation of the 'Kabbalistic Order of the Rose-Cross' was launched, the accepted head was certainly Guaita. The Supreme Council was composed of himself, Sar Péladan, Papus, Paul Adam and the Abbé Barlet, who was destined to succeed Guaita as head of the Order.

According to the occultist magazine *Initiation*, the Supreme Council consisted of twelve members, six of them known (the above list is therefore one short—perhaps Albert Jounet should be included) and six unknown, ready to restore the Order in any circumstances. Besides one degree, exclusively practical (whatever that might mean) there were two others, subsidiary and theoretical, in which initiation was given.

Every member took an oath of obedience to the directive
Council but his liberty was absolutely safe-guarded, so that
he might leave the society if he wished to do so, under the
sole condition of keeping secret the teaching received.

It might have been expected that Huysmans, with his
occultist preoccupations at this period, would have been
brought into contact with the members of the Kabbalistic
Order of the Rose-Cross. He must surely have heard of them
from the very beginning of his enquiry; there was much in
the character of Guaita to attract him and had he been alone
some understanding might have been arrived at. But at
Guaita's side was Sar Péladan, a man who might have been
created to excite in Huysmans every instinctive antipathy.
Huysmans called him, in an untranslatable phrase: '*Mage de
camelote et bilboquet du Midi*,' and to say that any man was
from the Midi was to place him outside the pale of any
possible sympathy.

What Huysmans does not seem to have known was that
Guaita and Péladan were even then parting company.
Péladan felt that Guaita's Order was insufficiently Christian,
and he broke away to found an 'Order of the Rose-Cross of the
Temple and of the Graal', more familiarly called the Catholic
Rose-Cross. What he wanted to do was to restore to the Church
the hidden wisdom which he thought it had lost; but his
Order was also a literary and artistic movement. He threw
himself into this with characteristic energy, organised ex-
hibitions of mystical art and performances of Mysteries, some
of which he wrote himself. Huysmans, however, embraced
in one common contempt all the varieties of Rosicrucians,
and when he established intimate relations with a known
occultist he chose the man they execrated most.

CHAPTER EIGHT

SATANISM AND MAGIC

———————— • ————————

In espousing the cause of the Abbé Boullan, Huysmans undoubtedly came down on the wrong side, for Guaita, whatever may be thought of his activities, was a scholar and a gentleman, Péladan in spite of his eccentricities was a writer of some merit, and Papus was *chef de laboratoire* at the hospital of La Charité. Boullan was a scoundrel, or a madman, or both.

His career was even more extraordinary than those of the others.[1] He was an unfrocked priest, formerly of the diocese of Versailles, and had even been the Superior of a monastic community. He was also the editor of the mystical review, '*Les Annales de la Sainteté*'. In the pursuit of his religious or editorial duties he fell in with a nun called Adèle Chevalier, who claimed to be *miraculée* and to have received special marks of the Divine favour, and Boullan took it upon himself to go to Rome to lay her case before the Holy Father. The Pope, however, refused to recognise the validity of the alleged miracle, and Boullan returned to Paris, disconsolate but not discouraged. At the instigation, he alleged, of the Virgin, he founded at Bellevue an institute known as '*L'Œuvre de la Réparation des Âmes*', and he took Adèle Chevalier with him. In their clinic, if one may call it so, they proposed to cure—

---

[1] See the very interesting article by Frédéric Boutet, 'Mages Noirs, Messes Noires' in *Œuvres Libres*, No. 51, 1925.

for a fee—the 'diabolic affections' of any who felt themselves to be in need of their services.

It sounds rather like psychoanalysis, *avant la lettre*, but Freud had not yet been heard of, and the public authorities, both civil and ecclesiastic, regarded the enterprise with a very suspicious eye. The Abbé Boullan and Sister Chevalier were prosecuted for fraud and *'attentat public à la pudeur'*, and the terms of the prosecution have a flavour of their own: 'Inasmuch as Boullan cannot have had conversation with the Virgin. . . .' A little later he was put under an interdict by the Archbishop of Paris for having claimed to cure a woman possessed of a devil by means of the seamless robe of Christ. He went to Rome to protest but found the Vatican no more sympathetic than it had been on the previous visit, and he was for a time imprisoned by the Inquisition. Released after a short detention, he travelled over Europe and at Brussels he fell in with Vintras.

Strange as may seem some of the characters we have been discussing, Vintras surpasses them all. He was equally remarkable for the details of his own career and for the influence he exerted on others. Yet he started in life with almost every possible handicap. He was born at Bayeux in 1807, the bastard of a poor working girl who was quite unable to support him. He was educated in summary fashion at a charity school and, when a mere child, was apprenticed to a tailor at Chevreuse. Giving up this employment he became a clerk in a bookshop in Paris, married a laundress as poor as himself, kept a stall in a fair, became a tout for a wine merchant, and finally a fireman in a little cardboard box factory at Tilly-sur-Seules.

So far his career might have been paralleled by that of a thousand poor devils living from hand to mouth and drifting from one casual employment to another. But Vintras was no ne'er-do-well. Although he could only just read, write and figure, he was a good workman, and was by nature gentle and pious. And in the summer of 1839, when he was thirty-two years old, he had a vision. The Archangel Michael appeared to him and told him that he had been chosen to be the reincarnation of the Prophet Elisha and to prepare the way for the Paraclete.

He was a man of imposing presence, tall and bearded. After his vision, he became extremely eloquent, speaking as if by inspiration upon the most recondite theological subjects. He spoke as in a trance, and could not afterwards remember what he had said, so that those who had been present had to repeat it to him. He preached the Gospel of Pity, maintained the angelic nature of all souls before their entry into the earth life, and the non-eternity of Hell. He preached—before it was orthodox to do so—the doctrine of the Immaculate Conception.

His influence was hypnotic and irresistible, and among those who became his disciples were priests,[1] as well as laymen, aristocrats as well as labourers, learned men as well as simple folk. He founded the 'Church of Carmel' and, in a sanctuary hung with red cloth, he celebrated, in French, a mass of his own invention, the 'provictimal sacrifice of Mary', in honour of the Virgin. The prayers of this ritual were full of an exalted mystical eloquence which had a profound effect upon those who were present. And in their excited imagination they heard voices, smelt delicious perfumes, and saw a flight of doves settling on the shoulders of the Hierophant. A shower of blood fell from the ceiling of the sanctuary, miraculous Hosts appeared of themselves upon the altar and floated in the air. And these Hosts bore the stigmata upon them, and letters of blood. Some of these bleeding Hosts were later to come into the possession of Huysmans.

The ecclesiastical authorities, perhaps understandably,

[1] One of them was the Abbé Léopold Baillard, the 'Apostle' in Maurice Barrès's *Colline Inspirée*.

have always looked with an unfavourable eye upon such manifestations. The Bishop of Bayeux seized some hundred of the bleeding Hosts, and Vintras was imprisoned for fraud. He had, however, the gift of bi-location and while supposed to be safely in prison at Rennes was able to appear nonetheless in the sanctuary and show himself to his disciples. When he was released from prison he returned to Tilly-sur-Seules and here, on the night of the Ascension, 1850, he had another mystical experience receiving 'by the direct influx of Christ confirmation of his consecration in the Ministry of Elisha'. This happened in the presence of a large audience which included seven priests. Henceforward he put aside the name of Vintras and called himself Strathanael, or Pierre-Michel, or Elisha. He conferred the priesthood upon a lady of Armaillé, whom he proclaimed to be the Joan of Arc of the New Dispensation. It is perhaps not surprising that he was, shortly afterwards, constrained to travel abroad.

He went to Belgium and then to London where he stayed for some time, and it was from here that he combated the Satanists. He learned, by means of his clairvoyant powers, that a Black Mass was to be celebrated in a lonely house near Paris on the night of 28th February, 1855. Jules Bois gives an elaborate account of this mass,[1] which he declares he had extracted from the archives of Vintras which came into Huysmans' possession, but as he himself admits, it has only a mediocre importance as a document, since Vintras did not claim to have been present, except in the spirit. But, to his own satisfaction at least, he succeeded in putting a stop to these impious proceedings. The celebrant found himself unable to consecrate and the young woman whose naked body presumably provided the altar, in the accepted manner of Black Masses, was struck dead.

Vintras apparently regarded the combating of the Satan-

[1] In *Le Satanisme et la Magie*, Paris, 1895, p. 233.

ists as the main business of his life, but there were some who declared that he was a Satanist himself. Among these was a certain Geoffroy, whose name in occultism was Jehovael, and who had formerly been a disciple. He accused his former Master of officiating at ceremonies in a state of nudity, of admitting women to the priesthood, and of being a homosexual. The way of the heresiarch is hard.

The fascination of Vintras was, however, so great that new disciples replaced those who had fallen away. After various journeys, including one to Brussels where, as we have noted, he fell in with Boullan, he went to Lyons and established there a Temple which existed for many years. Among his acolytes was no less a person than the Duke of Parma. Vintras died there in 1875 and was succeeded by Boullan, although some of the faithful refused to recognise the new pontiff and broke away.

As we have seen, Huysmans had been in correspondence with Boullan while writing *Là-bas*. The work began to come out as a *feuilleton* early in 1891, and in the summer of the same year he decided to pay a visit to Lyons to see 'Dr. Johannès' for himself.

Boullan lived in the Rue de la Martinière in a house which, according to Frédéric Boutet,[1] belonged to an architect, a good, simple-minded old man deep in alchemy, and paying little attention to his lodgers. Huysmans found there also a certain Monsieur Soidekerck, formerly a manufacturer of church ornaments who had been one of the disciples of Vintras. In addition he met two women who acted as mediums for Boullan: Madame Laure and Madame Thibault, the latter of whom was to play some part in Huysmans' own life.

In such a ménage extraordinary happenings might perhaps have been expected, nor is the expectation disappointed.

[1] *Les Œuvres Libres*, 51, p. 228.

A veritable battle of magicians is described by Jules Bois, basing himself on the evidence of Huysmans.[1]

Warning of an impending attack had been sent to Boullan three days before, 'according to the laws of Magic', although who formulated such laws and why the practitioners of magic should obey them is yet another mystery. He had also been warned, says Bois, by the twittering of birds; but it was his clairvoyant, Madame Thibault, who told him when the actual assault was about to begin. The worthy doctor rose up 'like a tiger'.

'Madame Thibault,' he cried, 'what are these workers of iniquity doing?'

'Father, they are placing your portrait in a coffin.'

'The Law of the Countersign and the *Choc en Retour* will punish them,' replied Boullan, and he gave the order to place the declaration of war he had received in a similar coffin and to bury it.

'Madame Thibault, what are these evil men doing now?'

'Father, they are saying a Black Mass against you.'

Boullan sprang to his feet (again!). Having put on the great red robe of Vintras, tied with a blue cord, and on the back of which was a cross upside down, to signify that the reign of the suffering Christ was over, Boullan, bare-headed and with bare feet—as he remained throughout the hostilities—chanted the Office of Melchisidek, as was required of the Elect of Carmel. Still the 'workers of iniquity' were not vanquished. Then the 'Father' performed the 'Sacrifice of Glory' in which 'the feminine rite, allied to the masculine rite, red wine mingled with white, created, according to the law rediscovered by Pasteur (shades of Pasteur!) a victorious

[1] He prefaces his remarks (*Satanisme et Magie*, p. 330) by saying that he is sure not to be contradicted by Huysmans who had himself been present. Huysmans had every opportunity of contradicting the story if he had wanted to do so, seeing that he wrote the preface to Jules Bois' book.

ferment, by which the impious altars were overthrown and the hierophants of Satanism struck dead'. At the moment of the consecration, Boullan, holding a fragment of a Host in each hand, invoked the Archangels and implored them to give him victory over his enemies, the Satanists.

It was an extraordinary spectacle, says Bois, still, presumably, quoting Huysmans, to see the little old man with his wolf's paw and his wild, prophetic eyes, defying with word and gesture the wicked occultists whom distance could not preserve from his just fury.

On another occasion Boullan had the worst of it. Not having received any previous intimation of an attack—it would seem that the Queensberry rules of Magic were not always respected—he was unprepared. Thuds were heard, like the blows of a fist on the face of the operator, and bumps appeared on his forehead. Boullan gave a great cry; he tore open his robe and showed on his chest a great bleeding wound.[1]

What are we to make of all this? Are we to consider it as the raving of lunatics, or as an elaborate mystification contrived by Boullan to impress the visitor, Huysmans or another? Perhaps he saw, in the visit of the already famous writer, a chance to justify himself, and to take revenge upon those who had tormented him, by Magic or otherwise. Certainly he took great pains to get Huysmans on his side, and even handed over to him, in addition to certain documents extracted from the 'Archives of Vintras', a number of the great heresiarch's 'bleeding Hosts'. These Huysmans used to brandish when he felt himself threatened by the machinations of the 'Satanists'.

And menaced he apparently was, for when he was back in Paris, Boullan, from Lyons, sent him an urgent message not, under any circumstances, to go to his office on the following

---

[1] Bois declares that he had this detail from the painter, Lauzet, who was present at these happenings in 1892.

day. He was then '*Chef de Division*' in the Ministry of the
Interior, and could presumably give himself leave if he
wished to do so. He accordingly stayed at home. That very
day, a heavy mirror, which hung immediately over his desk,
fell down and was shivered into fragments. It seemed likely
that had anyone been sitting at the desk he would inevitably have been killed. Such, at least, was Huysmans'
opinion and he held the Brethren of the Rose-Cross responsible. It was at this period of his life also that he was attacked,
just as he was about to go to sleep, by invisible fists which
beat him over the face. Boullan, with the aid of Madame
Thibault, his housekeeper and *voyante*, delivered him from
these also.

This protection, however, was soon to be taken away.
Boullan was making ready to leave Lyons for Paris, where he
had been asked to give a series of lectures on the Kabbala in
the *Salle des Capucines*. He felt that he was about to obtain
victory over his enemies and in a speech quoted by Jules Bois
he said, 'We speak of that which is known to us by our personal experience. For years we have undergone attacks by
means of Black Masses, and by bewitchments of every kind,
by poison, by the most dangerous proceedings, and in spite of
all, by the will of God, who alone is master of life and death,
we are on our feet, and in spite of cruel sufferances endured,
in good health after having overcome so many perils.' Next
day, before he could leave for Paris, he died suddenly.

Huysmans was profoundly shocked by this sudden collapse
of his friend. It was true that Boullan suffered from heart
disease and from a disease of the liver, but Huysmans had no
hesitation in ascribing his death to the magical machinations
of his enemies of the Rose-Cross.

Certainly the Rose-Cross had done all that it could to put
an end to Boullan's practices. Papus admitted later that, after
proper enquiry, the occultists of his circle had sent to the

ex-Abbé two formal letters calling upon him to cease his practices. Jules Bois was able to quote a remark of Guaita that his condemnation had been pronounced in the most formal manner.

Bois rushed into print with an article in *Gil-Blas*, in which he brought definite accusations against Guaita and Péladan. The Paris press took the matter up and *Figaro* sent a journalist to interview Huysmans. Huysmans was categoric. 'It is indisputable,' he said, 'that Guaita and Péladan practise Black Magic every day. . . . It is very possible that my poor friend Boullan has succumbed to their practices.'

The evening after this interview, Huysmans was more than ever persecuted by the kind of psychic attacks from which Boullan was no longer there to protect him. A touch of the sinister—or the ludicrous—is added by the statement that his favourite cat suffered also.

Stanislas de Guaita thereupon sent his *témoins* both to Huysmans and to Jules Bois. Frédéric Boutet must surely be right in declaring that these two challenges form a unique example in modern times of duels motivated by accusations of sorcery.

There was nothing of the fighting man about Huysmans. He declared through his own *témoins* that he did not hold himself responsible for the remarks of Jules Bois, and that he had never thought of impugning the honour of Monsieur de Guaita. Jules Bois, a younger and tougher man, was less accommodating, and his duel with Guaita actually took place.

It was fought with pistols at the Tour de Villebon. A nephew of Victor Hugo, Paul Foucher, journalist and novelist, who acted as Jules Bois' second, contributed a very curious account of the affair to the *Sud-Ouest Toulouse* for 12th May, 1894.

'I was one of the *témoins* of Bois, who said to me, as we were leaving for Meudon, where the encounter was to take place, "You will see something very singular happen. On both sides our partisans are praying for us and practising conjurations." Something strange did indeed happen on the road to Versailles. One of the horses in our landau stopped suddenly and began to tremble, then stagger as if he had perceived the devil in person. It was impossible to proceed. This trembling lasted twenty minutes.

'The duel, none the less, took place and, thanks to God, or perhaps the Devil, two bullets were exchanged without result. Such, at least, was believed, but several days later, when I was trying some shots for practice at Gastine-Renette's, the celebrated gunsmith said to me, "What happened the other day? The bullet of one of the adversaries did not leave the barrel. My employee noticed it when he was cleaning the pistols."

'I was sure that the pistol of Jules Bois had not missed. As for the pistol used by Monsieur de Guaita, it is quite inadmissible that neither he nor his witnesses, of whom one was an officer and the other was Laurent Tailhade, should not have noticed that the pistol did not fire. The occultists could therefore pride themselves on having terrified the horse of one of the adversaries, and having prevented the bullet from leaving the pistol of Monsieur de Guaita.'

Jules Bois has himself left an account[1] of his meeting with Guaita. 'It was,' he says, 'if I remember well, a bright afternoon. . . . He was silhouetted against a wall, pale, in a black coat, his hat pulled down over his eyes, his finger patient on the trigger. . . . He was already ill, his face puffy, his breath short, but his eye proud. His hair was blond, almost red, which gave him the look of a wild animal that our civilisation had made neurasthenic. . . . I remember his look and his almost desolated gesture when the smoke had blown away and we found ourselves both on our feet, much less moved

[1] In *Le Monde Invisible*, p. 28.

than our seconds, whom all this business of magic and strange incidents en route had made a little over-excited.'

Three days later, Jules Bois fought another duel, this time with Papus, at the Pré-Catelan and with swords. 'I remember', says Bois, 'Papus taking off his coat while the elegant horsewomen made a circle around us. I remember the swords, the gypsy eye of my adversary, the impatient wrinkle in his forehead, his beard and his jovial lips, his heavy build. He was a bull among these improvised evangelists.'

This duel also was not without its aura of magic. The horse in the carriage which was conducting Bois to the scene of the conflict, fell down. He took a second carriage. The second horse fell down like the first, the vehicle was thrown over and he arrived on the field scarred and bleeding. Paul Foucher, to whom we owe this account, adds, rather ironically, that 'happily, although the swords were magic, the wounds they inflicted were very slight and have long been healed.' In fact, Papus and Bois were shortly afterwards reconciled, nor do we hear of any more attacks on Huysmans on the part of the occultists.

Huysmans continued to believe that Boullan had been on the side of the angels. He even invited the redoubtable Madame Thibault to come and keep house for him in the rue de Sèvres. After some hesitation, she accepted this invitation and he actually allowed her to establish in his house a little chapel in which she officiated as a priestess of the rite of Vintras. It must have seemed to many that Huysmans was himself a Satanist and this accusation was actually brought against him and against his disciple Jules Bois, in consequence of which, as Bois humorously remarks, many worthy people in the Provinces and in Paris 'withdrew from him all their estime'.

The accuser, who professed to be defending the cause of Holy Church, was a certain Gabriel Jogand-Pagès, who wrote

PIERRE VINTRAS (ÉLIE-STRATANAEL)

From *Le Satanisme et la Magie*

SAR PÉLADAN

under the name of Léo Taxil, and whose early literary activities had not been of a nature to commend him to the Catholic Hierarchy. Works of his listed in the long-since defunct *Librairie Anti-Cléricale* include a *Life of Jesus* which is actually a satirical parody of the Gospels embellished with five hundred 'comic' designs, a *Bible Amusante*, a novel founded on the story of the seventeenth-century Jesuit Girarde and Catherine Cadière and entitled 'The Debaucheries of a Confessor', a work on the mythical Pope Joan, a 'grand historical romance' called 'The Pope's Mistresses', and an attack on Pope Pius IX for his 'debaucheries, follies and crimes'. He followed this with an assault upon the actual Pontiff entitled 'The Poisoner Leo XIII'. In addition he wrote a book on 'Contemporary Prostitution' which, for those with strong stomachs, is not without a certain sociological interest. *That* world at least Léo Taxil seems to have known well.

He had been a Mason, but was, for some unexplained reason, expelled from the order after receiving only the first degree. Soon afterwards he was received into the Catholic Church, and having been for so long a violent and scurrilous anticlerical became at one stroke a defender of the Faith. But the violence and scurrility remained. In collaboration with 'Dr. Bataille', whose real name was Hachs, he founded a kind of magazine called *Le Diable au Dix-neuvième Siècle*, and all who wished to be informed of the activities of the Prince of Darkness in the modern age became eager subscribers. The magazine found a particularly ready sale among the village curés who drew largely upon its contents for the exhortation of their flock. They were indeed of a nature to frighten any pious soul.

Taxil and Bataille distributed blows all round. More conscientious writers, such as Jules Bois, tried to draw a distinction between Satanism and Luciferism. The latter, he claimed, was a separate religion, the former merely Christianity upside down. The true Satanist was a superstitious and sacrilegious medium or a bad priest who found an extra spice in eroticism when it was accompanied by the profanation of holy things. Luciferism was a heresy: the last budding of the Gnosis, a revival of that Albigensianism which no persecution had quite succeeded in extirpating. The heresy of the Templars was the same, and in the nineteenth century its champion was Albert Pike. According to the most modern forms of the doctrine, Jesus began by being the disciple of Lucifer, but on Mount Thabor he signed a pact with Adonai, that is, the God of the Old Testament. Thus he merited the punishment of the cross.

Jules Bois claimed to know that Baphomet, the idol of the Templars, was still adored by the Luciferians under the name of Palladium and in a more refined form. For Baphomet was an androgyne image like the androgyne images of India (from which, no doubt, it was ultimately derived), but in the modern idol *le caducée de son ventre* had been replaced by the crucified rose, with at the foot, the Pelican 'in her piety', symbol, says Bois, at once touching and cynical, of man's multiplication of himself by the act of generation. This is the only sacrifice that Lucifer admits, a voluptuous sacrifice, a joyous immolation, an identification of duty and pleasure. Lucifer, he concludes, is none other than Pan.

Jules Bois' various writings attempt to be, and to a large extent succeed in being, an objective account of modern mystical and quasi-mystical movements. The object of Taxil and Bataille was very different. We may leave Bataille out of the picture if only because his works are so stuffed with absurdities that the most credulous reader might be excused from perusing them to the end. What are we to make of secret laboratories hidden in the Rock of Gibraltar and engaged in manufacturing poisons for the destruction of the

Catholic world? What are we to think about the alleged Satanic orgies of Queen Victoria? Taxil's accusations are a more serious matter if only because they were countenanced and encouraged by responsible members of the Catholic Hierarchy.

The explanation is a simple one: Taxil was endeavouring to fix the accusation of Luciferism upon Masonry. Now it is true that Catholicism had long regarded Speculative Masonry with horror, as a work of the Devil, but as Waite points out,[1] the devilry of which it was accused was of an intellectual and political kind. It was supposed to be materialist and revolutionary. The only accusation of actual diabolism, made by Mgr. de Ségur, refers to the year 1848 ('the Year of Revolution') when there was alleged to be a Masonic Lodge in Rome where the Black Mass was celebrated in the presence of men and women. The story, as Waite acidly remarks, 'rests on nothing that can be called evidence'.

Even Dom Benoît who published, in 1886, two large volumes entitled *Freemasonry and the Secret Societies*, brings no accusation of a defined cult of Lucifer, merely remarking that 'all divinities of Rome, Greece, Persia, India, and every pagan people, are the gods of Masonry'. Even Paul Rosen, a renegade Mason who, in 1888, brought out a work called *Satan and Co.*, knows nothing of Luciferism. Indeed he conceives the end of Masonry to be social anarchy, and the overthrow of monarchical government. He does, however, mention Albert Pike.

Albert Pike had been mentioned already in a book by Taxil called *The Brethren of the Three Points*, published in 1885, but he does not yet connect him with the alleged worship of Lucifer. His *Sœurs Maçonnes*, published in 1888, deals with diabolism and Luciferism but with no reference to Albert Pike. It was not until 1891 (the year of the publication of

[1] Arthur Edward Waite, *Devil-Worship in France*, London, p. 44.

Là-bas) that he brought out *The Mysteries of Freemasonry*
in which he professed to set out the whole story.

It was strange enough. Albert Pike was an American, born
of humble parents in the city of Boston in 1809. In spite of
financial difficulties he managed to graduate at Harvard
twenty years later. For a time he was a schoolmaster, but
soon abandoned teaching and, after exploring the Rocky
Mountains (quite a hazardous undertaking at the period), he
settled in Arkansas as a journalist, founded the *Arkansas
Advocate*, and was active in promoting the admission of
Arkansas into the confederation of the United States. In the
late 'forties he became interested in Masonry and pursued
the Craft with so much energy and ability that, in 1859, he
was elected Sovereign Commander Grand Master of the
Supreme Council of Charleston.

So far we seem to be on fairly firm ground. Albert Pike
was a real person and he was certainly Grand Master of the
Supreme Council of the Ancient and Accepted Scottish Rite
in Charleston. But now persists in intruding itself into the
narrative not indeed King Charles's head but the skull of
Jacques de Molay. And Jacques de Molay, as the world knows,
was the last Grand Master of the Templars, that Order of
soldier-monks who had done good service in the Crusades and
who, at the beginning of the fourteenth century, had established themselves all over Europe, as the surviving number of
their churches still makes plain. Their wealth and power
excited the alarm of the Papacy and the jealousy and greed
of the French King. They were accused of heresy, unnatural
vice and the worship of the idol Baphomet. Jacques de Molay
was arrested and under torture confessed. Then he retracted
his confession and the very same day the King of France,
Philippe le Bel, had him burnt alive. What happened to the
skull of Jacques de Molay between 1314 and the beginning of
the nineteenth century is not known, but (such is the story)

in the year 1801 a Jew named Isaac Long carried it to
Charleston together with the original statue of Baphomet,
and fortified by the presence of these sacred relics, set about
the reconstruction of the Scottish Rite of Perfection and of
Herodom under the name of the Ancient and Accepted Scottish Rite.

Certainly the Scottish Rite was established at Charleston at
this period, but no serious person any longer lends any
credence to the rest of the story. This much, however, must
be said: Speculative Masonry does represent the survival—or
the revival—of the Ancient Mysteries. Most Masons are not
occultists, but many occultists have been drawn towards
Masonry, and it is interesting to note that one of Albert Pike's
coadjutors in Charleston was a certain Phileas Walder, originally a Swiss Lutheran Minister, afterwards (it is said) a
Mormon, but certainly an occultist, and one who had been a
personal friend and disciple of Eliphas Lévi. Masonry is
certainly capable of an esoteric interpretation. Most Masons
seem unaware of this, and their organization is regarded by
them merely as a convivial brotherhood and a mutual benefit
society with certain curious old customs. Those, however,
who have a leaning towards mysticism soon discover that in
their rituals they possess a fragment of a universal symbolism,
some of which descends from a remote antiquity. This
mythical side of Masonry was set forth by Albert Pike himself in a book entitled *Morals and Dogma*, a work which may
be compared in some ways with Madame Blavatsky's *Secret
Doctrine*.[1] There is nothing startling in it to those acquainted
with modern Theosophy, Jewish Kabbalism, the rituals of
Tantric Buddhism or the doctrines of the Sufis. Of course, as

[1] *Morals and Dogma* is practically unobtainable. For a more popular
and accessible account of the same matter the reader is referred to
Symbolism of Freemasonry, or Mystic Masonry, by J. D. Buck,
Chicago. Third Edition, 1925.

it claims, of necessity, that mystical states can be attained by means other than those sanctioned by the Church, it may be thought offensive to Catholic opinion.

Taxil's accusations, however, went much further than this. According to him Pike became a man of such eminence in Masonry that the Italian patriot Mazzini entered into a secret partnership with him, and on the very day on which the Italian troops entered Rome,[1] they founded together a Supreme Rite and Central Organization of Universal High Grade Masonry. Pike, under the title of Sovereign Pontiff of Universal Freemasonry, became head of the Supreme Dogmatic Directory located at Charleston. Mazzini, at Rome, became head of the Supreme Executive under the title of Sovereign Chief of Political Action. The new organization was given the title of the Reformed Palladium, the Palladium being the term used for the Baphomet idol.

Shortly before his death Mazzini recommended to Pike that his successor in Rome, as chief of the Executive, should be a certain Adriano Lemmi. Pike agreed, and when he himself died, the Dogmatic Directory after the brief and inglorious pontificate of a man named Albert George Mackey, devolved also upon Lemmi. This however did not suit all the faithful and a number of them broke away, including a lady of the name of Diana Vaughan.

Not only was she dissatisfied with Lemmi, but she found herself developing a great veneration for Joan of Arc. She therefore repented of her connection with the Palladium movement and determined to expose her former associates to the indignation of the world.

In June 1895 Léo Taxil was able to announce in the *Revue Mensuelle* that Diana Vaughan had been received into the Catholic Church. With commendable speed—just one month later—she began the publication of her *Memoirs of an ex-*

[1] We begin to see where the shoe pinches.

150

Palladist. These were not, as Waite sarcastically remarks,[1]
a 'literary performance'. The style, nevertheless, had certain
characteristics which were surprising, to say the least. 'She
does not come before us (says Waite) with one trace of the
uncertainty of accent which might have been expected to
characterise the newly-acquired language, not merely of
Christian faith, but of its Roman dialect. We find her speaking at once, and to the manner born. Could anything, by
possibility, be narrower than certain perished sections of
evangelical religion in England, it would be certain sections
of ultramontane religion in France; but Miss Vaughan has
acquired all the terminology of the latter, all the intellectual
bitterness, all the fatuities, as one might say, in the space of
five minutes.'[2]

The contents of the work, and the claims made by Miss
Vaughan, were sufficiently remarkable. She was, according
to her own account, a descendant of the famous seventeenth-
century mystic Thomas Vaughan, 'Silurist', a name held in
reverence by all who care for English literature, and by all
who are capable of recognising the accent of true piety. Miss
Vaughan alleged that he made a compact with Satan in the
year 1645 (there is nothing like being exact in the little
matter of dates) and that he wrote the well-known alchemical
treatise, 'An Open Entrance to the Closed Palace of the King',
under the name of Eirenæus Philalethes.

Miss Vaughan further alleged that Thomas Vaughan con-
summated a mystical marriage with Venus-Astarte, and as a
personal friend of Oliver Cromwell was allowed to substitute
himself for the executioner who beheaded Archbishop Laud
in order that he might practise black magic with a handkerchief soaked in the victim's blood.

[1] Arthur Edward Waite, *Devil-Worship in France*, London, 1896, p.
165.
[2] *ibid.*, pp. 167, 168.

Waite[1] had no difficulty in demolishing this tissue of absurdities. Vaughan wrote under the name of Eugenius Philalethes, but never under that of Eirenæus Philalethes, who was a different person. He was never a friend of Cromwell, being indeed a High Churchman, and so much of a Royalist that he was ejected from his living on the suspicion of carrying arms for the King. Moreover he never travelled—the Venus-Astarte marriage is supposed to have taken place in America—and, in any case, the dates of his life do not fit the events of Miss Vaughan's narrative. It might have been thought that any reasonable being would have rejected her story out of hand, especially when it was stuffed out with an account of her own adventures which strains credulity even further.

She was born, she said, in Paris, the daughter of an American Protestant from Kentucky and a French Protestant lady. Her mother died when she was fourteen and her father returned with her to Louisville, where he had some property. He became affiliated to the Sovereign Rite of Palladium created by Albert Pike and in 1883 presided at the initiation of his daughter as apprentice. She soon rose in the Order, and on April 5th, 1889 was sufficiently advanced to evoke Lucifer in person. It is agreeable to be able to record that he appeared to her in no questionable shape but 'superb in masculine beauty'.

Did anyone take this nonsense seriously? Unfortunately they did. For now appears in the arena no less a person than Mgr. Léon Meurin, S.J., Archbishop of Port Louis in Mauritius. 'If you would be saved from the excesses of unseated reason,' wrote Huysmans, 'try Mgr. Meurin; read the Archbishop on Palladium.' The learned Jesuit's researches are embodied in a magnificent publication entitled *Freemasonry, the Synagogue of Satan'*, a work which is still quoted in anti-Masonic literature even today.

[1] *ibid.*, pp. 255–289.

He informs us that black magic was rife in Mauritius, and this we may well believe. The Christianity of the inhabitants of that island may be as skin deep as that of the inhabitants of Haiti.[1] If the Archbishop had concerned himself with the customs and practices of his own flock he might have made a serious contribution to scientific anthropology. But he was not interested in anthropology. He was concerned to show that Masonry was devil-worship, that it was Jewish in origin, that it was entirely in the hands of Jews, and that its purpose was universal dominion, the exaltation of Jewry and the destruction of Christendom. It is sad to think that a presumably pious and learned man should thus anticipate the language of Julius Streicher.

He made some very strange assumptions and even stranger blunders. He quoted Carlyle as an authority on the Kabbala. Having discovered that the degrees of French Freemasonry numbered thirty-three he pointed out triumphantly that this was the number of the divinities in the Vedas, and he even found an esoteric significance in the fact that a Masonic circular had been issued from No. 33 Golden Square, London, the 'square of gold' being also not without its meaning. He even reproduced as an authentic document a story called *Aut Diabolus, aut Nihil*, which had appeared in *Blackwood's Magazine*.

Léo Taxil was no doubt delighted with the reinforcements which came from so august a quarter. He had indeed every reason to be pleased with the reception accorded to his accusations by the Hierarchy. Eighteen ecclesiastical dignitaries, including cardinals, archbishops and bishops, congratulated him on his work. He was complimented by the Cardinal-Vicar of Rome; he even received the Pope's

[1] For a really objective and scholarly account of such matters see the work of another Jesuit: Joseph J. Williams, S. J. *Voodoos and Obeahs, Phases of West Indian Witchcraft*, London (1933).

benediction. And then, suddenly, in 1897, for reasons which must remain obscure, he announced that the whole thing had been a mystification, that Diana Vaughan was a fictitious character and that the Luciferian sect did not exist.

It made very little difference. One might almost say that the Taxil campaign was a symptom rather than a cause of the universal neurosis which seemed to afflict France, and especially Paris, in the last decade of the nineteenth century. We tend to look at 'the Nineties' through the eyes of Toulouse-Lautrec, and it seems to us a halcyon period when life was lived in public and gaiety reigned. But behind *La Goulue* and *Nini-patte-en-l'air* were more sinister figures and the general atmosphere of the *fin-de-siècle* was febrile in the extreme.

Politically France was unstable; it seemed hardly possible that the Third Republic should survive. The intellectual anarchism of writers like Paul Adam had bred real anarchists who had begun to throw real bombs. French chauvinism saw enemies everywhere, and yet France seemed to have no solid core round which Frenchmen could rally. Scepticism in thought and immoralism in literature appeared to have put an end to the old traditions. Most 'right-thinking' people were convinced that an active diabolism was threatening the very existence of Church and State.

Huysmans' own position was an uncomfortable one, for as the archives of Boullan had now come into his possession he must have realised that the man in whom he had put his trust was in reality far nearer in character to the imaginary Canon Docre than to an angel of light. Canon Docre indeed had been largely an invention of Madame de Courière who had filled Huysmans up with stories of a bad priest who lived at Bruges and officiated in the Chapel of the Holy Blood. There was also a hint no doubt of a certain Canon Roca, who really existed, a socialist priest who explained Christian doctrines by

Kabbalism and who had the odd notion—for a priest—of founding a paper called *L'Anticlérical*. It was not Canon Docre of *Là-bas*, but, in reality, his adversary Boullan who fed white mice with fragments of the Host, and who gave himself up to the secret rites of the incubus and the succubus. As Bachelin justly remarks,[1] 'his practices included everything: hysterical mysticism, erotomania, scatology, sadism and Satanism.' Huysmans must surely have been a little ashamed of having been taken in. The long confessions of Boullan and other satanising priests which came into his hands could have left no doubt in his mind. He burned them shortly before his death.

Meanwhile his thoughts were turning away from Occultism altogether. He was exploring quite a different aspect of the supernatural. He was already *en route*.

[1] Henri Bachelin, *J.-K. Huysmans, Du Naturalisme Littéraire au Naturalisme Mystique*, Paris, 1926, p. 207.

CHAPTER NINE

EN ROUTE

———————————— • ————————————

There is little doubt that in the years which followed
the publication of *Là-bas*, Huysmans was profoundly
unhappy and perplexed. His exploration of the slums
of occultism had led him to an impasse. Boullan and his
friends had seemed to offer a way of escape from the down-
to-earth Naturalism of Zola and his school, but they had led
him deeper and deeper into the mire. Where, and to whom,
could he turn? Occultism had at least done this for him: it
had opened his mind to the possibility of a Beyond, and it was
perhaps natural that Huysmans should find his thoughts and
desires turning to another alternative.

Several writers have pointed out the curious parallel between the evolution of Huysmans and that of Chateaubriand
nearly a hundred years before.[1] They had the same aesthetic
approach, even the same emotional reactions to religion,
which meant for them the Catholic Church. Chateaubriand's
René had 'frequently sat down in a deserted church' and
watched the sinners kneeling in penitence at the foot of the
altar. 'And none came away without a face more serene.'
'Ah!' he cries, 'who has not sometimes felt the need of self-
regeneration, the need to renew his youth in the waters of

[1] See the interesting chapter '*A Dieu par le Moyen Age*' in Henri
Bachelin's *J.-K. Huysmans, Du Naturalisme Littéraire au Naturalisme
Mystique*, Paris, 1926, p. 208.

156

this torrent, to steep his soul anew in the fountain of life! Who does not sometimes feel crushed by the burden of his own corruption and incapable of doing anything great, noble or just!'

Huysmans felt the same. He began to frequent the churches of Paris, at first as a spectator, or rather as an auditor, for he was converted to plainchant long before he was converted to Catholicism. He often turned in to St. Sulpice, because there was a trained choir there, and he went in the evening because it was not then so crowded and because 'the ugliness of the nave, with its heavy vaulting, vanished at night.' It was true he had often to listen to a sermon, unctuous and commonplace, but when the noise of stamping feet and the movement of chairs told him that it was over, there fell a great silence, broken by a prelude from the organ. And then arose, against the mere murmur of the music, the slow and mournful chant of the *De Profundis*.

'Resting on the low accompaniment of the organ, aided by basses so hollow that they seemed to have descended into themselves, as it were underground, they sprang out, chanting the verse *"De profundis ad te clamavi, Do—"* and then stopped in fatigue, letting the last syllables *"mine"* fall like a heavy tear; then these voices of children, near breaking, took up the second verse of the psalm, *"Domine exaudi vocem meam,"* and the second half of the last word again remained in suspense, but instead of separating, and falling to the ground, there to be crushed out like a drop, it seemed to gather itself together with a supreme effort, and fling to heaven the anguished cry of the disincarnate soul, cast naked, and in tears before God.'[1]

'Ah,' he cried, 'the true proof of Catholicism is its art.' And that art was a unity, a marvellous blend of music, architecture, sculpture, painting, all held together in one unique

[1] *En Route*, trans. by C. Kegan Paul, London, 1922, p. 2.

cluster of thoughts, all serving the same end. Plainchant it-self was a kind of architecture now curving in upon itself like sombre Romanesque arches, now mounting skyward in the soaring lines of the Gothic, breaking into flowery tendrils and tracery as fine as lace. What music could compare with the tenderness of the *De Profundis* chanted in unison, the solemnity of the *Magnificat*, the warmth and splendour of the *Laude Sion*, the enthusiasm of the *Salve Regina*, the sorrow of the *Miserere* and the *Stabat Mater*, the majestic omnipotence of the *Te Deum?* Compared with such music all the pert inventions of a Gounod were so many 'fonts of toilet water'.

Durtal, the name Huysmans gave to the hero of *En Route* and of all his later novels, Durtal, who hardly pretends to be anybody but the author himself, stays on until the church is about to close. He wonders why, while listening to the music, it did not occur to him to pray. But why should he? 'Pray indeed? I have no desire for it. I am haunted by Catholicism, intoxicated by its atmosphere of incense and wax, moved even to tears by its prayers, touched even to the marrow by its psalms and chants. I am thoroughly disgusted with my life, very tired of myself, but it is a far cry from that to lead-ing a different existence! And yet—and yet—. . . . If I am perturbed in these chapels, I become unmoved and dry again, as soon as I leave them. . . . My heart is hardened and smoke-dried by dissipation, I am good for nothing.'[1]

'I do not practise my religion,' said Durtal to himself, 'because I yield to my baser instincts, and I yield to these instincts because I do not practise my religion.' He realised that, alone and unaided, progress was impossible, but to whom should he turn for help? To a priest? But the priests he had known were 'so mediocre, so lukewarm, above all so hostile to mysticism' that he was afraid they would do him

[1] *En Route*, p. 15.

more harm than good. They would tell him, he felt sure, that he had no business with mystical ideas, they would try to convince him that art was dangerous, they would empty over his head their flowing bowls of veal broth. Huysmans, and hence Durtal, had a horror of the commonplace and the cliché, and pious books, and pious conversation, seemed to him to be full of both.

Then one day, in a bookshop in the Rue Servandoni he got into conversation with an old priest. It was a shop full of rare liturgical works and lives of the saints, and the priest was probably surprised to see him there. When he learned that Durtal was looking for works on St. Lydwine of Schiedam, he was interested at once, and the two men walked home together conversing about the extraordinary woman who suffered every conceivable ill of the flesh and who subsisted for thirty-five years on nothing but the wafer of the Sacrament.

This is the story of Durtal's meeting with the Abbé Gévresin, as told in *En Route*. In real life it happened somewhat differently, for fantastic as it may seem, the person responsible for bringing Huysmans into contact with the Abbé Mugnier, the original of Gévresin, was no other than Madame de Courière, the original of Madame Chantelouve. Thus she who had first led him in the direction of Satanism was now, by an extraordinary combination of circumstances, to be the means of putting him on the road to conversion.

The Abbé Mugnier was at that time *vicaire* of St. Thomas d'Aquin. He was an unusual kind of priest, for he combined holiness of life with an enthusiasm for some of the great figures of the Romantic Movement in French literature. He had an enormous admiration for Chateaubriand and Victor Hugo and he professed a personal cult for the memory of George Sand which was, to say the least, exceptional among his confrères.

Born at Lille in 1852, he was four years younger than

Huysmans. In 1864 he entered the Seminary of Nogent-le-Rotran. He was about to begin his studies at the *Grand Séminaire* of Chartres in 1870 when war broke out, and he was ordained priest the day after the proclamation of the Commune. He became *vicaire* of St. Nicolas-des-Champs in 1879 and in 1888 was transferred to St. Thomas d'Aquin.

It was at a charity sale in 1890 that he was presented to Madame de Courière. He probably did not know that she had just been released from an asylum at Bruges to which she had been confined for running naked through the public park. He was charmed to find that she shared his enthusiasm for George Sand, and he invited her to visit him in the now vanished presbytery of St. Thomas d'Aquin where he lived.

When she did so she spoke to him of George Sand's nephew, the sculptor Clésinger,[1] whom she had known in the last years of his life. She produced from the carpet bag which she continually carried all the latest books and current issues of the literary reviews. She was a writer herself and, through the influence of her lover Rémy de Gourmont, was a contributor to the *Mercure de France*.

One day she showed the Abbé an issue of *L'Echo de Paris* in which *Là-bas* was appearing as a serial. She confessed (as well she might) to knowing the author. He was, she said, a man of great talent who for some time had been lurking round churches and was looking for a priest in whom he could confide. The Abbé Mugnier had not then read any of Huysmans' works, but he had heard of him as a writer belonging to the Médan group, that is, as one of the disciples of Zola. That such a man should be troubled with religious scruples interested the good priest extremely. He accepted Madame de Courière's offer to bring them together.

---

[1] Jean-Baptiste Clésinger (1814–1883) was the lover of Madame Sabatier, the celebrated 'Présidente' whom Baudelaire hailed as his *Vénus blanche*.

They met for the first time on May 23rd, 1891, and the Abbé has recorded his first impression of a 'thin man, his head entirely shaved, with clipped moustaches and showing signs of the embarrassment that everyone feels in a place unfamiliar to him'. Having effected the introduction, Madame de Courière retired and the Abbé Mugnier and Huysmans were left face to face.

Huysmans came straight to the point. 'I have just published a Satanic book,' he said, 'full of Black Masses. I want to write a *white* book, but for that I must be white myself. Have you anything that will bleach my soul?' Then he added, under his breath, the phrase that was frequently on his lips: 'I have religious atavisms.' The Abbé Mugnier resolved there and then to accept the task which was proposed to him in so abrupt a fashion.

Durtal fell into the habit of calling on the priest and he was always warmly welcomed. But soon he began to wonder, characteristically, if the welcome was real. Since he did not call upon him for spiritual advice he was afraid of being in his way and taking up his time. He persuaded himself that he was acting with discretion in not going to see him until he had really made up his mind to be converted. But, left to his own devices, he felt miserable and astray.

Although he was not actually engaged in writing a book, he was still toying with the idea of a life of St. Lydwine of Schiedam, but doubted if, in his present state of mind, he could make any progress. The old dreams began to haunt him again, his obsessions once more took hold of him. A succession of licentious scenes played themselves out like a pantomime in his imagination. 'Nude figures danced in his brain to the tune of psalms, and he woke from these dreams weak and panting, ready, if a priest had been there, to throw himself at his feet with tears, just as he would have abandoned himself to the basest pleasures, had the temptation suddenly come to him.'[1]

He found indeed, as many have found before him, that the very sharpening of the sensibility which was the condition of his repentance, lent a new urgency to the desires of the flesh. There was at this time in his life, a woman whom he calls Florence. We know nothing about her except for the occasional hints we can find scattered throughout the pages of *En Route*. We know that she had adolescent haunches and a street-arab smile, and we learn, in another passage, of 'her strange tastes, her mania for biting his ears, for drinking toilet scents out of little glasses, for nibbling bread and butter with caviar and dates'. It doesn't sound very alarming or diabolical. But we can perhaps assume that Huysmans regarded her with so much horror because she lent herself to his fantasies; for there was nothing straightforward or robust about his eroticism, and, reading between the lines, we can be fairly sure that there was an element of perversity and fetichism in his love-making. Perhaps that explains the terrible hold Florence seemed to have had over him. During long walks through Paris in which he endeavoured to tire himself out, her image followed him. If he sat in a café it 'came between his eyes and the newspaper he sought to read, becoming ever more definite. He ended after hours of struggle, by giving way and going to see this woman; he left her overwhelmed, half dead with disgust and shame, almost in tears'.[2]

Yet still he was bound to her and, in an effort to free himself, he adopted the strange compromise, as he calls it, of visiting another woman he knew. The result was to intensify the obsession of Florence, and he continued his intimacy with her until one day, with a desperate effort, he 'extricated himself from the sewer and stood on firm ground'.

During this crisis he had avoided going to see the Abbé

[1] *En Route*, p. 19.   [2] *En Route*, p. 81.

Gévresin for he was ashamed to confess his state of mind, but at last, feeling a new attack coming on, he took fright and knocked at the presbytery door of St. Thomas d'Aquin. The Abbé received him with his invariable kindness and heard his story. He pointed out to him that, at least, he was now repentant, and Durtal replied:

'Yes, but what is the good of it, if one is so weak that in spite of all efforts one is certain to be overthrown at the first assault?'

The Abbé made a strange reply. He promised that in future, the greater part of Durtal's temptations would be remitted, that his burdens would be placed on shoulders more able to bear them. He believed, he said, that this mystical substitution was possible. 'The saints will enter the lists to help you; they will take the overplus of the assaults which you cannot conquer; without even knowing your name, from their secluded province, nunneries of Carmelites and Poor Clares will pray for you, on receiving a letter from me.'

This notion of mystical substitution, with its related idea of the 'Treasury of Merits', is always a little startling to the Protestant mind, and with reason, for it was one of the rocks on which the Church split in the days of Luther. Even Huysmans was 'stupefied' by it in spite of his Catholic background; but it excited his imagination and helped him to overcome his obsessions. From that very day the most acute attacks ceased. He wonders, in true Huysmans fashion, whether that cessation was due to the intercession of the cloistered Orders or to a change in the weather, for the stifling heat gave way to floods of rain. He was able to sleep better and dismiss Florence from his thoughts.

Meanwhile the Abbé Gévresin was biding his time. Knowing Durtal's passion for plainchant he suggested that it was only the Benedictines who were aware of the real tradition and, in Paris, the only place where it could be heard in all its purity was in the chapel of the Benedictine nuns of the Blessed Sacrament in the Rue Monsieur.

As the good priest had foreseen, this hint was more than enough for Durtal. On the following Sunday he hastened to the Rue Monsieur and found a small cruciform church with one of its arms prolonged into a hall, separated from the choir by an iron grating. Apart from two angels—'of which the execution was truly sinful'—he found little to offend his æsthetic sensibilities. 'The rest of the chapel was dim and not too afflicting to the eyes.'

Eagerly he watched as a young sacristan-sister saw to the candles. He noted that her features were 'sickly but charming' and concluded, with a somewhat morbid satisfaction, that her body was 'wasted by prayers'. Then all the nuns entered behind the iron screen, advancing two by two, turning to the altar and genuflecting—a procession entirely in black except for the whiteness of the head-band and the collar, and the glittering spot of the little monstrance on the breast.

But it was their singing that ravished him: the tenderness of tones that austerities had rendered seraphic, voices that caught fire as they unfolded, blazing in virginal clusters of white sound. After listening to the *Kyrie Eleison*, to the *Gloria in Excelsis* and to the *Credo*, he concluded that here was something quite different from anything sung elsewhere in Paris. Instead of the curls and fringes of the polished melodies to be heard at St. Séverin and St. Sulpice, here 'he found himself in the presence of a chant, thin, sharp and nervous, like the work of an early master, and saw the ascetic severity of its lines, its sonorous colouring, the brightness of its metal hammered out with the rude yet charming art of Gothic jewels.'

When next they met the Abbé told Durtal of the extraordinary lives led by these women, fasting continually, rising at two in the morning to sing Matins and Lauds, taking turns before the taper of reparation and before the altar. 'Woman is stronger and braver than man,' declared the Abbé. 'No male ascetic could lead such a life, especially in the enervating atmosphere of Paris.' He spoke of their absolute obedience, and of the terrible crisis they had to pass about the twenty-ninth year of their age. But carnal emotions were not, to speak correctly, the most difficult of the assaults they had to undergo. Their real horror was the wild regret for the maternity they would never know. 'The desolate womb of woman revolts, and full of God though she be, her heart is breaking.'

The conversation which follows is pure Huysmans; full of his delight in the excessive and the grotesque, full also of his grim, Hogarthian humour. We learn of the most extravagant practices, such as those of the venerable Mother Pasidée of Siena, who not only scourged herself with holly and poured vinegar into her wounds, but had herself hung upside down in a chimney with a fire of damp straw underneath; of Benedict Labre who picked up the vermin that fell out of his sores and put them back; of Suso who for eighteen years bore on his naked shoulders an enormous cross studded with nails. We hear also of the strange Order of the Daughters of St. Magloire who, before they were admitted, had to swear that they had lived a life of sin. They were then examined and if their intact virginity proved them to have lied, they were turned away.

Huysmans then makes the Abbé describe the life of those who *were* admitted. 'They were whipped, locked up, subjected to the most rigid fasts, made their confessions thrice in the week, rose at midnight, were under the most unremitting surveillance, were even attended in their most secret retirement; their mortifications were incessant and their closure absolute. I need hardly add that this nunnery is dead.' It is sometimes difficult to know when Huysmans is laughing at the reader—and at himself.

Durtal leaves, reflecting that he would like to found an abbey where there would be a good library and leisure to work therein, decent meals and plenty of tobacco and 'permission to take a turn on the *quais* now and then.' The Abbé Gévresin probably guessed his thoughts, but he knew also that he would be unable to resist the lure he had laid down for him, by mentioning that there was to be, next Sunday, in the chapel of the Benedictine nuns in the Rue Monsieur, a ceremony of 'Clothing'. It was to take place between vespers and benediction and would be presided over by the Abbot of La Grande Trappe.

Sure enough Durtal was there, and the description of the ceremony is one of the most successful of Huysmans' evocations. He describes the entry of the postulant, dressed as a bride, the shearing of her hair, her re-entry dressed as a nun, the Abbot's address, the *Te Deum*. Then, preceded by the cross and torch-bearers, the procession passes out of the church into the courtyard, in one wall of which is a folding door. The postulant stands in front of it, alone. She knocks on the door and it opens to reveal another large court, in which waits the community, in a semi-circle. And with alternating phrases of chanted Latin, the new nun moves slowly forward. The Mother Superior of the Convent comes to meet her— and the door closes.

It was on the way back from this service that the Abbé, who had also been present, unmasked his batteries. Echoing a remark of Durtal's about the beauty of the cloistered life he said that he himself had long wished to become a monk, and a member of St. Benedict's family. When he was younger and stronger he had always gone for his retreats to one of their monasteries, sometimes to the black monks of Solesmes or of Ligugé, sometimes to the Cistercians, the white monks of La Trappe. Both were branches of the same tree, but the Trappists interpreted the rule of St. Benedict, which was broad and simple, less in its spirit than in its letter, while the Benedictines did the opposite.

Durtal (that is, Huysmans) could never resist a discussion concerning the differences between the monastic orders, and seeing that he had his attention, the Abbé spoke of a small Trappist monastery near Paris, Notre Dame de l'Âtre (really Notre Dame d'Igny, near Fismes, on the confines of the Aisne and the Marne) which not only had saints among its children but was situated in a delightful solitude with ponds and immemorial trees.

Durtal objected that the Trappist Order was the most rigid that had ever been imposed on men. It was then that the Abbé delivered his final assault. He seized Durtal's hands and looked him in the face. 'It is there,' he said, 'that you must go for your conversion.'

Durtal immediately began to explain that he had neither the strength of soul nor the strength of body for such a course. Would he have to get up at two o'clock in the morning? Would he have to eat vegetables cooked in water?[1] The Abbé reassured him. He would not have to get up until three, or even four, o'clock and vegetables were only cooked in water on fast days. Durtal was still doubtful. He wanted, he said, 'a mitigated asylum, a quiet convent'.

The priest replied that if he sent him to the Jesuits he was quite certain he would not stay two days. He would find himself among amiable and clever men who would interfere with his life, mix themselves up with his art, examine his every thought with a magnifying glass. At La Trappe, on the contrary, he would be free to go and come as he wished; no-one would trouble him or question him. He would be able to decide to be converted or not, just as he wished.

Durtal felt quite dazed by this proposal. He was seized with

[1] In this particular difficulty of the monastic life Englishmen would appear to have an unfair advantage.

an almost physical anguish at the thought that the time had come when he must make up his mind. The Abbé, seeing that he was suffering, promised to pray for him, and Durtal, left alone, began to marvel at the priest's perspicacity. 'He recalled the strategic smiles, the ambiguous phrases, the dreamy silences of the Abbé Gévresin, he understood the kindness of his counsels, the patience of his plans; and a little put out at having been, without knowing it, led so wisely, he exclaimed in spite of himself: "This, then, was the design the priest was ripening, with his air of not concerning himself with it at all." '

The Abbé had not intended that Durtal should become a permanent inmate of La Trappe; he had suggested that he should go there for a week. Durtal continued to think of objections, some of them trivial, some of them real enough. He felt very deeply the squalor of the life he had been leading and the thought of confessing his sins 'to an old monk who emerges from an eternity of silence to listen' terrified him. 'The Eucharist also seems terrible. To dare to come forward, to offer Him as a tabernacle the sewer of self scarce purified by repentance, a sewer drained by absolution, but still hardly dry, is monstrous.'

The bad cooking and the getting up in the middle of the night might, on second thoughts, be endured, 'and no doubt I shall find some means of smoking cigarettes by stealth in the woods. After all, a week is soon over, and I am not even obliged, if I begin to feel ill, to remain a week.'

In the end, he decided to go, and in July 1892, 'with the good humour of a whipped dog,' he set out for La Trappe. Meanwhile the Abbé had written to the authorities asking them to allow their guest as much liberty as possible. The fact that he was a well-known novelist and *sous-chef de bureau* at the Ministry of the Interior was not mentioned.

There is little doubt that part of the interest of *En Route* for the general public lay in its picture of life in a monastery. The laity, even in Catholic countries, knows very little of such matters, and with Huysmans they were at least sure that everything would be minutely observed and accurately set down. He had not been a *Naturaliste* for nothing, and he did not cease to be one when he went to La Trappe.

Even more interesting is the analysis of his own sensations, when he made his first contact with the Trappists. He describes his arrival, his reluctance to ring the bell, the silent doorkeeper, his introduction to Father Etienne, the Guest Master, the 'cell' into which he was shown.

He found pens and writing paper laid out for him—perhaps the Abbé Gévresin had let a hint fall after all—and two books: *The Introduction to the Devout Life* by St. Francis de Sales, and St. Ignatius Loyola's *Spiritual Exercises*. He also found a card setting forth the 'Exercises of the Community': the whole day from two o'clock in the morning to eight o'clock at night accounted for. He also found the rules for those like himself who were merely making a retreat. He was to rise, as the Abbé Gévresin had promised, not at two o'clock in the morning but at four. He concluded that this was 'an almost possible hour'.

Then he began to read the notes on the back of the card:

'Those who are not bound to say the Breviary will say the Little Office of the Blessed Virgin.

'The Retreatants are requested to make their Confessions at an early date, in order to have their mind more free for meditation. . . .'

The confession! That was the rub. He had not yet made up his mind that he was going to confess at all. The good monks were certainly taking a great deal for granted. However when he met Father Etienne again he asked to see the confessor on the following evening.

Father Etienne showed him the room where he would dine,

in company, it seemed, with a certain M. Bruno, a person who had renounced the world and lived enclosed without, however, having taken the vows. 'He is what our rule calls an Oblate,' said Father Etienne, and this was probably the first time Huysmans had heard a term which was to occupy so much of his thought for the rest of his life.

M. Bruno proved, as Father Etienne had suggested, a learned and a holy man with whom it was a pleasure to converse—for conversation was permitted during the meal—and Huysmans took to him at once. His real name was Charles Rivière. He had lived the greater part of his life at Rheims where he was engaged in the wool trade. Like Huysmans he never married and when his mother died in 1892 he entered the monastery of La Trappe d'Igny as an Oblate. He remained friendly with Huysmans and paid him several visits in the closing years of the latter's life. He himself died at an advanced age in 1912.

In the book he serves as a kind of *raisonneur* to explain to Durtal the details of the monastic life which the newcomer could not be expected to know. Durtal was relieved to find that the dinner was not too inadequate, consisting of two poached eggs, a bowl of rice, another of French beans and a pot of honey. When it was over M. Bruno told him that he had twenty minutes in which to walk in the garden before compline.

Huysmans excelled in describing religious services and this, his first among the Trappists, was no exception. He was impressed by the rapid declamation of the Office and the almost hypnotic effect of the responses, by the great shout of '*Salve Regina*'. And, suddenly, at the word '*Maria*', the chant ended, the tapers were extinguished and all the monks fell on their knees. Then, as 'the Angelus unfolded under the arches the separate petals of its clear sounds, they prostrated themselves, their faces buried in their hands.' Durtal concluded that the true creator of plainchant could be none other than the Holy Ghost. When the service was over he said goodnight to M. Bruno and returned to his cell.

The night that followed was terrible. It was as if the Devil was making a final assault upon his soul. He woke trembling from a succession of nightmares. All his old erotic dreams returned to trouble him, but with a force and urgency that he had never known before. All the imaginary caresses which in real life could only follow one another were, in the dream, united in a single moment. It seemed as if a fluid form was only just vanishing as he awoke and 'this being was felt near him so distinctly, that the sheet, disarranged by the wind of the flight, was still in motion, and he looked at the empty place in terror. It reminded him of the stories he had read of the Succubus, and also of the occasions when he had been with Madame Chantelouve.

Fearful of falling asleep again, he looked at his watch. It was two o'clock. He went out into the garden to smoke a cigarette and, seeing a light in the chapel, entered it quietly. He almost fell over a prostrate body and saw to his astonishment that the floor of the sanctuary was almost covered with human forms, 'lying in the attitudes of combatants mowed down by grapeshot, some flat on their faces, others on their knees, some leaning their hands on the ground as if stricken from behind, others extended with their fingers clenched on their breast, others again holding their heads or stretching out their arms.'[1] And all in absolute silence.

Durtal saw that some of them were in ecstasy, and he cried, within himself: 'Oh, to pray like these monks!' Then he found himself praying, sinking down on the pavement, humbly asking pardon for having soiled by his presence the purity of the holy place. It is impossible to read this passage in *En Route* without being convinced of the desperate sincerity of the man who wrote it.

[1] *En Route*, p. 171.

The mass ended at six o'clock and Durtal walked in the woods for a while, before breakfast, collecting his thoughts. He was almost happy until, in conversation with Father Etienne, the latter remarked that a monk would be waiting for him at ten o'clock to hear his confession. Durtal's agony of mind returned. He remembered that he had never confessed since his childhood and did not even know how a confession was made.

It was not necessary to search his conscience: 'without any need of probing it his life sprang out in jets of filth . . . he recalled to mind how he had sought after monstrous iniquities, his pursuit of artifices aggravating the malice of the act, and the accomplices and agents of his sins passed in file before him.' He remembered that 'demoniacal adulteress' Madame Chantelouve who had drawn him into sacrilege. 'And in her turn, Florence appeared with her little street-arab smile, and her childish haunches.'

When, at last, he found himself in the presence of the confessor he completely lost his head. The words would not come; he broke down and wept, and, seeing his condition, the monk said, 'Your soul is too tired for me to fatigue you with questions. Come back at nine o'clock tomorrow.'

Durtal got through the day somehow. He read the Penitential Psalms and the life of St. Angela of Foligno. She too had been a sinner, a woman of many lovers and shameless life. But she was converted, assumed the habit of the Third Order of St. Francis, begged in the streets and washed the sores of beggars. In the end she was rewarded with visions of Christ. Durtal was comforted, but felt compelled to add that the conditions of the Blessed Angela were more favourable than his. 'Living in the thirteenth century she had a shorter journey to make to approach God, for since the Middle Ages each century takes us further from Him.' She lived in a time full of miracles and overflowing with saints, whereas he lived in an age when miracles were rare, and in Paris where saints scarcely abounded.

As the hour for confession once more approached his terrors returned. But the Prior—for such the confessor was—showed him great tenderness. Durtal began by accusing himself of the ordinary faults of mankind: want of charity, evil speaking, lying, vanity, anger. The monk interrupted him to ask if all his debts were paid and he was able to answer yes. 'Have you belonged to any secret society? Have you fought a duel? I am obliged to ask these questions because they are reserved cases.' The penitent answered 'No', although, as we have seen, he had come very near to doing both. When he came to the sins of the flesh he trembled and was silent. 'Must I go into the details?' he asked.

The confessor replied that it was not necessary, if he would answer one or two questions: had he been guilty of solitary vice or of sins committed between persons of the same sex?

'Not since I left school.'

But he admitted every possible excess in his relations with women, and, with a great effort, confessed that he had from curiosity assisted at a Black Mass, and that afterwards, without wishing it, he had defiled a Host which Madame Chantelouve had concealed about her. The Prior asked him if he had continued his relations with her afterwards, and he replied 'No'.

Then the Prior, after a little speech in which he warned him of the dangers of falling back, raised his arms, clad in the ample white sleeves of his habit, and uttered the three words: *Ego te absolvo*. Durtal burst into tears.

There can be little doubt that in this account of Durtal's confession and absolution we have an authentic fragment of Huysman' autobiography. This is what makes it so moving. And the effect is not diminished by his frank account of all the difficulties (one can hardly call them religious difficulties) which immediately presented themselves. He found that on the following day, when he had hoped to be given Holy Communion, there was no monk available to conduct the service. There was only a visiting priest, a fat, jolly man who retailed funny stories, and to whom Durtal had taken an instant dislike. It was in vain that he told himself that the character of the intermediary was of no importance—and, after all, the priest, for all he knew, might be a holy man— his sense of disappointment remained.

Then there was the question of the rosary. The Prior had instructed him to get one, and to say 'ten' as his penance. Durtal drove himself to distraction wondering whether he had meant ten beads or ten whole rosaries. The latter would mean five hundred prayers on end. Yet just ten beads seemed a most inadequate penance for all his sins. Besides, he confessed that he had such an instinctive repugnance against 'these drops of elevation taken in globules' that he could hardly bring himself to say the rosary at all. In the end he decided to swallow the larger 'dose' (his own word), and found himself 'stupefied' in the process.

Finding him distracted the good M. Bruno fetched the Prior, who assured him that he had meant ten beads. He told him to say no more, but he ordered him to communicate without fail on the following day. And he found, after all, that the service was conducted by a monk.

Certainly everything was done to help and cherish this strange penitent, and when he left La Trappe he did so with real regret. He had been there a week, but in that week how much had happened. Now he had to take up his life again in Paris, attend his office in the Ministry, meet his friends— but not, of course, Florence—and do his best to maintain himself in Grace. He was a new man. It was yet to be seen how much of the old man—of letters—remained.

CHAPTER TEN

THE MIRACLE OF CHARTRES

———————————— • ————————————

Huysmans had come back from La Trappe converted,
but happiness still eluded him, and the account of
his condition which he puts into the mouth of his
character Durtal is both sincere and pathetic. 'On his return
to Paris from La Trappe he had fallen into a fearful state of
spiritual anæmia. His soul kept its room, rarely rose, lounged
on a couch, was torpid with a tepid languor still lulled by the
sleepy mutter of mere lip-service, and prayers reeled off as by
a worn-out machine of which the spring releases itself, so that
it works all alone with no result, and without a touch to start
it.'[1]

A strange association presented itself to his mind between
the *Revelations of St. Teresa* and Poe's *Fall of the House of
Usher*. In Durtal, the Chambers of the Soul were deserted
as after a long mourning; but in the rooms that remained
open, phantoms of sins confessed, of buried evil-doing,
wandered like the sister of the tormented Usher. Durtal, like
Edgar Poe's unhappy sufferer, listened with horror to the
rustle of steps on the stairs, the piteous weeping behind the
doors. . . . How worm-eaten, how arid were the poor recesses
of his soul! He wondered, with anguish, whether they would
not end like the Manor in Edgar Poe's tale, by crumbling

[1] *The Cathedral*, by J.-K. Huysmans, translated from the French by
Clara Bell, London. (Kegan Paul, Trench, Trübner and Co.) 1898.

175

suddenly, one fatal day, into the dark waters of the pool of sin which was undermining the walls.'

And yet, since his return, 'the most persistent miscreant of them all', which had tormented him so long, the sin of the flesh, at last was silenced, and left him in peace. 'La Trappe', he cried, 'crushed me! It cured me of sensuality, but only to load me with disorders of which I knew nothing before I submitted to that treatment! It is humble itself, but it puffed up my vanity and increased my pride tenfold—then it set me free, but so weak, so wearied, that I have never since been able to conquer that inanition, never have been fit to enjoy the Mystical Nourishment which I nevertheless must have.'

He realised that he would never be able to adopt, for himself, the austere Rule of the Trappists, but he could, at least, write an account of his conversion. The book was to be called *La Bataille Charnelle* (it was only later that he changed the title to *En Route*) and he would write it, of course, in his office, grumbling the while at the occasional interruptions of official business. Even Huysmans could not entirely divest himself of his duties as a Government employee.

Paul Valéry has left an amusing snapshot[1]—if it be not blasphemy to call anything of Valéry's a snapshot—of Huysmans in his office at the Ministry of the Interior. He was in 1892, when Valéry visited him, *sous-chef de bureau* in the *Sureté Générale*, and complained bitterly of the annoyance caused to him, in his official capacity, by the anarchists. It was at the height of the period of bomb-outrages; President Carnot had only recently been assassinated, and the Press was highly critical of the alleged incapacity and inaction of the *Sureté Générale*.

'Some *Préfet*,' complained Huysmans, 'informs me that his local *anarcho* has disappeared. When that happens it costs France thirty thousand francs.'

[1] Frédéric Lefèvre, *Entretien avec Paul Valéry*, Paris, 1926, p. 41.

Valéry expressed his astonishment and Huysmans explained that it was necessary to telegraph a description of the suspect to the police of the world. Valéry suggested that it would be simpler, and cheaper, to give ten thousand francs to the anarchist. Huysmans smiled and said that that solution hadn't been thought of.

The functionary-novelist had other troubles due not to his official position but to his fame as an author. *Là-bas* had just been published when, one day, his clerk handed him a card embossed with a coronet, and on which he read the name of a nobleman quite unknown to him. When the door was opened there appeared a gentleman in a state of acute embarrassment. He was wearing an overcoat with an astrakhan collar and held in his red-gloved hands a top-hat *d'une provenance assez lointaine*. He seemed to have the utmost difficulty in expressing what he had come to say. Finally he uttered the mysterious words: 'Monsieur, the Countess is below.'

It appeared that the Count and Countess had journeyed in their antique carriage from some remote part of France solely in order to see Huysmans, for the lady had insisted that nothing could make her happy unless he would use his influence to get her admitted to a Black Mass. Huysmans' reaction was to have the unhappy husband thrown out of his office.

On another occasion he was visited by a man in cyclist's knickerbockers and a check cap who claimed to be the Archbishop of Colombo. It was true he was in disgrace and had been interdicted by the Church. But he still wore an enormous amethyst on his finger as a sign of his ecclesiastical dignity, and he could still—since the sacraments are indelible—ordain priests, which he was very willing to do for a consideration. Such priests could then supply real consecrated Hosts for the practitioners of Black Magic. It is small wonder that Huysmans kept two green files in his office labelled respectively *raseurs* and *tapeurs*.[1]

Among Huysmans' visitors at this period of his official life was Gustave Coquiot, his ardent disciple, to whom we are indebted for so many intimate pen-pictures of the writer he admired so much. He called upon him first one evening in April 1892, apparently not yet having made his acquaintance and not knowing how he would be received, just as Huysmans had called on Zola a generation before. He climbed the narrow staircase in the Rue de Sèvres, knocked at Huysmans' door and when it was opened by the writer himself proffered his letter of introduction. Huysmans received him amiably, although he was not very talkative, and the young man nearly ruined everything by praising Sar Péladan, as a man of talent in spite of his odd behaviour. As we have seen Sar Péladan was, both as an occultist and a 'man of the Midi', one of the people Huysmans most cordially detested. However the *gaffe* was smoothed over, and Coquiot invited to come again.

He returned frequently, although he could not help contrasting the reception he sometimes encountered with that accorded by Mallarmé, his other idol, courteous and calm, where Huysmans was bitter and restive. But Huysmans' bark was worse than his bite, and even his constant complaints of the life he was compelled to live away from the cloister could not conceal his real joy at finding himself back in Paris in his comfortable apartment full of books and bibelots where, at ease in his slippers, under the lamp, smoking innumerable cigarettes, and with his cat Barre-de-Rouille beside him, he could work in peace.

On the walls were many pictures: watercolours by Forain, curious works by Raffaëlli, Seurat, Cézanne, Bresdin and

[1] If a personal note may be permitted, the present author could name another senior Civil Servant who finds it necessary to keep on his desk a permanent file labelled, concisely, 'Lunatics'.

Constantin Guys, engravings by Peter Breughel, Israel van
Meckenen, Dürer, Teniers, Hogarth, Lucas van Leyden,
Daniel Hopfer and Piranesi. The only name which surprises
in this list is that of Piranesi. One would not have expected
his grandiose evocations of Roman ruins to appeal to Huysmans. All the rest reflect very faithfully both his enthusiasm
for the Impressionists, of whom he had been so powerful a
champion, and his passion for the grotesque, especially the
Flemish grotesque. It is interesting to compare this decor of
1892 with the one described by Dom Besse two years later,
when everything had become much more ecclesiastical.

Huysmans lived very simply. A 'daily help' cleaned his
rooms, blacked his boots and prepared his fire. He did everything else himself, even to checking his laundry. Coquiot
does not tell us if he cooked, but it seems unlikely. He probably followed his life-long practice of having all his meals in
restaurants. The young disciple frequently accompanied him
to the *Petite Chaise*, 36 Rue de Grenelle, where he took his
breakfast, or on his walks along the quais.

'When I had the joy of accompanying him,' he says[1], 'we
invariably began our walk at the Pont Neuf, and, after a
glance under the bridge, the picturesque aspect of which
always captivated him, we went on slowly towards the Pont
Royal. But how many books he handled before arriving there
and how many characteristic things he had to say, how many
remarks about the authors whose works were displayed on the
bookstalls . . .

'At the Pont Royal the Seine was always so pretty, so
inviting that we never failed to follow it to the Place de la
Concorde. And the boats and the men unloading them, the
dogs bathing in the river, all these amused us, until the
moment when I felt that he wished to be left alone—until
the moment when I watched him go away, very straight and

[1] Gustave Coquiot, *Le Vrai J.-K. Huysmans*, Paris, 1912, p. 25.

very thin, without a gesture, in his eternal tall hat with the flat brims.'

Sometimes Coquiot would make his way to the Ministry itself and would drop in with a friend to find Huysmans surrounded not only by his official files but by his own books and the classified notes of his (private) work. He never failed to greet them with some sarcasm at the expense of the Administration, and of his colleagues who were all, according to his account, pedantic numskulls (*solides cuistres*). From time to time he had to send in a report from which his chiefs estimated his zeal, intelligence and general conduct. This does not seem in the least unreasonable although the young disciples were naturally scandalized.

For his chiefs Huysmans was obviously a man of small account. They had heard that he was a writer, vaguely affiliated to the Zola school, but as he remained an employee, it was obvious that he could not be very successful. They were therefore both astonished and scandalized when, in September, 1893, he was suddenly made a Chevalier de la Légion d'Honneur. Many of his superiors had been coveting the cross for years and now Huysmans had received it over their heads!

Huysmans merely smiled his sardonic smile and went on with his book. The Abbé Mugnier had not lost sight of his penitent and he suggested that for some of the theological passages it would be wise to enlist the help of a clerical friend. This friend was the Abbé Ferret, priest of St. Sulpice. He was a year younger than Mugnier but they had been fellow-pupils at St. Sulpice between the years 1871 and 1876. He was a man of piety and learning, and some commentators have thought that his influence on Huysmans was even greater than that of the Abbé Mugnier himself.

Huysmans' conversion had created considerable interest in the world of letters, and in 1894, before the publication of

En Route, he was asked to write a preface for the *Poésies Religieuses* of Verlaine. Huysmans took a high line and some of his remarks were more calculated to frighten the pious than to convince them of the reality of his conversion. He hailed Verlaine as the great Catholic poet of modern times, and called upon the Faithful to be thankful for the sins and errors of the recently departed poet, for without them he could never have written such exquisite verse. He goes on to remark, characteristically, that the only Catholic writers of talent were the converts, for they were the only ones who had gained sufficient experience of life to know what they were talking about. And, if this were true, how grateful Catholics should be to those who had become champions of the Faith at such peril to their own souls!

Such remarks were not likely to be accepted with unlimited enthusiasm by the clergy and the more docile members of their flocks. Some pious people began to doubt whether the ex-disciple of Zola had ever really been converted at all, and these doubts were not entirely dissipated even by the publication of *En Route*. In fact the book reawakened the suspicions of those Catholics for whom the spiritual odyssey of Huysmans was nothing but 'literature', a kind of mystification similar to that of Léo Taxil. Even Lucien Descaves, one of Huysmans' intimates, was not quite convinced that the Master was serious,[1] and Gustave Coquiot dared to express the same sentiments to Huysmans himself. A few days before the two men had been together in the church of St. Germain-des-Prés and Huysmans had launched out into one of his usual diatribes against the stupidity of the Catholic clergy in all matters connected with art. There were plenty of such diatribes in *En Route* and they were not calculated to appease the Catholic press.

Huysmans tried to defend himself against the attacks to

[1] See *L'Événement*, April 25, 1891.

which he was subjected. In a letter[1] he begs his correspondent not to forget when reading *En Route* that the book was not intended primarily for Catholics but for the intellectual world of Paris. He believed that there was in this world a misdirected current of mysticism, and that his book might help to canalize it, and that one had to keep the attention of such a public. For this reason, it was necessary to put aside all pious chit-chat and to concentrate upon the *'haute mystique'*. It was also necessary to tell the truth about the clergy, and naturally enough they were not very pleased. The book, claimed Huysmans, was absolutely sincere, a real confession of the soul, as well as an attempt to exalt the splendour of the liturgies, the admirable art of the Church. Huysmans' main fear was that by this book of *'Catholicisme Enragé'*, he had excited against him all the Jews and Freemasons who governed France.

The good monk to whom this letter was addressed was still not satisfied. He would have liked the author to suppress certain pages offensive to pious sentiment, and Huysmans defended himself in another long letter. 'They that are well,' he declared, 'have no need of the physician, but they that are sick.' But it was impossible to treat the sick with innocuous remedies. What they needed was an emetic. With characteristic phrase, he even goes so far as to refer to his book as *un vomitif d'âme* and claimed that *En Route* had already caused conversions and was continuing to do so from day to day.

Gradually the feeling changed. The Abbé Mugnier rallied his forces. He spoke of the book to his parishioners at St. Clotilde; he even induced Marshal MacMahon to carry copies to his country estate and distribute them to the guests at his shooting parties. What the guests thought of this method of literary propaganda is not recorded.

[1] February 25th, 1895, quoted by Dom A. du Bourg, in his *Huysmans Intime*, Paris, 1908.

The Miracle of Chartres

The Abbé Klein, writing in *Le Monde*,[1] declared: 'The conversion of the writer Durtal is serious.' The Catholic journal *Études Religieuses* maintained that 'in this curious, profound and moving book, there is the history of a soul hating evil, triumphing over it and moving upward to the light.' The *Revue Thomiste* was equally favourable and even Mgr. d'Hulst, who had not been spared some very disobliging remarks in *En Route*, remarked that there are states of soul which cannot be invented. Meanwhile, as a good literary man, Huysmans had already begun to think of his next book. He had plunged deeply, not only into the works of the mystical writers but into the history of Catholic art. And the more deeply he penetrated the more he became convinced that Catholic art (by which he meant, of course, Gothic art—he would probably have detested Rome if he had ever gone there) was almost entirely a monastic creation. The monks it was—the Benedictines—who had presided over the flowering of Romanesque into Gothic.

Later researches have only served to confirm this opinion. Indeed, thanks to the monumental work of Emile Mâle,[2] we can trace the development step by step and can realise that it all stemmed from St.-Denis, where, early in the twelfth century, Abbot Suger began to reconstruct his basilica on a new principle. In 1144 the great church was completed, a miracle of lightness combined with strength, a mathematical harmony of slender columns and delicate traceries which was to establish the type of ecclesiastical architecture for four centuries. St.-Denis has been called the grandmother of cathedrals. 'It is from St.-Denis,' says Anthyme Saint-Paul,[3] 'from its monastic church that is derived the characteristic cathedral-type, of which Amiens is the culmination.' From

[1] March 12, 1895.
[2] Emile Mâle, *L'Art religieux du XIIe Siècle en France.*
[3] A. Saint-Paul, *Architecture et Catholicisme*, Paris, 1905.

St.-Denis is derived the tripartite form of the façade, together with the sculptured symbolism that enriches it.

Suger, the Abbot, was a real creator in this field. 'Thanks to Suger reappeared the symbolic opposition of the Old and the New Testament; the Tree of Jesse was probably born at St.-Denis; it is here also that the parable of the Wise and Foolish Virgins was associated with the Last Judgment. The most ancient example of God the Father, his arms outspread and supporting on his breast the Son on the Cross, is to be seen at St.-Denis. The Middle Ages imitated this theme for centuries. Perhaps we should also credit Suger with that beautiful scene of the Coronation of the Virgin which the Middle Ages loved so much.'[1] All this wonder, this miraculous blend of true piety and the extreme of æsthetic sensibility, had been the work of monks, or of those working under their direction. And all these monks had belonged to the Order of St. Benedict. Surely it was in this Order if any that he, Huysmans, could find a refuge.

But strange as it may seem, until the very eve of the publication of *En Route*, he had not met any Benedictines, although he had attended some of their services in the Rue Monsieur before his departure for La Trappe. Even now his first meeting was almost an accident; certainly it came about in the curiously roundabout way in which everything seemed to happen to Huysmans. He had a friend called Gustave Boucher who kept a bookshop on the Quai Voltaire. They had known one another since 1890, at which time they were both deeply immersed in occultism, and indeed it was Boucher who had introduced him to some of the more curious 'spiritualist' circles. But Boucher, like Huysmans, had now put occultism behind him and had renounced the Devil and all his works.

[1] Dom Philibert Schmitz, *Histoire de l'Ordre de Saint-Benoît*, vol. VI, p. 55.

While Huysmans was finding his salvation at La Trappe d'Igny, Boucher was in retreat at Ligugé, and here he fell in with the Abbé Mugnier who happened to be paying a visit to the Benedictine monastery. It was natural that they should speak of Huysmans, and they did so in the presence of Boucher's spiritual director Dom Besse.

Dom Besse was no ordinary monk. He was passionately devoted to art and literature and dreamed of making his Order the centre of artistic creation which it had been in the Middle Ages. It seemed to him, as he listened, that Huysmans was a man after his own heart and he determined to visit him next time he was in Paris.

'Guided by the bookseller,' says Dom Daoust,[1] 'the monk gaily climbed the five flights of the Rue de Sèvres and reached the bachelor's abode under the roof. We can imagine this decisive meeting without difficulty. From the moment he entered Dom Besse felt at home in this medieval hermitage: the walls were hidden by rows of books and reproductions of the Primitives. And this library looked like an oratory with its saints forming a pious circle round you, while the mantelpiece, cluttered with chalices, relics and a censer, lying on a chasuble with a white cross, resembled an altar.'

Huysmans was equally delighted with his visitor. With his massive but muscular frame and his air of rude health he brought a breath of fresh air into the apartment. Under the name of the Abbé Felletin, he is described for us in '*L'Oblat*'. 'Robust, the blood near the surface of the cheeks and making them look like the peel of apricots, the nose protuberant and mobile when he smiled, the eyes light-blue and the lips full, this monk exuded an atmosphere of tranquil piety, the joy of a healthy and unselfish soul, a soul that smells good.'

[1] Joseph Daoust, *Les Débuts Bénédictins de J.-K. Huysmans*, Saint-Wandrille, 1950, p. 9.

No man could have been less like Huysmans himself with his scraggy figure, his thin face, his pointed pepper-and-salt beard, his suspicious, unquiet eyes; but the monk and he took to one another at once. They plunged into a discussion of monasteries, liturgies, mysticism. It was Dom Besse who did most of the talking. From his vast store of learning he spoke eloquently of the services of the medieval Benedictines to all the arts: architecture, sculpture, music, letters, science. Now science had been abandoned to the laity and all the arts of the Church had suffered a sad decline. The Benedictines had already reformed the liturgy and revived the Gregorian chant. It remained for them to do the same for painting and sculpture.

All this was so much in line with the tenour of Huysmans' own thoughts that it would have been strange if he had not caught fire. And then the monk revealed the purpose of his visit. He had been entrusted by his superiors with a mission. He had been put in charge of the project of restoring the ruined Abbey of St. Wandrille, in Normandy. To the rhythm of the purest Gregorian its walls should be built anew until, its façade rich with statues and its walls decorated by a new Angelico, there should arise a splendid basilica, worthy rival of Cluny and Vézelay. Before he parted Dom Besse had Huysmans' promise to visit St. Wandrille as soon as an opportunity arose.

His first visit was in July 1896 in the company of Boucher. He found Dom Besse established, with a handful of young monks, in a group of buildings on the bank of the Fontenelle. It was true that there was nothing very medieval about some of them. The entrance gate was pure Louis XV. Huysmans' 'cell' was a vast apartment more reminiscent of the *Ancien Régime* than of the Middle Ages. But there was a cloister and an ancient chapter house which served as a chapel. It was true that the music did not reach the standard Huysmans would have liked; but he was in a mood to be pleased and found the *Kyrie*, 'exquisite, profound, grave and tender', and the *Credo* 'charming'.

He was delighted with the refectory in spite of the meagre fare. It was the first time he had ever been present at a monastic repast, for at La Trappe the guests took their meals apart from the monks. Dom Besse himself intoned a superb *Benedicite*, and a reader in a pulpit chanted the psalms.

Huysmans thought that at last he had found the retreat of his dreams. He assisted at the Offices, he examined the old buildings with their mutilated statues and sculptured capitals. He walked in the park, wandered down long alleys of secular trees, a carpet of dead leaves under his feet. He studied the mystics. He talked to Dom Besse.

The latter showed him, 'under the mantle', a copy of a recently printed work by Madame Cécile Bruyère, Abbess of Solesmes, entitled *'De l'Oraison d'après la Sainte Écriture et la Tradition monastique.*[1] Why 'under the mantle'? Because, confessed Dom Besse, the writings of the Abbess contained 'some daring propositions which had not been read without displeasure at Rome'. For his own part he did not care very much either for the Abbess or her book. Huysmans, however, was immensely taken with it, particularly with a passage about the assaults of the Devil, which seemed to him to re-count his own struggles to escape from the obsessions of Satanism. Madame de Bruyère's book *On Prayer* was a favourite with him for the rest of his life. He mentions it with great respect in his own writings, but makes out that it was first shown to him by the Oblate, M. Bruno, at La Trappe. The reason for this curious transposition is that, when he came to write, St. Wandrille was too painful a memory. For the moment his only regret was that he had to leave so soon. He

[1] The first edition, *communication essentiellement privée*, was brought out at Solesmes in 1886.

left on 8th July, having stayed a week. It was necessary for him to take up again the dreadful burden of his life in Paris.

He visited St. Wandrille again towards the end of September and in company with Dom Besse looked at some of the antiquities of the neighbourhood. They went to Caudebec and to Joumièges, and at the latter place walked in the great triple alley of trees which gives so exact an image of the nave of a great church with its side aisles, a nave supported by great pillars and roofed in by leaves. He agreed with Chateaubriand that it must have been by such a spectacle that man was first inspired to invent the Gothic arch.

He returned to Paris once more enchanted. Dom Besse was both an artist and a saint, and the young men who were helping him the future hope of art and sanctity. Several of them visited him in the Rue de Sèvres, and their coming and going served to maintain his enthusiasm at fever-heat. St. Wandrille was *his* abbey and within its walls he had passed the happiest hours of his life.

And then, out of a clear sky, came the thunderbolt. Those who had sent Dom Besse to St. Wandrille began to wonder whether they had not, after all, made a mistake. It was not that they doubted his enthusiasm; it was precisely his enthusiasm they were afraid of. For in his grandiose projects the good monk had completely neglected the practical side of affairs. He had spent money lavishly, too lavishly, on things which were not immediately necessary for the establishment of a monastery. Suddenly came the news that he had been deposed and, worse than that, exiled to the monastery of Silos in the mountains of Old Castile. Some of his young helpers, discouraged, abandoned the monastic life altogether.

Dom Besse obediently packed his bags and left for Spain, without a word of complaint. But for Huysmans the shock was terrible. 'Everything is ruined,' he cried. 'The future is darker than ever; my dream of a haven is lost.'[1] It is a sign of the bitterness of his disappointment that he does not mention St. Wandrille in any of his books, and that he never visited the place again.

He tried to console himself by attending midnight mass, on Christmas Eve, at Chartres, a cathedral which was to occupy an increasing part of his attention for the next few years. He was beginning to toy with the idea of writing a great Catholic trilogy of which *En Route*, already published, should form the first part. That work had dealt largely with the *mystique* of the Catholic Church; the two books to follow should deal respectively with its symbolism and its liturgy. The second book was now his immediate concern and, looking about for a thread on which to string the story, he hit upon the idea of having as its 'hero', not a man, but a building, a cathedral. And what cathedral could be more suitable for such a purpose than Chartres?

He had by this time visited most of the cathedrals of Northern France, but neither Rheims, nor Amiens, nor Beauvais, nor Notre Dame de Paris seemed to him to sum up in themselves the ideas he was trying to express. Chartres was unique. Here, better than anywhere else, could be studied that strange flowering of the Gothic which is the glory of the Middle Ages. The thought moved him to some of his most eloquent passages.

'Really, when one comes to think of it, a cathedral is a superhuman thing! Beginning, in our land, from the old Roman crypt, from the vault which seems, as it were, crushed like the soul itself by humility and fear, and bowed before the infinite Majesty whose praise they hardly dared to sing,

[1] Huysmans' actual language was much stronger: 'C'est l'avenir plus noir qu'avant, l'illusion d'un havre foutue! Dire qu'il ne restera rien debout, dans ce s— de temps!' Daoust, *op. cit.*, p. 35.

the churches gradually grew bolder; they gave an upward spring to the semi-secular arch, lengthening it to the shape of an almond, leaping from the earth, uplifting roofs, heightening naves, bursting out into a thousand sculptured shapes all round the choir, and flinging heavenward, like prayers, their rapturous piles of stones.'

The Romanesque, he decided, was the La Trappe of architecture, sheltering the most austere Orders, kneeling in ashes and, with bowed heads, chanting in an undertone none but penitential psalms. The Gothic was the abode of less rigorous and more artistic Orders. 'Bowed shoulders are straightened, downcast eyes are raised, sepulchral voices become seraphic. It is, in fact, the expression of the spirit.' The Romanesque, in a word, was allegorical of the Old Testament, and the Gothic of the New, and here, at Chartres, the work was, so to speak, in two volumes, since upon the Romanesque crypt rested the Gothic church.

In *La Cathédrale* Durtal spends three months at Chartres. The real Huysmans never stayed so long, or indeed for any length of time. Instead he paid it occasional visits. The bibliophile Georges Landry had been for some years one of Huysmans' closest friends. Landry, in his early days, had shared a room with Léon Bloy and had known Barbey. By 1884 we find Huysmans dedicating *A Rebours*, '*A mon ami Landry*'.[1] It was with him that he journeyed to Chartres for the mass at dawn. The two friends arrived during the night, attended the early and the later mass, had a pleasant *déjeuner* and returned to Paris the same afternoon.

Huysmans' description of the great cathedral in the early hours of the morning is justly famous. He pictured the mighty church as a dark forest into which no ray had yet penetrated, and in which as the dawn began to break it became even

[1] Landry died in a *maison de santé* in 1924, aged 70. See Lucien Descaves, *Le Journal*, July 21, 1924.

more difficult to discern the surrounding shapes. Gradually he could make out, in the thinning gloom, the immemorial trunks of fabulous white trees, the spring of their branches still invisible. Then great sword-blades gleamed, sword-blades without hilts or handles, shining through the dark, and enormous shields riddled with holes, the great rose-windows of the transepts.

That on the north was the first to come to life, rosy fires and the lurid flames of punch gleaming in its hollows while below, in the middle blade, was seen the gigantic image of a negress robed in green with a brown cloak. Then the other rose was lighted up, and in the blade below it appeared a woman in myrtle-green and brown holding a child.

'And it seemed as if the sun, as it mounted higher, followed the growth of the Virgin, taking its birth in the window where She was still a babe in that northern transept where St. Anne, her mother, of the black face, was seated between David and Solomon, each against a background of purple, to prefigure the royal birth of the Son . . .

'And at the end of the apse, quite high up, there was another Mary, triumphant, looking down the sacred grove, supported by figures from The Old Testament and by St. Peter. And it was She again who in the south transept faced St. Anne, Sho, now a woman and herself a mother . . .

'The sheltering forest had vanished with the darkness; the tree trunks remained but rose with giddy flight from the ground, unbroken pillars to the sky, meeting at a vast height under the groined roof; and the forest was seen as an immense church blossoming with roses of fire, pierced with glowing glass, crowded with Virgins and apostles, patriarchs and saints . . .

'As it reached the chancel, the light came in through brighter and clearer colours, through the blue of translucent sapphires, through pale rubies, brilliant yellow and crystalline white. In the very centre of the cross the sun pierced clearer glass, less storied with figures, and bordered with almost colourless panes that admitted it freely.

'At last, in the apse, forming the top of the cross, it poured in, symbolical of the light that flooded the world from the top of the Tree; and the pictures were diaphanous, just lightly overlaid with flowing lines and aerial tints, to frame in a sheaf of coloured sparks the image of a Madonna, less hieratic and barbaric than the others, and a fairer Infant, blessing the earth with uplifted hand.'

La Cathédrale, however, could not consist entirely of purple passages, however splendid, and Huysmans' avowed intention in writing it was to set forth a system of Christian symbolism, as exemplified in the construction and decoration of the great church. In this he was not wholly successful. The study of medieval art was still in its infancy and he cannot be blamed for not making use of researches which in his day had hardly begun. He was compelled to fall back on the writings of medieval symbolists in whose works the science of symbolism is so overlaid with pious fancy that the mind becomes weary of strained resemblances and arbitrary parallels. To be told that the roof of the church symbolizes charity because it covers a multitude of sins is to be edified but little and instructed not at all. To be informed that the robes of the priest are long to symbolize his long perseverance in the Faith is to learn nothing of the origin and meaning of ecclesiastical vestments.

It may as well be admitted that Huysmans found some difficulty in filling up the pages of *La Cathédrale*. There is, strictly speaking, no story. The two priests who are introduced, in order that Durtal may ask them questions and secure answers, never really come to life. Indeed there is no very convincing character in the book except that of Madame Bavoil. She appears again in *L'Oblat* and there is so much

CHAPEL OF NOTRE DAME SOUS TERRE, CHARTRES

THE ABBÉ MUGNIER WITH THE LITTLE DAUGHTER OF THE
COMTESSE DE CASTRIES
From *Deux Amis: J. K. Huysmans et l'Abbé Mugnier*

life in her that it is thought she must have been founded on a real personage. As Seillière remarks, she has characteristics which could hardly have been invented. Perhaps some of them were borrowed from the astonishing woman who kept house at Marseilles for the Abbé Boullan and whom Huysmans, as we have already seen, installed for a while, after Boullan's death, in his own apartment in the Rue de Sèvres.

We do not know what became of Boullan's Madame Thibault. She could hardly have remained with Huysmans after his conversion, for although her mysticism was extreme, it could not, on any count, have been called orthodox. Even Madame Bavoil's mysticism, although firmly in the framework of the Church, was certainly a little odd. She was in constant communication with Jesus and all the Saints, consulted them on all occasions and heard their voices in reply. She had a passion for the more bizarre of the mystical writers, in particular for Jeanne Chézard de Matel, who lived at the end of the sixteenth century and founded the religious Order of the Incarnate Word. She had made pilgrimages all over Europe, on foot and begging her way, and when she became too old for such strenuous exercises found other penances, such as fasting and (strangely enough) depriving herself of the Eucharist, even at Easter, in obedience to her 'Voices'.

The mystery is deepened for a moment by the strange fact that on Huysmans' tomb in the Montparnasse cemetery occurs, with the names of various members of his family, that of

'Vᵛᵉ. Alavoine, née Bavoil (1800–1881).'

It is rather as if the astonished visitor should find inscribed on the monument of Dickens the name of Sarah Gamp. The explanation, however, would seem to be quite simple. The widow Alavoine, whose maiden name was Bavoil, was presumably a connection of the Huysmans family, and Huysmans used the name (he always had the greatest difficulty in thinking of names for his characters) precisely because he thought it was extinct. In any case, the date of her death (1881) precludes her from being either the real Madame Thibault or the imaginary Madame Bavoil.

The latter, in Huysmans' narrative, had found it extremely difficult to discover a sympathetic confessor. The ordinary curé, faced with her account of celestial voices and her refusal to communicate except by their permission, was apt to lose patience and turn her out of the confessional. Then one day, by chance, or rather by inspiration, she entered the church of Notre Dame des Victoires in Paris and found, in the Abbé Gévresin, a priest who was willing to listen to her. He did more: he took charge of the direction of her soul, and when shortly afterwards his niece died he installed her as his housekeeper. All this had happened ten years before the story opens. Recently the Abbé Gévresin had become a Canon of Chartres, and when he set up house there he took Madame Bavoil with him.

We do not know if the real Abbé Gévresin (i.e. the Abbé Mugnier) *had* a housekeeper. We do know that he was never Canon of Chartres, and never lived there; and that all this is a literary device for allowing our author to put the machinery of *La Cathédrale* in motion. In this, as we have already noted, he was not very successful.

The real interest of the book is that it reveals the conflict raging in Huysmans' own mind, between the Catholic mysticism to which he had now given his formal assent, and the mystique of beauty from which he could not shake himself free. He was trying—desperately—to be a good Christian, but he continued, as a writer, to be a *Naturaliste à la Zola*.

He was, in fact, engaged on an impossible task, and his subconscious recognition of this goes far to explain the acerbity of his judgments. He looked about him at the kind of literature which the clergy recommend to the faithful and he found in it nothing but an unheard of ignorance and an instinctive hatred of Art. It seemed to him as if there were a conspiracy among the Christians of his period to destroy all initiative, all independence. He found nothing but pious chit-chat, 'improving' little tales, written in a glutinous style in which there was neither juice nor savour. And all this in order to preserve the flock from the least possibility of temptation. Keep them in ignorance, such was the notion, and then these poor sheep will never acquire any taste for forbidden fruit. How much better it would be to put vice plainly before them! Let literature deal with every subject however scabrous, let no sin be unpainted, no depth of the human heart unexplored!

This is certainly the doctrine of *Naturalisme*, but it was not likely to find favour with the bishops. The Middle Ages, cried Huysmans through the mouth of Durtal, was not afraid of coarse words nor even of obscene images, as the gargoyles on medieval cathedrals bear witness. Why must modern Catholics be so namby-pamby? He was inclined to blame such a development on Jansenism (that Protestantism inside the Church) which, nearly triumphant in the seventeenth century, has never ceased to exercise its influence. And he complains that all the great literary movements of modern times —Romanticism, Naturalism—have happened outside the Church, and in the teeth of its opposition.

The Catholic critic, Ernest Seillière, has some pertinent things to say about this contention.[1] '*Parbleu*,' he cries, 'that was precisely their object and aim, since they both (the second being but a disguised form of the first) based themselves on the direct negation of the psychological principle of Christianity which is called Original Sin.' Rousseau's doctrine of the inherent goodness of mankind, his notion that you

[1] Ernest Seillière, *J.-K. Huysmans*, Paris (1931), p. 250.

have only to leave men to themselves to see them getting better and better, not only produced the literary movement of Romanticism, but also the excesses of the French Revolution and the progressive debasement of manners. The Middle Ages might be brutal and coarse, the seventeenth and eighteenth centuries vicious, but they all acknowledged the existence of a standard. The essence of Romanticism was to deny that standard, and the practice of Naturalism was to tread it under foot.

Perhaps we, of what Seillière calls the eighth '*génération Rousseauiste*' are not quite so certain of the inherent goodness of man as those who lived before the First World War. If we cannot accept the doctrine of Original Sin on the word of Bossuet we can do so in the name of Freud. But it is perhaps a little unfair to tar—or whitewash—Huysmans with the brush of Rousseau's optimism. It was precisely because he did not share it, because he always looked on mankind— including himself—with an aversion bordering on disgust, that he was able, unlike Zola and the rest, to become a Catholic novelist.

And now a deeper question obtrudes itself. Is there such a thing as a Catholic novelist? Does not the novel itself spring by lineal descent from the romance of the troubadours? Is not the Albigensian heresy imbedded in its very heart? The modern clergy do not think so. Otherwise they would not hope to find edification for their flock in the novels of some modern English writers. It has been left to one of the greatest Catholic novelists of France to wonder whether the writing of novels be not incompatible with being a Christian at all.

The question never presented itself to Huysmans in quite so precise a form, and yet he was destined to give great offence to some of his fellow Catholics by every one of his books. *La Cathédrale*, which was published in February 1898, might have been considered harmless enough, yet

Huysmans learned through his friends in the Bishop's Palace at Poitiers that several Cardinals in Rome were determined to have the book put on the Index. On the advice of Dom Delatte, Abbot of Solesmes, Huysmans wrote to the Prefect of the Congregation of the Index, Cardinal Steinhuber, to say that he submitted himself to the judgment of the Church, and asking him to specify which passages of the book had been found objectionable. Fortunately, perhaps, he did not receive a reply, for aid was about to come to him from a very unexpected source.

It so happened that he had known in Paris the pious and sympathetic Marquise de Sainte-Foix. This *grande dame* now wrote to Huysmans from Algiers where she was then living. She had heard that his book[1] was about to be condemned, and she asked him if he had any friends in Rome. If not she knew a lady who would intervene on his behalf. Not only had she made conversions through the book but she was, both by family connections and personal acquaintances, very powerful at the Vatican.

Shortly afterwards Huysmans received a letter from this lady, who was none other than the foundress and Prioress of the Carmel d'Alger. Before becoming a Carmelite she had been Princess Bibesco, and she certainly intervened to some purpose. The Index ceased all proceedings against *La Cathédrale*, not, however, without reluctance, as can be gathered from the letter written to her by one of the Cardinals, in which he says that in defending Huysmans she was a hen hatching the egg of a duck.[2]

La Cathédrale came under fire from the anticlerical camp also, some of his official chiefs, who were Freemasons, regarding

---

[1] She uses the plural 'livres', so perhaps not only *La Cathédrale* was threatened.

[2] Rancœur, *Correspondance de J. K. Huysmans avec Madame Cécile Bruyère*, p. 80.

the book as a frank piece of *propaganda Fidei*—as indeed it was. The Abbé Mugnier is, however, mistaken[1] in implying that Huysmans was compelled to resign from the Ministry in consequence. Huysmans asked to retire in February 1898 when he had completed thirty-two years' service. After noting this fact concerning '*M. Huysmans, sous-chef du 4ᵉ Bureau de la Direction de la Sûreté générale*', the Senator Edgar Millaud remarks in his souvenirs[2]: 'It seems that he paid no more attention to the *Sûreté générale*, to departmental business, to public assistance or to the government of prisons, than to the affairs of the Grand Turk. While he was writing *A Rebours* he never opened a single letter from the Ministry or wrote a line for the Administration which paid his wages.'

We have, however, a slightly different account from M. E. Ogier,[3] later Minister for the Liberated Regions, but in Huysmans' time employed as what we should call Establishments Officer in the Ministry of the Interior. 'Huysmans,' he wrote, 'was a rigorously conscientious employee, not only in the matter of punctual attendance at his office, but also by the strict performance of the tasks confided to him. To tell, the truth, they were not very difficult. Huysmans' duties were concerned with the expulsion of undesirable aliens and the service never worked more smoothly than in his time.' This would seem, even by Huysmans' own confession, to be somewhat too rosy a picture. He never made any secret of writing his books in official time. M. Ogier continues: 'Touched by a kind of moral instability, and by a hatred of Paris and the world, he came to see me and asked me as a personal service to "liquidate his retirement".'

The *rond-de-cuir* was free at last. No more was the re-

[1] In his preface to Huysmans' *Pages Catholiques*, Paris, 1899, p. 10. The phrase reads: 'Il dut résigner ses fonctions au lendemain de *la Cathédrale*.'

[2] *La Nouvelle Revue*, August 1st, 1920.

[3] *Mercure de France*, November 1st, 1920, pp. 857–858.

luctant functionary compelled to make his daily pilgrimage to the Rue des Saussaies, no more was the man-of-letters disturbed by the necessity of dealing with undesirable aliens. Huysmans was free, and according to the evidence of his most intimate friends was still dreaming of the cloister, still hoping to find a refuge where religion could be practised and art enjoyed under one roof. If only Dom Besse were still at St. Wandrille. . . .

But could this combination be found nowhere else? St. Wandrille was a mere colony of Ligugé, and Ligugé itself a daughter-house of Solesmes. Solesmes was the centre of the great Benedictine revival in the nineteenth century. *There* were monks to be found who lived for the revival of medieval art, who studied illumination, and glass-painting, and goldsmiths' work and architecture. There the Rule of St. Benedict was kept in all its purity; there the Offices of the Church were conducted with all the ancient pomp. 'And if you want to hear the real, authentic Gregorian chant,' said one of his clerical friends (but they must all have said it) 'you must go to Solesmes.'

CHAPTER ELEVEN

THE HOUSE OF BENEDICT

———————— • ————————

Solesmes, the great Solesmes, was the creation of a single man. At the beginning of the nineteenth century, when the revolutionary flood was starting to subside, there remained, of all the hundreds of Benedictine monasteries throughout Europe, a mere thirty. When Napoleon made his peace with the Papacy and re-established the cult, some of the monks hoped that their troubles were over, but the Emperor was not well disposed to a revival of monastic life. With the regular clergy he knew where he was; they could, he hoped, be integrated with the State-structure he was intent on building. But monks, with their independence of the bishops, were another matter. At best, they did not fit into the pattern; at worst, they owed obedience to the superior of some Order which might not even have its headquarters in France.

The restoration of the Monarchy improved the situation very little. Some of the monks had found a place in the regular hierarchy and were by no means anxious to set up their monasteries again. Others tried, but failed. It proved impossible for a time to re-establish the famous Congregation of St. Maur. Even under the reign of Louis Philippe religious houses for men had no legal standing; but the government was tolerant, and there was one young man who was determined that the ancient glories of the Benedictine Order should be revived in France.

200

The House of Benedict

His name was Prosper Guéranger. He was born in 1805 at Sablé-sur-Sarthe, entered a seminary while still a youth and was ordained priest in 1827. For a time he was administrator of the *Missions Etrangères* in Paris, but he returned to his own district in 1830 to devote himself to historical studies. He had a passion for ecclesiastical history and for a time had no other ambition than to be elected to a chair at the Grand Seminary at Le Mans.

Among the religious monuments of the neighbourhood was the ruined Abbey of Solesmes, about an hour's ride from Sablé, and this relic of the past excited the imagination of the young priest. It had been founded in 1010 as a priory dependent on the great Abbey of St. Pierre de la Couture at Le Mans, had survived two pillagings during the Hundred Years War and during the Wars of Religion in the sixteenth century. It had been rebuilt several times before it was suppressed, with the rest of the monasteries, in 1791.

From that time it had been in private hands and now Prosper Guéranger learned that its lay owners were about to demolish the old buildings entirely. He was determined that they should not do so, set about collecting enough money for its purchase and succeeded so well that he was able to buy the entire property in 1833. Three years later, with the approval of the Bishop of Le Mans, Solesmes was re-established as a Priory under the Benedictine rule. At first the little community consisted only of Dom Guéranger and five companions, of whom three were priests. Only one of them persevered to the end. However, other candidates came forward and in 1837 he felt sufficiently sure of himself to go to Rome and obtain Papal approval of his 'Constitutions'.

Later in the same year Solesmes was elevated to the rank of an Abbey and made chief of the 'Congregation of France of the Order of St. Benedict'. By superhuman efforts Dom Guéranger overcame the difficulties which beset his infant foundation; the number of monks increased to such an extent that he was able to establish two daughter-houses, Ligugé, founded in 1853, and Marseilles in 1865. In the following year he established, in Solesmes itself, the nunnery of St. Cécile. At his death in 1875 Pope Pius IX issued in his honour the brief *Ecclesiasticis viris*. Dom Guéranger had certainly deserved well of the Benedictine Order and of the Church.

In his early years at Solesmes Dom Guéranger's idea of the Benedictine life was much more limited than it afterwards became. At first he envisaged his foundation as a kind of university in which each monk would devote himself to some intellectual pursuit, but gradually, although he never lost his passion for study, he came to hold a rather different view of the monastic ideal. Learning was now no more the end, but the means of attaining to the highest degree of spirituality.

The enthusiasm of Dom Guéranger was largely instrumental in the establishment of a feast of the Church which modern Catholics take for granted. He published the Latin text of St. Gertrude's *Exercises*[1] with a French translation and an introduction expounding the ideas of this Benedictine nun, who lived in the second half of the thirteenth century at the nunnery at Helfla in Saxony and was conspicuous for her devotion to the Sacred Heart. This devotion was already established in Benedictine and Cistercian monasteries, but was as yet little known to the outside world. It received a great impulse during the seventeenth century through the vision of Margaret Mary Alacoque of the nunnery of Paray-le-Monial. In 1697 the Holy See granted a special office to the

---

[1] The *Exercises* were seven in number and are concerned with the purification and sanctification of the soul from baptism till death. They had immense influence, particularly in the sixteenth century, when St. Teresa took St. Gertrude as her model and guide.

Order of Visitandines to which she had belonged, but refused a feast common to all with special Mass and Office. It was Dom Guéranger who, in 1852, supplicated Pope Pius IX to extend the feast to the Universal Church and this was done four years later. It is now, of course, one of the most widespread of Catholic devotions.

The work, however, to which Solesmes owes its world-wide reputation is the restoration of Gregorian chant, that ancient music of the Church which took shape at least as early as the sixth century. The honour of having been responsible for the final arrangement of the Roman chant is traditionally given to St. Gregory the Great (A.D. 540–604), and the weight of modern critical opinion is that this attribution is not unjustified. We know from his early biographers that he personally supervised the Roman choir-school and had a hand, to say the least, in the revision of the music. It was therefore rightly called Gregorian and, surviving all the tumults of the Dark Ages, it was heard in all the Churches which sprang up in Europe in the period of Romanesque and early Gothic architecture.

But already, by the thirteenth century, it had become corrupted by contact with the new polyphony and with secular music, and had already lost its freshness and its power of developing along its own lines. At the Renaissance the old tradition was almost lost and the ancient manuscripts could no longer be interpreted. Pope Gregory XIII entrusted the great Palestrina with the task of reform, but he was unsuccessful and in the three centuries which followed things went from bad to worse. Only in certain Benedictine foundations was there any attempt to preserve or restore the ancient music of the Church. Dom Pierre Benoît de Jamilhac of the Congregation of St. Maur published in 1673 a work entitled *La Science et la Pratique du plain-chant*, and just a hundred years later Dom Martin Gerbert brought out his treatise *De cantu et musica sacra.*[1] All this, however, was without much influence in the general practice of the Church.

The final restoration of Gregorian chant in the nineteenth century was the work of the Benedictines, particularly those of the Congregation de France, and it was thanks to Dom Guéranger that the study of the ancient melodic texts was put on a scientific basis. The task begun by Dom Jansions and Dom Pothier was continued by Dom Mocquereau and his collaborators, and in 1889 the work entitled *Paléographie Musicale* began to be published, reproducing in phototype facsimiles the chief musical manuscripts of the Middle Ages. The influence of the movement thus inaugurated was immense, and spread far beyond the confines of the Benedictine Order. Indeed it would be little exaggeration to say that there is hardly a Catholic—or High Anglican—church in the world which has not felt its impact.[2]

Dom Guéranger was also the creator of what is called the 'liturgical movement'. In the early centuries of the Church the liturgical unity, the universal use of the Roman Rite, which modern Catholics take for granted, was unknown. There were variants everywhere, some of them valuable and beautiful, like the Ambrosian Rite of Milan. Most Anglicans who are interested in such matters at all know that their own liturgy is derived not from the Roman Rite but from 'the use of Sarum'.

In France the ancient Gallican liturgies gave place in the time of Charlemagne to the Roman usage and this reigned

[1] See Dom Philibert Schmitz, *Histoire de l'Ordre de Saint-Benoît*, Paris, 1949, vol. VI, p. 138. See also P. Aubry, *La Musicologie mediévale*, Paris, 1900.

[2] It would be out of place in a work like the present one to attempt even to list the vast number of works on Gregorian which have come into existence, since Dom Guéranger's day. There is an extensive bibliography in A. Gestoué's *L'Art grégorien*, Paris, 1910. See also N. Rousseau's *L'Ecole grégorienne de Solesmes*, Tournai, 1910.

uncontested with minor variants until the seventeenth century. In the seventeenth and eighteenth centuries many of the bishops took it upon themselves to 'reform' the liturgy in their own dioceses and sometimes they introduced 'Gallican' and even Jansenist innovations. There was complete confusion, to such a point that sometimes priests in the same diocese were using different breviaries.

Dom Guéranger tried to put an end to this liturgical chaos and in doing so he was naturally compelled to stress the pre-eminence of the Roman Rite, as having the four essential qualities of a true liturgy: antiquity, universality, authority and unction. But he came to deplore the fanaticism of some of his disciples. He regretted the disappearance of some of the ancient local liturgies, he helped the Cistercians to retain their antique usage, and at the end of his life adopted the '*rite monastique*' at Solesmes.

His views were expounded in a work which might well in itself have been a monument to any man. The first volume of his *Année liturgique* appeared in 1841. Many more followed and by the end of the century his work had been translated into almost all European languages and more than half a million copies had been sold. The vast literature of liturgiology which has come into existence since his day did so under his inspiration, direct or indirect, and much of it was the work of the monks of Solesmes or of their allied houses.

Solesmes indeed became the centre not only of the study of the liturgy but of its practice, and it was this over and above his desire to listen to plainchant in its purest form that drew Huysmans to Solesmes. It was its religious æstheticism that attracted him, a religious æstheticism in which some Catholic writers have found much to criticize. Ernest Seillière calls it 'that curious translation of Christian mysticism into terms of ancient formulæ, a translation naturally pleasing to the century of Romanticism, for it sought, by primitivism, to reconstruct a Middle Ages almost purely illusory, indeed factitious'.[1]

This was not Huysmans' opinion. In the essay entitled *Le Luxe pour Dieu*[2] he hails Solesmes as '*Notre Dame des Arts*' and defends it warmly. Many people nowadays, he remarks, have acquired the habit of proclaiming that they see the point of institutions like St. Vincent de Paul or the Little Sisters of the Poor, but not of the Carmelites and the Trappists. Still less are they able to understand the Benedictine idea which is *le luxe pour Dieu*, the attempt to surround the Saviour with all the luxury and all the *comfort* possible.

Dom Guéranger himself, if he had still been alive, might well have been surprised by such a notion, as by the passage in *La Cathédrale* in which Huysmans develops the same theme. 'The aim', he remarks, 'of the true son of St. Benedict is to chant the Divine praise, to serve his apprenticeship here for what he will do On High, to celebrate the Glory of the Lord in terms inspired by Himself, in the language which he himself has uttered by the voice of David and the Prophets. It is a work of joy and peace, a foretaste of the jubilation of the Beyond, a work which approaches him to that of the pure spirits, in a word the most noble work there can be on earth.'

Dom Guéranger indeed would have been not only surprised but deeply grieved if he could have foreseen the extravagant lengths to which some of his ideas were to be pushed by the inheritors of his mantle. As we have noted, he had founded the nunnery of St. Cécile in close proximity to his monastery, and at his death the Abbess was a certain Madame Cécile Bruyère, the future authoress of the celebrated work *On Prayer* which so much impressed Huysmans when it had first been brought to his notice at St. Wandrille.

[1] Ernest Seillière, *op. cit.*, p. 304.
[2] Published in *De Tout*, 1900.

This extraordinary woman was Dom Guéranger's own protégée, almost his own creation. She was born in 1845 in Paris, but her father, a celebrated engineer who had been largely responsible for transforming Le Mans into a modern town, had a country house not far from Solesmes, and it was there that she spent much of her childhood. Under the influence of Dom Guéranger she turned to religion. Although proud, jealous, irritable and excessively romantic, she was extremely intelligent and the Abbot of Solesmes soon began to think of her as the future head of his nunnery. She was the youngest of the six women who in 1868 took their vows as Benedictine nuns, but in spite of her youth she was elected Prioress of the new foundation and soon made her influence felt.

Dom Guéranger himself was not entirely exempt from a high-flying mysticism, and a thirst for the marvellous which is never without its dangers. His devotion to St. Gertrude has already been mentioned, and he found in the new Prioress one who delighted even more than he did in her visions and ecstasies. St. Gertrude relates that sometimes Jesus pressed his lips to hers ten times during the recital of a single psalm, and if such things had happened once, Madame Bruyère[1] saw little reason why they should not happen again. She saw even less reason why they should not happen to her.

Dom Guéranger was—justifiably—proud of his foundation. Madame Bruyère believed that Solesmes was the very heart of Christendom. There, and there only, was the pure doctrine and the true practice to be found. 'Our principles', 'our ideas': such phrases were constantly on her lips. Indeed there was nothing in her upbringing or in her surroundings to supply the humility which was so conspicuously lacking from her natural character. She had adopted Dom Guéranger's noble

---

[1] In law, of course, she was Mademoiselle Bruyère. She was 'Madame' by virtue of her office.

ambition of making the Benedictine Order, and Solesmes in particular, the centre of regeneration for the whole Church, and of that Church she regarded herself as one of the four supporting columns, the other three being Dom Guéranger, Pope Pius IX and Cardinal Pie, Bishop of Poitiers.

Of these Dom Guéranger was the first to die, and on his death bed he recommended his monks to the care of the Abbess, probably meaning to express no more by this than a general hope that the two religious establishments should continue in good relations and give one another any help that was necessary. But Madame Bruyère interpreted his dying wish in a very different sense. The new Abbot, Dom Couturier, was a pious and modest man, and she was soon able to twist him round her little finger. He allowed and even advised his monks to place themselves under her spiritual direction.

She must have been a woman with an extraordinary power of personality, for, shortly after the election of Dom Couturier, she received a visit from a former monk of Solesmes who had now been elevated to the purple: Cardinal Pitra; and this Prince of the Church, after long conversations with her, decided that she was a saint and accepted her as his spiritual directrice. The results were unfortunate. She told him, and her entourage, that he would be the next Pope and, bitterly disappointed that Leo XIII was elected instead, she encouraged him to issue a manifesto criticizing the policy of the new Pontiff which nearly lost him his hat.

She soon saw that she could do little with Dom Couturier himself: he was 'too unmystical', so she set herself to undermine his authority by imposing her will on certain of his monks. She chose Dom Logerot and Dom Fromage. They both became her fanatical devotees and it was through them that her ideas were relayed to the monastery. She was, they insisted, an indubitable saint. She was constantly surrounded by a choir of infant angels who dictated her writings, including the work *On Prayer*, but who sometimes made so much noise that she had to order them to be quiet. She had the gift of bilocation, that is of being in two places at the same time, like St. Dominic and St. Joseph of Copertino. This phenomenon, known to occultists as 'the wandering of the astral body', has often been recorded in the lives of saints and mystics.[1] Madame Bruyère used it to fly to the assistance of the Pope when he was in difficulties.

'The Devil was attacking him,' she remarked on one occasion, 'but I stood firm. It was a hard struggle; I suffered terribly for a week; but now victory has been gained; I feel better.'

The Pope in question was, of course, Pius IX; she would never have gone to the trouble of bilocation for Leo XIII.

One of her strangest claims was to have shared in the birth-pangs of the Blessed Virgin, and not in the birth-pangs only, but in all the other physical sensations of motherhood from conception to the suckling of the child. Some of the phrases which she allowed, and even inspired, her disciples to use about her in their talks to the novices take leave not only of all common sense but of all decency.

Perhaps this is going too far. Perhaps we are wrong in finding such phraseology somewhat startling. The mystics of all religions—Christian, Hindu and Muslim alike—have sometimes indulged in imagery drawn from ordinary sexual experience, and in language as physiological as that employed by Madame Bruyère. Perhaps there is no other language in which high mystical states can be expressed, and if modern sceptics find it shockingly inappropriate, it is not, perhaps, because they think nobly of religion but because they think meanly of sex.

[1] Those who wish to try it for themselves are recommended to consult *The Projection of the Astral Body*, by Sylvan J. Muldoon and Hereward Carrington, London, 1929.

Be that as it may, it is at least doubtful if the monks of Solesmes were benefited by the state of excitement engendered by Madame Bruyère's activities. The very novices were never allowed to forget the close proximity of the neighbouring convent and they were even encouraged to follow their 'sisters' in every detail of their lives. Dom Logerot described with complacency their hair-shirts and their hair-girdles, and even the washing of the same, impregnated with blood and sweat. He even let it be known that there was in the convent a certain cell with the name of 'Blue-beard' where the nuns were in the habit of scourging themselves and which the Mother Superior had to have white-washed every year to efface the blood spattered upon the walls. The effect of such discourses on young men who had taken vows of perpetual chastity must have been deplorable.

Another of the Abbess's aberrations was to promote what one can only call mystical love-affairs between the monks of Solesmes and the nuns of her own establishment. She would discover spiritual affinities and encourage correspondence between the twin souls. Had he known Dom Couturier would never have allowed it, but he had in his innocence given his monks a general permission to correspond, and Madame Bruyère saw to it that the majority of the letters did not pass through his hands. She let him see one or two from time to time to keep him quiet.

Her own dealings with the monks of the neighbouring abbey were equally peculiar. She had a number of spiritual sons, and her relations with them she described as so many 'maternities'. She felt herself pregnant of them, gave them birth, fed them at the breast, etc. 'You are my own. Come on my knees. Sleep in my arms. Henceforward I will look after you. You will drink at my breast my own substance.' She even said that some of her children scratched her breast so cruelly that the milk they took was tinged with blood. As for

Dom Caseus (the latinization of the monk's real name which was Fromage), he was a '*pisseux*'. 'One could not hold him for an instant without being wetted.'

Certainly some of the Abbess's remarks sound like extracts from a psycho-analyst's casebook; as when she said of one of her protégés: 'What a sweet baby! One changes his nappies,[1] one coaxes him and caresses him. Why, at thirty years old, hasn't he put off, with his former existence, his masculine sex? What joy, what sweet delight if he could put on the nun's veil!'

All these dangerous eccentricities, however, were unimportant in comparison with the damage which Madame Bruyère was doing to Solesmes by dividing the monks among themselves. Under the strong hand of Dom Guéranger Solesmes had been a unity, a solid phalanx of the Church Militant. No doubt there had been disagreements between individuals, but these had never broken the ranks. Now the community was split in two.

A young man of twenty[2] who became a novice at Solesmes in 1887 has left us an account of his first disillusionment. For some months he had lived through what he describes as a mystical honeymoon, until one of the other novices took it upon himself to explain the situation to him. The congregation, he told him, was divided into two opposing camps, the '*Jeunes*' and the '*Anciens*' who were also known as the '*Céciliens*' and the '*Anti-Céciliens*'. The '*Anciens*' had nearly all been the companions of Dom Guéranger. They wished the Benedictine Order to consecrate its energies, in the tradition of St. Maur, on learning and the writing of books. The '*Jeunes*' wanted to cultivate the contemplative life of personal sanctification. Dom Logerot, who had been Director of

[1] The original, to avoid misconception, reads: '*Quel charmant bébé, on l'enveloppe de langes, on le câline, on le caresse*', etc.
[2] Albert Houtin, *Une Vie de Prêtre*, Paris, 1926.

Novices since 1879, was the chief of the '*Jeunes*'. It was confidently expected that when the Abbot, Dom Couturier, died, and he was already an old man, Dom Logerot would succeed, but even this was by no means certain, for the party of '*Jeunes*' was itself divided between his claims and those of Dom Delatte. Their rivalry, and that of their adherents, caused yet another cleavage in the ranks of the monks.

What the young man did not then know was that the succession had already been decided by Madame Bruyère. Dom Logerot, in spite of his frenzied partisanship, had fallen from grace. Dom Delatte, who, when he first presented himself at the monastery, had been rejected by Dom Guéranger, had finally entered it through the good offices of the Abbess and had quickly been promoted to the post of Prior. When Dom Couturier died in 1889, Dom Delatte was elected Abbot although by so small a majority that Madame Bruyère vowed vengeance against those who had opposed her will. Sooner or later they were all transferred to other monasteries.

Dom Delatte seems to have been completely her creature. He even undertook in her company a journey to England, and although they were accompanied by another monk and another nun, this voyage caused malicious tongues to wag.[1] The Abbess was determined to set up a nunnery in close proximity to the monastery at Marseilles and she was eagerly seconded in this by Dom Delatte. The Abbot of Marseilles, in spite of the admiration he still felt for her, was compelled to point out that local opinion would not permit it. Rumours of the situation at Solesmes were already beginning to filter through.

Indeed, news of the eccentricities of the Abbot and Abbess was bound to reach an ever wider and wider circle, and the ecclesiastical authorities became alarmed. Even those who,

[1] Unjustifiably, no doubt, but it would have been wise to have avoided even the appearance of *inconvenance*.

like the Archbishop of Bourges (Mgr. Marchal) and the Bishop of Rosea (Mgr. Jourdan de la Passadière) were particularly devoted to the memory of Dom Guéranger, began to wonder if all was well at Solesmes, and in 1891, these two members of the Hierarchy, together with Dom Gauthey and Dom Bourigaud, '*visiteurs canoniques*' at the Abbey, imposed upon two monks, who had been in the past 'directed' by the Abbess, the obligation of conscience to set down in writing all they knew. The two monks, whose names were Dom Coutel de la Tremblaye and Dom Sauton, obeyed, and their report made very strange reading, so strange that the Bishops thought it their duty to forward it to Rome.

The Vatican, while justifiably proud of the grand tradition of Catholic mysticism, has always tended to look upon contemporary mystics with a suspicion bordering on dislike. The case of Solesmes was very carefully considered and in April 1893 the Holy Office intervened. Dom Delatte, the Abbot, was summoned to Rome and, to the distress of his supporters, was forbidden to re-enter France or to have any communication with his monks until further order. He was directed to live meanwhile in the monastery of Subiaco. The Prior, Dom Cabrol, was deposed from his office and all relationship between the male and female religious at Solesmes was ended. The nuns were placed under the jurisdiction of the Ordinary, their confessors and almoners to be found in future among the diocesan clergy. The oldest monk at Solesmes, Dom Gauthey, was appointed interim administrator and Superior General of the Order.

These were merely provisional measures. The Holy Office next instituted a doctrinal prosecution against the Abbot and the Abbess, and it seemed for a moment that the orthodoxy of Solesmes would be irretrievably tarnished and the work of Dom Guéranger ruined. But the Benedictines had powerful friends. Among the nuns were two princesses of the House of Lœwenstein-Lichtenstein and they invoked, for the protection of their Abbess, the intervention of the Queen of Spain and the Emperor of Austria. The quarrel was thus transferred from the doctrinal to the diplomatic sphere. Pope Leo XIII decided to restore both the Abbot and the Abbess to their functions, but they were in future to hold their places *ad nutum Sanctæ Sedis*, at the pleasure of the Holy See. This meant that, if there was any further trouble, they could be deposed without ceremony.

There the matter might have rested had it been possible to keep the whole affair secret from the secular Press. This was perhaps hardly to be expected and, on November 13th, 1893, an article appeared in *Le Matin*, giving a most sensational and scandalous account of what was supposed to have taken place at Solesmes. Edouard Drumont, who regarded himself as the great Catholic publicist of the day, but is now chiefly remembered for his ferocious antisemitism and the unedifying part he played in the Dreyfus affair, replied to *Le Matin* with an article in his own paper *La Libre Parole*. This consisted of a panegyric of the Abbot and Abbess and a violent attack on the two monks who had denounced them to the Holy Office. As we have seen, they had done nothing of the kind. They had merely obeyed their ecclesiastical superiors in preparing a report, and Dom Bourigaud, Abbot of Ligugé, wrote a letter of protest to *La Libre Parole*.

Then came the news of the re-instatement of Dom Delatte as Abbot of Solesmes, and most people, ignoring the niceties of the terms under which he had returned, regarded this event as a complete victory. What the general public did not know was that on November 22, the Holy Office, with the approval of Leo XIII, had summarized the mystical ideas of the Abbess in Five Propositions and that in December all the monks and nuns at Solesmes were ordered by the Pope to sign a formula disavowing them.

This tended to accentuate the existing divisions among the monks. Those who did not belong to either the '*Anciens*' or the '*Jeunes*' and who had taken no part in the controversy, were offended at having to disavow opinions they had never shared; the '*Céciliens*' were annoyed at this plain mitigation of their triumph, and their opponents professed to believe that the reinstatement of Dom Delatte was only a temporary measure.

Dom Chamard, the Prior of St. Maur, between whom and the Abbot of Solesmes there was perpetual rivalry, was completely disconcerted by the latter's return. When he found that his own monks welcomed the news he treated them as rebels, only to be treated by them as a rebel against his Superior General. St. Maur only recovered its peace by the transfer of Dom Chamard, in May 1894, to the Monastery of St. Wandrille.

No hint of this background of tumult is to be found in Huysmans' references to Solesmes. He had intended to go there in October 1895, but a *fâcheux influenza* had prevented him from doing so. In December 1896 we find him writing: 'I went to Solesmes this year and passed very sweet hours there. Perhaps at the end of next year, I shall pass no longer hours but years.'

Everything indeed was done to make him feel at home. The monks were delighted to have attracted the now famous writer to their abbey, perhaps hoping that he would provide a continual propaganda on their behalf, and even do something to 'rehabilitate *Madame l'Abbesse*'. He continued to be the fervent admirer that he had always been since her treatise *On Prayer* had first fallen into his hands. It was true, he remarked, that her writings had come under some suspicion on the part of the Vatican, but this was quite unjustified, since they were 'founded upon the surest principles of the mystical tradition, learnedly esoteric, no doubt, but completely orthodox'.

Huysmans was here laying down the law with a

vengeance—'*on ne sait trop en vertu de quelle compétence*', as
Seillière rather acidly remarks. But as a matter of fact the
treatise *On Prayer* shows little trace of the sexual fantasies in
which Madame Bruyère was wont to indulge in her conversation and more intimate writings. Unkind critics have suggested
that if it is 'founded upon the surest principles of the mystical
tradition' this is due to the excellent memory of the Abbess for
the writings of earlier mystics. None the less the book has continued to be reprinted as a work of edification to this day.

Even the fact that her book had been criticized gave her a
point of contact with Huysmans, for had not his own works
had a similar reception from the pious and timid? We may be
sure that she spared no pains to impress him and gain his
confidence. She certainly succeeded, for Huysmans never
ceased to speak of 'the good Abbess of Solesmes' with the
highest respect. In a letter to the Prioress of the Carmel
d'Alger,[1] he cried: 'Her Abbey of St. Cécile is a marvel;
everything goes wonderfully and she is adored by her nuns.
To understand plainchant, it is there one must go. I remember one night of my existence which will remain for me sub-
lime. It was the eve of the Feast of the Dedication, at Solesmes.
The good Mother said to me, "Come, this evening,[2] to
Matins; the porteress will be warned." I went and found in
the dark church, near to the altar, a little table with a lamp
prepared for me. The veil of the cloister was lifted and there
appeared the whole choir with the Abbess at the back. There
followed admirable chants, voices such as one hears no more,
and the beauties of the liturgy seemed to me, in this setting,
so striking that I wept, in my little corner.

'They are real artists. And there are among the sisters those

[1] Quoted by Lucien Descaves, *Deux Amis, J. K. Huysmans et l'Abbé
Mugnier*, Paris (1946), p. 51.
[2] Not of course 'this evening', but in the early hours of the following
morning.

who illuminate manuscripts as in the Middle Ages . . . There
is in this cloister the complete blend of the highest aristocracy
and the simplest of women. The nieces of the Emperor of
Austria, the Queen-Mother of Portugal, who is an *oblate*, and
holy women of the bourgeoisie and the people.'

As for the Abbess, 'she is an admirable and very holy
woman. I revere and love her infinitely—and I am sure that
she loves me too; for she has cut herself in pieces to be useful
and agreeable to me.'

It seems, however, that he only had one private interview,
for he was probably speaking of her when he wrote to the
Abbé Mugnier:[1] 'One evening, a sweet and terrible evening,
a saint whom I saw for the first and last time—for she is forever behind the bars of a cloister—told me the truth about
myself and pointed out to me, quite sternly, the unresisted
torpor of my poor condition. Then she showed me something
else: the beauty of a soul transfiguring a plain face, thus
giving the lie to all those imbeciles of the Beaux-Arts. She
prays for me, I know, above all for my entry into the cloister.'

No ordinary woman could have made such an impression
on a man of Huysmans' stamp. But, as we have seen, she was
no ordinary woman, and it is tempting to wonder what would
have happened if he had known her a few years earlier, in the
full crisis of her high-flying mysticism. Perhaps, as a com-
panion to *Là-bas*, we should have had a work entitled *Là-
haut* and Madame Bruyère might have shared in the fictional
immortality of Madame Chantelouve. After all, some authentic saints have been very peculiar. It is only fair to add that
in the letters which were exchanged between Huysmans and
Madame Bruyère from 1896 to 1903 there is little trace of the
mystical extravagance for which she has been blamed.[2]

[1] Descaves, *op. cit.*, p. 39.
[2] See 'La Correspondance de J. K. Huysmans avec Madame Cécile
Bruyère, Abbesse de Sainte-Cécile de Solesmes', by René Rancœur in

The Abbot himself, Dom Delatte, was no less welcoming than the Abbess, and one night, after compline, he invited Huysmans to his room and pressed him to enter the noviciate. His cell, he told him, was ready; he had only to say yes. Huysmans almost yielded. But not quite. As Dom du Bourg remarks,[1] 'a disgust of life, the ardours of piety, the aspirations of artistic dilettantism for the beauties of the liturgy and of Gregorian chant are not sufficient to constitute a vocation.'

To say truth he was never happy at Solesmes. He never felt at home, and in the opening pages of *L'Oblat* he analyses his sensations with his customary candour. 'Solesmes is the only place,' he had cried in the first flush of his enthusiasm. 'The monastic life is only possible for me there!'

And yet he was compelled to admit that every time he left the abbey and was seated in the carriage which was carrying him to the station at Sablé, he breathed again as if an insupportable weight had been lifted from him, and as soon as he was installed in the train he could not help saying to himself: '*Mon Dieu*, what luck! I am free!' And yet he regretted losing the life he had lived there.

He found it difficult to understand these inconsistent impressions and feelings. Certainly, he told himself, Solesmes is unique; religious art shines there as nowhere else; the plainsong is impeccable; the offices could not be celebrated with more perfect pomp; nowhere else could he find an Abbot of the calibre of Dom Delatte, or musical palæographers more ingenious and more learned than Dom Mocquereau or Dom Cagin, or monks more kind and helpful; and yet, and yet—.

La Pensée Catholique. Cahiers de Synthèse, 13, Paris, 1950. Nineteen letters and two postcards of Huysmans are preserved in the archives of St. Cécile, and eighteen letters and three cards of the Abbess in the Collection of M. Lambert.

[1] Dom A. du Bourg, *Huysmans Intime*. In *Le Bloc Catholique*, Paris, 1908.

What then? The reply was a revulsion of his whole nature, a kind of instinctive dislike of the monastery with its illuminated façade, throwing into deeper gloom the secular buildings round it. He felt like a cat looking for a lodging, advancing cautiously, ready to turn tail at the slightest alarm.

And yet he agreed that it did not make sense. There was no shadow of proof that the inside of this cloister was untrue to its exterior. Yet the impression remained. He tried to reason with himself, to ask himself what he found displeasing. He could only answer: nothing—and everything.

For one thing, Solesmes was too big. The very size of the monastery with its army of monks and novices made impossible the charming intimacy of an establishment like La Trappe d'Igny. With its immense buildings and the perpetual crowd that filled them it could not help being a kind of barracks. Its very Offices resembled a parade with the Abbot like a general surrounded by his staff.

And what could one say of the so-called recreations where everyone felt himself under surveillance and was perpetually on his guard? Or of the lack of solitude, the delicious solitude of La Trappe being quite impracticable at Solesmes where there were neither woods nor lakes and where even the garden was flat and denuded, without a curving path or a corner where one could gather one's thoughts together, unregarded, without witnesses, alone?

He was compelled to admit that a vast organization like Solesmes could not be kept in being without a discipline almost military in its character. Solesmes was the very centre of the Benedictine revival. It was the Headquarters, sending out its officers on mission to less fortunate monasteries. And was not the reluctance with which these men departed the best possible tribute to the house of Dom Guéranger?

One of the monks, consulted by Huysmans in his difficulties, replied: 'But where would be the merit if we did not suffer from being part of a crowd, from being no more than one small pebble on a mighty beach'.

Huysmans—or Durtal speaking for him—admitted the justice of this remark: 'You are quite right,' he said, 'but what I want is something different.' To put it plainly, he wanted incompatible things. He wanted the sensations of a monk, and the privileges of a literary man in order to describe them. Would the Abbot, he wondered—with all his largeness of mind—allow him to write his books in peace, without trying to exercise some kind of control over their content? The mere thought that he might interfere—and, after all, the previous writings of Huysmans had not been such as to give the pious an unlimited confidence in their innocuousness—prevented him from writing anything at all. No sooner had he settled down to a chapter than he was interrupted by one of the innumerable Offices. Such a life was all very well when one was collecting the material for a book; but for writing it, no! Huysmans was, in fact, the incurable literary man, and it may well be doubted whether such men can ever wholly adopt the religious life with all its disciplines and abnegations.[1] At all events, Solesmes did not prove to be the haven that Huysmans had dreamed of. He had stayed at La Trappe for a week; he stayed at Solesmes for little more than a fortnight all told. He returned to Paris discouraged and unhappy, but he returned. There only, it seemed, he could get on with his books.

[1] Such a statement may be challenged by a recent example. But Thomas Merton would seem to be a much less complex character than Huysmans and even here there is something slightly disconcerting in an 'Elected Silence' which expresses itself in so voluble a literary output.

CHAPTER TWELVE

THE THIRD TRY

———————————— ● ————————————

Back in Paris once more Huysmans attempted to resume the layman's life to which he seemed condemned; but he could not forget his dreams. Which way was he to turn? He had gone to La Trappe to be converted, and converted he had been. But he had realised from the first that the asceticism of that rigorous community was beyond his powers of endurance. Then he had tried, with what high hopes, Solesmes; but when it came to the point of really becoming a monk there, he had shied away like a frightened horse. In his own account he could neither understand his repugnance nor deny that such repugnance existed.

There is, however, a tradition at Solesmes which may throw some light on the matter. It is said that the Abbot, after declaring that he would be glad to welcome him in the community, had asked him if he was prepared to make one supreme sacrifice. Huysmans asked what the sacrifice was to be, and the Abbot replied: 'Give me your pen.' If this is a true story it is easy to understand Huysmans' state of mind. Dom Delatte had tried to argue with him. 'Your reason tells you,' he said, 'that the monastic life is superior to all other kinds of life, and that it will assure your eternal salvation. That argument should be enough to put your will at the service of your reason. Take this step and God will help you.'

But the more he pondered this argument the less

convincing he found it. It seemed like an invitation to throw
oneself into the water in order to learn to swim, and it was in
this state of uncertainty that he paid a visit to yet another
monastery, that of St. Maur, in the *département* of Maine-et-
Loire. There he asked for a confessor, and was sent to Dom
Logerot, to whom he unfolded his difficulties. Dom Logerot
wisely told him that it would be better for him to remain a
layman and as such to live in a cloister, or in its immediate
neighbourhood. He mentioned several men who had taken
this course, and Huysmans, no doubt, thought also of M.
Bruno, whom he had met at La Trappe.

As far as his conscience was concerned, Huysmans was reassured, but he was nonetheless in despair. He had so long, in
his own words, been tormented by the vocation of the cloister,
and he found it hard to envisage life in Paris with nothing to
look forward to. He was afraid also of a mysterious Spanish
lady who, he said, was truly diabolical and had vowed to ruin
him. We shall hear more of this strange personage later. She
was yet another of the extraordinary women who seemed
fated to be found in Huysmans' path.

The material prospect was not much happier. His pension
as a civil servant, together with a little money he possessed
from other sources, was hardly sufficient to enable him to live
in Paris in comfort; yet he detested the idea of writing for the
papers. If once he began to do so, he saw that his life of St.
Lydwine would be indefinitely postponed.

He saw no one, except on Sunday evenings, when he
usually invited some of his friends to dinner. His most frequent visitors were Forain, Girard, Lucien Descaves, Landry,
and the Abbé Mugnier. The party also included very often
Jean de Caldain, his most faithful disciple, who asked him
one evening why, since he lived a life nearly monastic, he
did not choose to do so in a real monastery. But he had already
tried several monasteries and found they did not suit him.

The Third Try

He began to dream of a kind of lay monastery, if only such a thing were to be found, an association of artists and writers devoted to the task of raising Catholic art once more to the eminence it had once enjoyed. 'Such an institution', he wrote,[1] 'would scarcely be possible except in Paris or its neighbourhood, for the men of letters, historians, learned men, specialists in the study of various sciences, as well as painters, sculptors, architects, and craftsmen of all kinds, would need to keep up their connections with publishers and dealers and to visit the libraries and the museums, It would be necessary to arrange life in such a way that each could see to his affairs and do his work without being continually interrupted by Church services. The time-table would be easy to establish: prayers and mass early in the morning: complete liberty during the day—vespers at five or six for those who were able to attend—and compline for everybody, in the evening.

'I do not hide from myself, however, that if such a project were to succeed it would encounter every kind of opposition, but it seems to me impossible, in spite of all mockers and ill-wishers, that it should not take shape one day, for it is, as they say, in the air. Too many people await it, desire it, too many people who cannot, by reason of their occupations, their health, or their way of life, intern themselves in a monastery, for God not to give them a haven, a port where those souls who are obsessed by their longing for the cloistered life might drop anchor, and living out of the world might work near to Him and for Him, in peace.'

Huysmans speaks as if he knew hundreds of people who were only too anxious to adopt such a mode of life, but when it came to drawing up a list of names he could not think of any. 'I know one man of letters,' he said, 'and that is myself. But when I come to think of it, that is about all. Is there a single painter? Where can one find him?'

[1] In the closing pages of *L'Oblat*.

'Pardon! There is Dulac!' said Jean de Caldain.

'That's a bit much,' replied Huysmans, smiling. 'I should certainly be curious to see the works of your Dulac.'

'Good! You shall see them.'[1]

Two days later Jean de Caldain and the sculptor Pierre Roche brought Dulac to see Huysmans.

Charles-Marie Dulac was quite a young man. Having been born in 1865, he was in his early thirties at the time of his first visit to the Rue de Sèvres, and Huysmans was at once struck by the frankness and simplicity of his manner. 'He had,' he said,[2] 'an absolute transparency of soul and a sincerity now only to be found in the monks of certain cloisters. Perfectly at ease everywhere, as if he were in his own house, he looked at you while talking with eyes of an extraordinary purity.' He was plainly a dedicated soul.

He had begun his artistic career with a wall-paper manufacturer and had worked as a painter of theatrical scenery. But his real passion was for landscape and this became even more pronounced after his conversion, which had happened some five or six years before his meeting with Huysmans. It was his custom to travel about the country painting, lodging by preference in monasteries and convents such as St. Wandrille.

Dulac had travelled also in Italy and had lived there for three years with the Franciscans. He had wished to be one of them but had realised that *his* prayer was to paint. He had therefore contented himself with becoming a member of the Third Order of St. Francis. 'Dulac', remarks Huysmans, 'was Franciscan in the marrow of his bones. He was so in his way of life, in his thoughts, in his private devotions, in his paint-

[1] The conversation is reported by Gustave Coquiot in his *Le Vrai J.-K. Huysmans*, Paris, 1912, p. 207.

[2] In the preface which he wrote for the posthumous exhibition of Dulac's works. Reprinted in *En Marge*, Paris (1927), p. 148.

ing . . . he cherished poverty, despised advertisement, nourished himself like a hermit, lay down on whatever monastic beds he could find and painted only for God.' He seemed to Huysmans the very incarnation of his dream. Dulac had brought with him some of his *lithographies mystiques*, and the older man was moved to enthusiasm. Yes! this was the man he had been looking for in the project he had at heart. Jean de Caldain should join them too for he was very skilful in pulling lithographic proofs. And there was, for chaplain, the Abbé Ferret, who had played such an important part in Huysmans' own conversion. It only remained to decide on the situation of this new kind of monastery.

Such was the dream, but its realisation would require far more funds than Huysmans had at his disposal. Yet perhaps something less ambitious would suffice; perhaps it would be possible to establish a colony of writers and artists in the shadow of a monastery already existing. La Trappe was too austere; Solesmes was too big and was for other reasons impossible; St. Wandrille would have been ideal, but his dream of establishing himself there had been shattered by the departure of Dom Besse. He finally chose Ligugé, and there are several somewhat conflicting accounts of how he came to do so.

Gustave Coquiot declares that the Abbé Ferret brought to Huysmans' apartment a certain M. and Mme. Léon Leclaire, who had already had connections with Ligugé, and who painted the monastery in glowing terms. It was, they said, the oldest in France, having been founded by St. Martin in the fourth century. Its situation was pleasant, for it stood on the bank of the little River Clain, which meanders through the flat landscape of Poitou. In the seventh century it had become a centre of light and learning for the whole district, and although it was destroyed by the invading Muslims and later by the English, it had always risen again. Its latest revival was in 1853, when the Bishop of Poitiers established in the ruins a small company of monks from Solesmes. It was now one of the most flourishing Benedictine houses in France.

Huysmans' own account is slightly different. In a letter to Madame Cecile Bruyère, he says that it was his friend Gustave Boucher who invited him to Ligugé. Boucher had been there for some time, editing a local paper. He had a spare room in his lodging, and invited Huysmans to stay there. Huysmans made the acquaintance of some of the ecclesiastical officials of the district, and one of them, Canon Perret, said to him one day, 'There is a delightful piece of ground, with a little river, and old pine trees, not far from the station. It is for sale, you ought to buy it. Build a little house and finish your days in peace.'

At first Huysmans was staggered by this suggestion, but then he remembered his dream. If he really wanted to live as a layman in the shadow of a monastery, this was his chance. What was impossible at Solesmes was here easy; the country was charming, the great town of Poitiers was quite near, the railway service to Paris was excellent. Here he might indeed live in peace, and write his books. Besides, living here would be much cheaper than in the great capital. So the matter was decided, or rather, it was decided for him, for Canon Perret bought the piece of land forthwith in Huysmans' name. Coquiot says that the Leclaires provided a considerable part of the funds.

Huysmans characteristically took fright. He had always detested the provinces. Would he be able to work at Ligugé? Would he have access to all the books he needed? He feared that the reality would be inferior to his dream. Gradually, he allowed himself to be persuaded on condition that he was to bear half the expense himself. An architect was approached, an architect who had already erected a number of conventual buildings. His plans were approved and the construction put

in hand. The house was to be given the name of La Maison
Notre-Dame.

Huysmans thought of new possibilities of disappointment.
How would the monks receive these unofficial lay brothers?
Would they allow them to worship in the Abbey Church?
Even this difficulty was surmounted, surmounted in fact
before it arose, for it turned out that the church, although
used by the monks, actually belonged to the parish. Everything was settled and the construction of the house began.

And then, in September 1897, the Abbé Ferret died. This
was a shattering blow, but worse was to follow. Soon afterwards, Dulac, the *petit frère* of the whole enterprise, followed
him to the grave. Huysmans had seen in him, 'the incon-
testable hope of mystical painting in our time.' Then Jean de
Caldain, having lost his friend Dulac, decided not to go to
Ligugé. The project of a colony of writers and artists devoted
to the service of God had to be abandoned. The house, however, was nearly ready, and Huysmans, with many a doubt,
decided to go. It was arranged that he should live on the first
floor; the Leclaires were to occupy the *rez-de-chaussée*.

In a letter to Madame Bruyère, Huysmans describes himself as living at Ligugé in a hurly-burly of hammerings. He
blames the inconceivable indolence of the local workmen for
the delay in getting himself installed. He had also found, to
his horror, that the architect, thinking to please him, had
transformed a little arcaded corridor in front of the house into
a Moorish gallery, 'the Alhambra in Poitou!' It had been
necessary to destroy these ridiculous additions. He had
amused himself by dedicating each of the pillars to a friend,
and decorating them with symbolic flowers, carved in stone.
'Still,' he declares, 'life was infinitely sweet. He was with
excellent people and good Christians, and moreover—the
inevitable barb—he did not have to see much of them.'

He was still somewhat shaken by an incident which had

taken place just before his departure from Paris. His satanic Spanish lady, of whom we have heard before, had succeeded in slipping into his apartment with two removal men, and had created a terrible scene. She told him that she had just paid a visit to Bruges in order to solicit the help of the demoniac priest whom he had painted in *Là-bas* under the name of Canon Docre. However, their combined enchantments had had no bad effect. But he was very much alarmed lest she should follow him to Ligugé on her way to join her husband in Spain, and create a scandal. However, the Virgin had taken the matter in hand, and got him out of his difficulties, 'as usual'.

In the same letter we hear the first rumble of the storm which was soon to break. A regular campaign against the monasteries had been organized by the Dreyfusards. Huysmans was still in touch with some of his ex-colleagues at the Ministry of the Interior. It seemed that Solesmes had had a good report, but Ligugé, owing to the machinations of the local Prefect, who was a Freemason, a very bad one. It was all very disquieting. The letter concludes with a disobliging reference to a certain Madame Godefroid, who poisoned the atmosphere of the church with a strong scent of musk. Huysmans was later to think more highly of this lady, and to draw her portrait under the name of Mlle. de Garambois, in the pages of *L'Oblat*.

In that novel he paints a complete picture of life at Ligugé, where he stayed for just over two years; although we have to make certain adjustments and corrections before we can take the book as a straightforward, autobiographical record. He does not speak of Ligugé but of Val-des-Saints, a monastery which is supposed to be situated near Dijon, instead of near Poitiers. He does not mention the Leclaires, indeed he does not seem, in the end, to have been on very good terms with them, in spite of their kindness. Perhaps it needed more Christian charity than Huysmans could muster to share a house with anyone. He writes as if the whole house was his, and the garden also.

He introduces a character called M. de Lampre, a pious but crusty old gentleman who lives in the neighbourhood and helps the monastery in every way. This does not prevent him, however, from uttering, from time to time, the most scathing criticisms of the monks for their torpidity and the slackness of their devotions. M. de Lampre was perhaps founded upon some local original, but his purpose in the book is plainly to act as a kind of *dédoublement* of the author, and to say all the things that Huysmans thought but did not like to put into the mouth of Durtal, that is, himself.

M. de Lampre has a niece, a certain Mlle. de Garambois, a pious old maid who 'conceals in the ample body of a mature woman a young soul, all white, the soul of a child'. She causes much amusement both in the village and the abbey by her mania for wearing always the liturgical colours appropriate to each day. She is a living service book, a walking calendar, the standard bearer of the regiment. When she wears red ribbons everybody knows it is the feast day of a martyr, or that of a confessor when her ribbons are white. She sometimes regrets that the choice is so limited. She does not mind in the least when people laugh at her. Her good humour is constant and her bounty indefatigable.

She has only one fault: she is a gourmet, even a gourmand. She knows as much about cookery as she does about the Offices of the Church. She had intended to be a nun and had served her noviciate at the Abbey of St. Cécile at Solesmes, but the life had proved too hard. She had fallen ill and had been advised by her doctor to abandon it. She had, however, become an Oblate, a member of the Third Order of which Huysmans was always dreaming, and now lived in the shadow of the cloister. She has chosen Ligugé because she wishes to be near her uncle.

These two characters, uncle and niece, provide the light relief of Huysmans' *L'Oblat*. Huysmans had a grim, sardonic humour of his own and there is one delightful scene in which M. de Lampre is entertaining Mlle. de Garambois and Durtal to luncheon. The host, with infinite precaution, is drawing the cork of a magnificent old Pommard. 'Look,' he says, 'it is like pouring liquid jewels into the glass.'

'And he blames me for my gourmandise,' cries Mlle. de Garambois.

'Niece,' replies the old man gravely, 'Great wines are the products of monasticism, like architecture, illumination, and all that is beautiful and excellent, here below. Clos Vougeot and Chambertin were cultivated, one by the monks of Cîteaux, the other by the monks of Cluny; the Cistercians possessed vineyards in the districts of Corton and Romanée.' And he cites a whole list of other famous wines, both Burgundies and Bordeaux, which owe their quality to monastic cultivation. 'It is quite natural,' he continues. 'Wine is a sacramental substance. It is exalted in many pages of the Bible and Our Lord did not find any more noble substance into which to transform his blood.' Mlle. de Garambois pretends to take up this idea with enthusiasm, but complains that her uncle has, perhaps, not accepted, in all its completeness, the liturgical point of view. Seeing that the whole idea of the Benedictines is to celebrate the praises of God with the utmost pomp, should they not use the finest wine for the Sacrament, and would it not be a work of piety on the part of M. de Lampre if he were to make over for the service of the altar the contents of his excellent cellar?[1] 'You would give me by so doing a splendid example of contempt for the pleasures of the table which would, no doubt, be very profitable to me.'

[1] It is surprising that, at this point, Huysmans who was himself something of a connoisseur, should mention Montrachet and Pouilly which, being white wines, are surely unsuitable for such a purpose.

'Ah,' he replies, 'I see what you are getting at; *la gourmandise pour le Bon Dieu!* Very well! I have no intention, under the pretext of honouring the Most High, of offering distractions to his priests during Mass. Sin for sin, it is much better, all things considered, that the sin should be mine, for it is much less grave and less offensive to God, at table, with a glass in our hand, than at church, with a chalice. With your permission, I will therefore keep my wines, in the interest of Religion itself, and I am sure that your good sense, when you have considered the matter, will bear me out.'

Huysmans carries over from *La Cathédrale* the character of Madame Bavoil who, on the death of her old master, has entered Durtal's service. There was, in reality, no Madame Bavoil at Ligugé (in his letters Huysmans complains of the difficulties of obtaining tolerable service), but she continues to live in the pages of *L'Oblat*, and the author even extracts some amusement from her encounters—both theological and gastronomic—with Mlle. de Garambois.

Of course the book does not consist entirely of these *hors d'œuvres* as some captious critics called them. It is a serious attempt to describe the life at Ligugé of a man who, while not quite a monk, most certainly was very assiduous in his devotions. There are, it need hardly be said, some excellent descriptions of religious services, there are some little landscape paintings perhaps surprising in the townsman that Huysmans had been all his life. There are long dissertations on gardening, not so much in the horticultural as in its liturgical and symbolic aspects, there are lengthy discussions with the monks on questions of Church history, particularly as regards the Oblature. If he could not be a monk Durtal would at least be an *Oblat*, a member of the Third Order, and he wanted to be properly received.

After a year's residence in the shadow of the cloister, the simple ceremony took place. In Latin question and answer

Durtal and the Prior repeated the necessary formulæ and then Durtal signed a parchment setting forth his act of profession, and ceremoniously displayed it held open on his chest, to all the monks seated in their stalls. Durtal was deeply moved, but his emotion does not prevent him from finding fault with the music of the High Mass which followed. Even in such moments as these he was a difficult man to please.

He had come at last to a safe lodging, to the haven so long desired; and he had no sooner reached it than the refuge itself was threatened. The storm which had so long been brewing burst overhead.

Huysmans had, throughout his life, taken no interest in politics: he regarded the whole realm of public affairs with a kind of angry disgust. Unfortunately, politics tend to infringe, sooner or later, on the lives of even the most retiring of men. If the political acumen of Napoleon III had been a little greater, Huysmans would never have been a soldier. And now, at the end of his days, politics once more were to break up the mould of his life. He was in the position of a man who had taken refuge from the world in some Pacific island only to find himself involved in the Second World War.

He himself hardly seems to have realised what was happening. After his conversion he tended to envisage the world of men as divided into two camps. On the one hand were the enemies of the Church, and on the other, its friends. The friends were by no means all white, but the enemies were all black. In reality, as always, the problem was not quite so simple.

The Revolution, beginning with an attack on the privileges of the clergy, had finally tried to root out Catholicism altogether. By the beginning of the nineteenth century it was plain that this attempt had failed and Napoleon and the Vatican came to terms. The Concordat of 1801 re-established the cult and restored the hierarchy, but the nomination of bishops remained in the hands of the Government. The Government naturally appointed 'Gallicans', that is, men who accepted this semi-independence of Rome and who tended to magnify their own authority at the expense of both the Vatican and of their own inferior clergy.

Ultramontanism, the protest against this state of affairs, was originally something quite different from what it afterwards became. The original Ultramontanes were, indeed, men like Montalembert, Dupanloup, and Lacordaire: the 'Liberal Catholics' who regarded the later development of their theories with horror. The new Ultramontanes were Louis Veuillot, who assumed the direction of *L'Univers* in 1843, Mgr. Pie, who was appointed Bishop of Poitiers in 1849, and Dom Guéranger, whose work at Solesmes began at the same period. Their aim was to exalt the Papacy at all costs, and so far from thinking that the Church should take no part in politics, they regarded politics as the Church's concern—its concern, and no one else's.

They detested the Revolution and all its works. Some of them, like Louis Veuillot, thought for a time that they could make an ally of Napoleon III, but his Italian campaign put an end to such hopes. Mgr. Pie was a fanatical Legitimist. He regarded with an equal hatred the Republic, the Empire, and the House of Orleans. He desired to see the grandson of Charles X restored to the Throne of France.

Pope Pius IX had begun by holding certain 'Liberal' ideas, but the events of 1848 frightened him into reaction. The Encyclical *Quanta Cura* of 1864 made his position quite clear; and to it was annexed a *Syllabus Errorum* (based largely on a similar document prepared by the French Ultramontanes), in which it was denied that 'the Roman Pontiff can and ought to effect a reconciliation and alliance with progress, liberalism and modern civilisation'. The culmination of the process came in 1870 when, on the very eve of the extinction of the Temporal Power, the Pope declared himself Infallible.

The Doctrine of Infallibility has been so often abused and ridiculed that it is, perhaps, as well to set down its definition as voted by the Vatican Council: 'The Roman Pontiff, when he speaks *ex cathedra*, and when, in the exercise of his office as pastor and teacher of all Christians, he defines by virtue of his supreme apostolic authority the doctrine concerning faith and morals to be held by the universal Church, is, by the divine assistance promised to him in the person of St. Peter, possessed of that infallibility wherewith the Divine Redeemer willed that His Church should be endowed in defining doctrine concerning faith and morals: and that for this cause such definitions are irreformable of themselves and not because of the consent of the Church. And if any (which God forbid) should presume to contradict this our definition, let him be anathema.'

This claim is obviously a much more limited one than many Protestants profess to believe. What it says in effect is that, in future, no General Council can over-rule a Pope. As far as the laity and the outside world in general are concerned, it claims no more than has always been claimed by the Church. It merely decides with whom the final decision shall lie. None the less, it caused great offence and aroused much opposition even among Catholics themselves. Most of those who, like Newman, had opposed it, submitted; but a large number of German Catholics refused to do so, and left the Church.

The opposition it aroused among Catholics, however, was nothing to what it provoked outside the Church. It sounded like a declaration of war, as, indeed, in a sense, it was. The French Republicans, in particular, felt themselves threatened. They felt that they had in their midst a well-organised and formidable body vowed to the destruction of their regime.

Hence the dramatic force of Gambetta's slogan: 'Clericalism
—that is the enemy!'

It was hardly surprising that the anticlerical parties should
band themselves together, even if some of them made strange
bed-fellows. In the years following 1870 there was an enormous development of French Freemasonry, which cutting
itself off from English Freemasonry, proclaimed itself bitterly
hostile to the Church. Its Grand Master at this critical period
was Crémieux, and Crémieux was a Jew. The clerical party
also closed its ranks and its opposition to Freemasonry became
increasingly tinged with antisemitism.

And then, in 1878, Pius IX died, and the new Pope—to
the hardly concealed disgust of some of the Ultramontanes—
was Cardinal Pecci who took the name of Leo XIII. He was a
man of outstanding intellect as well as being an astute states-
man. He saw that it was largely the uncompromising Royal-
ism of the French Catholic leaders that had determined the
Republicans to break the power of the Church. As early as
1879 he had come to the conclusion that the Legitimist cause
in France was lost, and he deliberately pursued a policy of
reconciling Catholics to the Republic, even if it meant putting
some of the writings of the Ultramontanes on the Index.
After 1883 there was a better atmosphere in France.

Trouble, however, broke out anew. Many of the Republican politicians lacked probity; corruption was widespread
and, in 1883, a major scandal involved the President himself.
This added new fuel to the fire of antisemitism, although
neither President Grévy, nor his guilty son-in-law Wilson
were, in fact, Jews. Edouard Drumont's brilliant, bitter
pamphlet *La France Juive*, which appeared in 1886, excited
public passions still further, and many of the Royalists and
Catholics began to dream of a *coup d'État* which should deliver them from the Republic altogether. Unfortunately the
man who seemed indicated to carry it out was a poor creature.

General Boulanger was never anything but a blown-up balloon, and when the Government stood firm and threatened him with a trial for high treason, the whole enterprise collapsed.

The failure of Boulangism was a victory for the Republicans, but they had hardly had time to congratulate themselves before another financial storm—the so-called 'Panama Scandal'—threatened, once more, to sweep them out of office. Two years later the Dreyfus Affair divided France into two hostile camps.

All but a few country curés are now convinced that Dreyfus was innocent of spying on behalf of Germany, but his trial in December 1894 was conducted in an atmosphere of public hysteria that made any reasoned judgment impossible. He was found guilty and degraded with every mark of obloquy— his officer's epaulettes torn off, his sword broken—in January of the following year. In March he arrived at Devil's Island where he was to spend many weary years before his innocence was established. Not all of his accusers were scoundrels; some of them were merely wilfully blind. It was enough for them that Dreyfus was a Jew.

The Church cannot be held responsible for the condemnation of Dreyfus, except in so far as the French Catholics had promoted antisemitism in general. Of the two most guilty men, Colonel Henry was a Freethinker and Esterhazy only nominally a Catholic. But Drumont's paper *La Libre Parole* was bitterly anti-Dreyfus, and *La Croix*, the organ of the Assumptionists, only slightly less so. In spite of the fact that the Pope took a different view,[1] in the eyes of the Republicans the Church was implicated and many of them determined to make an end of clericalism once and for all.

[1] When interviewed by *Figaro*, he remarked, of Dreyfus, 'Happy is the victim whom God judges righteous enough to assimilate his sacrifice to that of His Son.' *Figaro*, March 15th, 1899.

It is against this background that we must see the Law of Associations. The project was initiated by the Prime Minister Waldeck-Rousseau, but the anticlerical majority in his own party stiffened its provisions and the law as finally promulgated on July 2nd, 1901, went far beyond what he had intended. It laid down that no religious congregation might be formed without an authorization given by a legislative act; that no branch establishment might be formed except by virtue of a decree of the Council of State; that no-one might direct or teach in an educational establishment of any kind if he belonged to an unauthorized religious congregation; and that any congregation formed without authorization should be declared illegal and its members punished.

The Pope protested, and Waldeck-Rousseau replied, almost apologetically, that he intended to apply the law with moderation. The Pope, as if to show the moderation of his own intentions, declined to forbid the congregations to apply for authorization. He left each congregation to decide for itself. In the end the vast majority of the religious houses—615 of them—submitted to the Government. But 86 male and 150 female congregations refused and these included the Jesuits, the Carmelites and the Benedictines.

The Benedictine House of Ligugé therefore began to make its preparations for departure. The Abbot had already taken the precaution of renting a château near Moerbeke in Belgium, and had despatched the cellarer and the hotelier to make preliminary arrangements. The monks followed in groups, leaving just enough of their numbers to continue the offices until they could be re-started in exile. Soon the monastery was almost empty. Huysmans was profoundly depressed.

It was not even as if the peasants of the neighbourhood had shown any signs of regret at the departure of the monks. On the contrary, they had made a tumult outside the monastery and at the Maison Notre-Dame, shouting 'Down with the Benedictines', and dancing the carmagnole. Huysmans reflected bitterly that they had been corrupted by the local Prefect who was, of course, a Freemason.

He decided that in the absence of the monks there was nothing to keep him at Ligugé. He had always disliked the provinces. He would try to find some corner in Paris where he might be quiet. The Prior suggested that he might take refuge with the Benedictine nuns in the Rue Monsieur. He could have a room, at a cheap rate, and he would be able to assist at the offices and hear excellent gregorian. Huysmans thought it might serve his turn.

Durtal speaks for his creator: 'The experience is over. Val-des-Saints (Ligugé) is no more. I was present at the burial of the monastery; I was the grave-digger of its services. That is what my oblature has amounted to; for there is no more point in it now that I am plucked from my cloister.'

His sadness turns to revolt. 'One must admit that life is very strange! Providence caused me to spend two years here, only to send me back like a fool, to Paris. Why? I do not know, although, no doubt, I shall know, one day. I can't help feeling all the same that something is wrong, that I have got out at some intermediate station instead of continuing my journey to the end. Perhaps I was too presumptuous.

'But all the same, O Lord (and I ought not to say this), I am beginning to be a little suspicious of You. It seems to me that You ought to have led me to a sure haven. I arrive—after what weariness!—I sit myself down—and the chair breaks under me. Is the bad workmanship of earth echoed in heaven? Does the Celestial Cabinetmaker also produce cheap chairs that collapse as soon as one sits on them?' A great discouragement settles upon his spirit. 'I tremble,' he says, 'at the idea of returning to Paris, in the tumult; what a misery! Instead of a peaceful property of my own I shall find the domino boxes of a block of flats, with the menace above and below of women letting themselves go on pianos, and brats noisily dragging chairs about all afternoon and yelling, without anybody making up his mind to strangle them, all night. In summer the room will be overheated, suffocating; in winter, instead of my flaming pine-cones, I shall be looking at a miserable stinking flame through the mica window of the stove. Instead of the horizons, I shall no doubt have a row of chimney-pots. Bah! I was already used to a vista of clay chimneys pushed through zinc roofs against a background of grey skies. I shall get used to it again; I shall get back into my old habits.

'And then . . . I have many things to expiate. If the divine rod is got ready, let us offer our backs; let us show at least a little good-will. And yet one cannot always be, in the spiritual world, like the man in the material world—the husband of the laundress or the midwife, who gazes into vacancy, twiddling his thumbs.

'Ah, my dear Lord, give us the grace not to try to bargain with Thee thus but to put our own will behind us once for all, to live in fact, no matter where, so long as it is far from ourselves and near to Thee.'

CHAPTER THIRTEEN

THE MYSTERY OF
SUFFERING

———————————— • ————————————

I n spite of the laments of Durtal at having to leave Ligugé,
those who were the intimate friends of Huysmans are
clearly of opinion that he would not, in any case, have
stayed there much longer. He had no real love of the country,
he detested 'the provinces' in all that the word implies, he
disliked the local inhabitants, he had even begun to fall out of
love with the monks.

Gustave Coquiot[1] says that he felt around him an atmosphere of hostility it was impossible to mistake. It was inevitable that it should be so. The monks did not understand his
extremely personal attitude to religion; they were shocked by
his freedom of speech. From the literary point of view the
law against the monasteries was a God-send to Huysmans.
It enabled his experiment in oblature to end with a bang
instead of a whimper. He came back to Paris, says Coquiot,
exhausted and cast-down but yet with the firm, if unacknow-
ledged, conviction that he really couldn't live anywhere else.

Hearing of his return, François Coppée offered him an
apartment in the house where he lived himself: No. 12 Rue
Oudinot. It was a pleasant apartment with the use of a garden
and at a reasonable price, and Huysmans was ready to move

[1] Gustave Coquiot, *Le Vrai J.-K. Huysmans*, Paris, 1912.

in. Unfortunately the proprietor, on hearing that a famous novelist was about to become his tenant, put up the rent.

We know that the Prior of Ligugé had proposed that he should take refuge with the Benedictine nuns in the Rue Monsieur, and this he now decided to do. He did not like the room that was offered to him, but Jean de Caldain, whom we have already seen performing kindly services for him, pointed out that he had only a few steps to go in order to reach the chapel; and there was room for his books. Huysmans was installed.

He tried to count his blessings. The fact that the gate was shut at nine o'clock at night excused him from all invitations to dine out. In fact, from this point of view he was better off than he had been at Ligugé; the monastic atmosphere was more pronounced. All the passing Benedictines looked in (there were many of them in Paris owing to the upheaval) and one of these, Dom Dubourg, formerly Prior of the Paris Benedictine house of St. Marie, was actually lodged in the room above. He became Huysmans' confessor and friend.

While still in his own monastery Dom Dubourg had heard of Huysmans' conversion and had read *En Route,* as he confesses, with a mixture of admiration and repugnance. He was moved by its apparent sincerity and outraged by its realism, and for long he was unconvinced that the conversion was real. His doubts vanished when he met the author, although he was still puzzled by the contrast between Huysmans in private life, simple, natural and affable, and the creator of so many strange characters and shocking situations.

It is doubtful if the good Prior ever quite resolved this difficulty, or ever fully understood the man he was dealing with. 'Certainly,' he says, in the series of articles which he contributed after Huysmans' death to the monthly review *Le Bloc Catholique,*[1] 'if it had been in his power, he would

[1] Reprinted in Dom H. du Bourg, *Huysmans Intime*, Paris, 1908.

have been happy, like Paul Féval, to consecrate the remains of a vanished fortune to buy up, in order to destroy them, the works of the past and so to appease his conscience. Certainly he would have cried, like that other convert Adolphe Rette,[1] "This is today one of my greatest afflictions—and I conjure all Christians into whose hands may fall any of the writings in which I strayed in this way to destroy them by fire. It would be a good deed."

'But for Huysmans, who had sold to a publisher his entire literary output, it was impossible to make these posthumous reparations.'

With all respect to the Prior of Sainte-Marie, this is nonsense. A man's *œuvre* is a unity and to truncate and emasculate it is to deprive it of all meaning. Huysmans was too much the literary man in the very fibre of his being to countenance anything of the kind. It is true that when he republished *A Rebours* he added a preface explaining how different was now his position, but he republished it all the same.

Still, if the monk did not fully understand the *oblat* he loved him, as can be seen quite plainly through the veil of the slightly pompous and old-fashioned diction of *Huysmans Intime*. His presence in the Rue Monsieur was a great consolation, for the novelist found his new quarters anything but cheerful. The whole house was sad and sunless, and the room was bitterly cold. Meals were taken in the guests' refectory and they were not very good meals. It would surely have been more surprising if they had been. One day a fire broke out in one of the chimneys and Huysmans saw, in imagination, his whole library consumed. It was plain that he would never be happy there and his friends set about finding him somewhere else to live.

It had to be on the Rive Gauche, for he had a horror of the

[1] Author of a work entitled *Du Diable à Dieu*.

fashionable quarters, with their palace hotels, blatant theatres, brightly lit shops and cafés. Besides, none of the churches on the Rive Droite knew anything about plainchant. In the end lodging was found for him at No. 60 Rue de Babylone and, in October 1902, after less than a year in the convent, he moved in.

While still living in the Rue Monsieur, he had busied himself with correcting the proofs of *L'Oblat*. The book appeared in January 1903, and at first the Catholic reactions were entirely favourable. The Abbot of Ligugé from his exile in Belgium sent his thanks for a complimentary copy. The Abbot of St. Maur de Glanfeuil, the Abbot of St. Wandrille, the Prior of Kergouan conveyed their felicitations; the monks of Solesmes had eagerly 'passed the book from hand to hand', the Prior of Farnborough announced his intention of reading it in the refectory 'even during Lent'.

But soon another note was sounded, and the Abbot of Ligugé felt compelled by the clamour of some of his own monks to issue a formal statement in the monastery journal, the *Bulletin de Saint-Martin*, regretting that certain ecclesiastical dignitaries and worthy layman also had been caricatured in Huysmans' pages. The statement was reported in *Le Temps* and was preceded by the record of a conversation with Dom Roche, a Benedictine who had visited Ligugé while the author of *L'Oblat* was there.

Dom Roche declared that Huysmans had never belonged to the Order of St. Benedict and knew nothing whatever about it. How should he, since his so-called conversion was merely a matter of an exacerbated sensibility and an artistic dilettantism? There was much more in the same vein and Huysmans thought it necessary to reply immediately in a letter to *Le Temps*, in which he tries to make out that the monastery of the Val-des-Saintes in the novel is quite different from the real Ligugé. He ends his letter by accusing the

Benedictines of lacking all humility and being unable to support any criticism, however mild.

In the end, by the efforts of Dom Besse and other friends, the trouble was smoothed over and Huysmans entered once more into the good graces of the Benedictines—at least until his next book should appear. Such a book was indeed almost completed.

He had spent much of his leisure at Ligugé working on his projected Life of St. Lydwine of Schiedam. The subject had long been in his mind, for she was one of his favourite saints, and even before his conversion he had been collecting materials. He had turned the pages of Gerlac, Brugman and À Kempis. He had come across a nineteenth-century hymn, preserved by the Bollandists, formerly sung in honour of Lydwine in Holland and Belgium:

> *Miræ patientiæ*
> *Vixit in hoc tempore,*
> *Nimiæ miseriæ*
> *Particeps in corpore.*
> *Non murmur resonat,*
> *Non querimonia,*
> *Sed laudem personat*
> *Devota Lydia.*

He had even found in a Jansenist breviary of the eighteenth century an *Office Propre de la Bienheureuse Lidwine.* It was not until 1892 that an *Office de Sainte Lidwine* was conceded to the churches of Holland by a decree of the Sacred Congregation of Rites.

His taste always had a bias towards the bizarre, not to say the macabre. He was chiefly interested in saints whose lives had something extraordinary about them, something extravagant, the victims of suffering almost beyond human imagination: St. Lydwine, St. Colette, St. Françoise Romaine,

244

the Blessed Jeanne de Maillé: living effigies of the Passion and bearing its marks in their own flesh. He liked his saints to be sick and was fond of repeating the remark of St. Hildegard that 'God does not inhabit healthy bodies'. On this count at least St. Lydwine was the perfect subject, for she is said to have suffered from every disease known to the Middle Ages except leprosy. She was also particularly dear to Huysmans as a native of those Low Countries for which he had always an atavistic tenderness.

Lydwine was born at Schiedam in the closing years of the fourteenth century. She was very beautiful but lost her good looks through illness at the age of fourteen. Shortly afterwards she fell, while skating on the frozen canals, broke a rib, and for the rest of her life was bed-ridden. The most horrible ills assailed her, her wounds festered and worms bred in her putrefying flesh. Her right arm was eaten away with erysipelas so that only a single muscle held it to her body, her forehead was a gaping scar, she became blind in one eye and with the other could only bear the dimmest of light.

Then the plague ravaged Schiedam, and she was the first victim. Two boils formed on her body, one under her arm, the other over the heart. 'Two boils, it is well' she said to the Lord, 'but three would be better in honour of the Holy Trinity.' Immediately a third boil broke out on her face. She still thought herself too fortunate and entreated God to allow her to expiate, by her sufferings, the sins of others. Her prayer was answered, and for thirty-five years she endured every imaginable ill, taking no food but the Eucharist, and living in a cellar, fetid in summer and so cold in winter that her tears were frozen on her cheeks.

But the Lord rewarded her with visions of His glory, sent angels to minister to her and communicated her with His own hand. Her festering sores exhaled delicious perfumes, and when she died her former beauty was miraculously restored to her. Crowds came to see her and all who were sick were healed.

Such was the story which Huysmans set himself to tell in terms of the Naturalism he had learned from Zola; and the result is enough to turn the strongest stomach. And yet the conscientious reader is compelled to admit that the method, in the end, succeeds. For Lydwine becomes, unlike most of the subjects of the hagiographers, a real person. The reader is compelled to accept her as he accepts a character in a realistic novel, to regard her, as Huysmans did, with a growing tenderness, to take part in her sufferings, to share her faith.

The doctrine of mystical substitution fascinated Huysmans as we can see by the conversation which he puts into the mouths of Durtal and the Abbé Gévresin in the early pages of *En Route*. He calls it 'that miracle of perfect charity, that superhuman triumph of Mysticism', and he made it, as he had always intended to do, the central theme of his Life of St. Lydwine. But perhaps he could never have written of it with so much conviction if he had not now begun to suffer the physical agonies which were to be with him, in ever increasing measure, until the day of his death. An author must always, to some extent, identify himself with his principal character, but to have the right to identify himself with St. Lydwine, Huysmans must himself suffer. While he was still unconverted he had complained of neuralgia; when he was at Ligugé he had to make several visits to Poitiers in order, as he imagined, to have his teeth attended to. Now that he had returned to Paris the pain had grown worse, and whether he knew it or not, what he was suffering from was cancer of the mouth.

Occultists believe that cancer is not a disease of the physical body but of the etheric double,[1] and some of them went so far

[1] Dion Fortune, Psychic Self-Defence, London, n.d., p. 39.

as to suggest that such was the suitable punishment of one who, by the words of his mouth, had 'revealed the mysteries'. It was hinted that the enemies of the black magicians were always punished. President Carnot had closed the Luciferian Temple in the parish of St. Sulpice, and had been assassinated a few days later. He too had been regarded as a traitor, for he had confessed when interviewed by *The Times* that while he practised Catholicism for reasons of State he was, in reality, a spiritist. Huysmans himself was by no means free from such notions for in a letter to Madame Bruyère he speaks of a diabolic action which he does not completely understand, but one thing is certain: 'the abominable Taxil lied more when he said that the Masonic Luciferian Cult did not exist than when he told all the stories which fooled the Catholics. It is certainly to that we must look for those who are directing the movement against the Congregations and the Church.'[1]

Be that as it may, the Republican Government of France was still pursuing its anticlerical policy. Having disposed of the monasteries it was now moving towards its final objective, the abolition of the Concordat, the separation of Church and State. Pope Leo XIII had foreseen the development and by his policy of *Ralliement* had tried to prevent it; but, on July 20th, 1903, the great Pontiff died.

His most likely successor seemed to be Cardinal Rampolla, Papal Secretary of State, who was known to favour his old master's views, and to share his friendly attitude to France. The French Foreign Minister Delcassé asked the French Cardinals to vote for him and he would probably have been elected but for the existence of that curious anomaly the 'Austrian Veto'. A friend of France was considered to be, ipso facto, an enemy of the Triple Alliance. Accordingly, at the third scrutiny, the Cardinal of Cracow, in the name of the

[1] Rancœur, *op. cit.*

247

Emperor Franz Josef, pronounced the veto and the election of Rampolla became impossible. The French Cardinals, however, were sufficiently strong to prevent the election of any Austrian candidate and in the end the Conclave elected the unpolitical Cardinal Sarto, Patriarch of Venice, who assumed the name of Pius X. The new Pope was a sincere and pious man—he has recently been canonised—but he abandoned the conciliatory policy of his predecessor towards the French Republic, and the separation of Church and State became inevitable.[1]

Huysmans took the most pessimistic view of these happenings, and in July 1904 we find him writing to a monk in exile to lament that the famous Abbaye-aux-Bois had been compelled to close its doors and that other convents were threatened. Soon, he feared, there would be only the parish church left—'until that is closed in its turn'.

He was made more unhappy still by his private troubles. He had already fallen out of love with his apartment in the Rue de Babylone. The neighbours were noisy, dragging furniture about above his head, singing and banging on a piano at all hours. Life was impossible, and yet he could not face the task of moving.

Once more Jean de Caldain came to the rescue and found him another apartment, this time at No. 31 Rue St. Placide. It was on the fifth floor and from the windows of the little dining-room one could see the tower of St. Germain-des-Prés and those of St. Sulpice. Huysmans established himself in what was to prove his last lodging. Dom du Bourg has described a visit to Huysmans in his final eyrie. Toiling up many steps, for there was no lift, one found immediately on the other side of the front door an antechamber full of works of art, and, beyond that, the study, *'cabinet de travail et de*

---

[1] The Separation Law was finally promulgated on December 9th, 1905.

prières, à l'aspect grave et religieux.' The walls of the room were completely concealed by bookshelves on which were arranged, carefully bound and dusted, the trophies of his many expeditions along the bookstalls of the Quais. There were works of history and archæology, works of literature, and a remarkable collection of mystical authors. In all corners of the room and on the mantelpiece were statues of wood and stone, '*aux poses naïves et hiératiques*', reliquaries and censers still smelling of their ancient incense: a miniature museum of the art and faith of the Middle Ages.

When the visitor entered he found Huysmans seated at his worktable, covering with his nervous and incisive handwriting large sheets of paper, arranged with the exactitude and regularity of the former bureaucrat. He rose, taking off his large horn-rimmed spectacles, and greeted the visitor with a friendly smile. His conversation was easy and natural, punctuated by occasional sallies of mordant wit, underlined by the gleam in his blue eyes and the malice of his smile. His judgments of men and things were as ever without indulgence, and he was given to sudden bursts of indignation, especially against those savants who by their Higher Criticism were undermining the simple faith of the Christian world.

Huysmans had no sympathy whatever with the Modernists. Once he had accepted Catholicism he had accepted it *in toto.* Indeed, as Rémy de Gourmont remarks,[1] 'not only was there no hesitation and no heresy in his faith, but he sought out, in the most obscure corners of his religion, everything that was most extraordinary, most extravagant, most impossible. Recognised mysteries and acknowledged miracles did not suffice him.' He had shown as much in his Life of St. Lydwine. And now he had still one more book to write, and preoccupied with the miraculous, and obsessed as he was with

[1] Rémy de Gourmont, *Promenades Littéraires I*, Paris, 1886, p. 27.

the problem of suffering, it was perhaps inevitable that he should choose to write about Lourdes.

Perhaps the choice was not wholly his, for it is easy to imagine the Abbé Mugnier making the suggestion. It is true that there was already a considerable number of books about Lourdes, but none was entirely satisfactory. As early as 1862 the Abbé Fourcade had brought out his *L'Apparition à la Grotte de Lourdes*. Henri Lasserre's ambitious work, *Notre Dame de Lourdes*, appeared in 1870 and was still regarded by many Catholics as the most complete and trustworthy account. Twenty years later came Zola's *Lourdes*. It was a by no means unsympathetic study, but it was not likely to be welcomed by the faithful, on account of its scepticism. Huysmans, the converted disciple of Zola, might well have seemed the ideal person to produce a work acceptable to Catholic opinion and yet avoiding the extravagances of Lasserre.

Huysmans deals with Lasserre in a characteristic passage. After marvelling that Jesus should condescend to make use of 'the wretched arts of human commerce' by 'adopting the repulsive tricks which we employ to float a manufacture or a business (phrases hardly calculated to reassure the pious) he wonders whether 'this may not be the sternest lesson in humility ever given to man, as well as the most violent reproof hurled at the American abominations of our day'. And he concludes that God 'adopted strong measures from the first. He raised up a man whose book, translated into every language, carried the news of the vision to the most distant lands . . . To the end that this work should stir up the masses, it was necessary that the writer destined to the task should be a clever organiser, and at the same time a man devoid of individuality of style and of any novel ideas. In a word, what was needed was a man devoid of talent: and that is quite intelligible, since from the point of view of appreciating art the Catholic public is still a hundred feet beneath the profane public. And our Lord did the thing well: he selected Henri Lasserre.'[1]

Informed Catholic opinion was quite aware that Lasserre's book was unreliable. The Jesuit Father Cros had in 1884 made a careful collection of the evidence of the affair of the Grotto and had confronted Lasserre with documents disproving what he had written concerning the behaviour of the civil authorities.[2] Father Cros offered to suppress the book he had written himself if Lasserre would alter certain passages in his own work. On his refusal Father Cros read the relevant passages to the priests of the Grotto. As a result his book was suppressed,[3] and did not finally appear until forty years later.[4] If Huysmans knew of its existence, he had certainly never read it.

The story of Bernadette (now St. Bernadette, for she was canonized in 1933) is so well known that a short summary is all that is here necessary. Marie-Bernarde, to give her her baptismal names, was born at Lourdes in 1844, the eldest daughter of a poor and improvident couple called Soubirous. At the age of ten she was a victim of the cholera and this left her delicate and ailing. On February 11th, 1858 she went with her sister and another girl to the grotto at Massabielle near the little town (at that time, indeed, Lourdes was little more than a village), and there had a vision of the Virgin. On later visits the Virgin spoke to her and said: 'I am the Immaculate Conception.'

The terms in which the Virgin announced Herself have given rise to considerable controversy. Catholic writers maintained (quite rightly) that no child of fourteen could possibly

[1] *The Cathedral*, by J.-K. Huysmans, translated by Clara Bell, London, 1898.

[2] See Edith Saunders, *Lourdes*, London, 1940, p. 265.

[3] See Abbé Domenech, *Lourdes, Hommes et Choses*, 1894.

[4] L. J. M. Cros, S.J., *Histoire de Notre-Dame de Lourdes*, 3 vols., 1925–6.

have invented such a phrase, and they argued, therefore, that Bernadette had really received a message from On High. Sceptics declared that it must have been the result of priestly inspiration, possibly unconsciously given, in the confessional or in the lessons on the catechism which Bernadette is known to have received. The Papal Bull, *Ineffabilis Deus*, declaring *de fide* the dogma of the Immaculate Conception, had been published in 1854. All Catholics had, of course, accepted it, but what if the Virgin Herself should come down from Heaven and confound the unbelievers by putting, so to speak, her own seal on the doctrine?

No one has ever impugned the perfect sincerity of Bernadette herself, no one, that is, since the very first days of her visions. She convinced even the civil authorities (and some of the equally sceptical ecclesiastical authorities) that for her at least the experience was a real one.

The local inhabitants needed no convincing. They began to flock to the grotto in ever increasing numbers. Soon the whole province was involved, and news of the new sensation filtered through to Paris. Louis Veuillot, the influential editor of *L'Univers*, visited Lourdes in person and the article he wrote for his paper spread the story of Bernadette to every quarter of France. The most distinguished visitors began to arrive, to the joy of M. Peyramale, the local curé, and it became obvious that Lourdes was destined to become one of the most important centres of pilgrimage in history.

In 1861 the Bishop of Tarbes bought the grotto for a thousand francs; two years later he obtained permission to build a chapel there. In 1864 a life-sized statue of the Virgin was placed in the niche and everyone was pleased except poor Bernadette who declared that it bore no relation whatever to her vision. The spring which flowed in the grotto was enclosed in pipes.

Now it was M. Peyramale's turn to be disappointed. The

ecclesiastical authorities took the grotto out of his charge and gave it to the Missionary Fathers of the Immaculate Conception, already established at Garaison, a village near Lourdes, where the Virgin had appeared to a shepherdess, two centuries earlier. Just as the physical earth has areas where the crust is thin, so there are volcanic regions in the geography of the soul, places destined to the eruption of non-rational forces.

One of these regions was undoubtedly the foothills of the Pyrenees. Huysmans begins his book by listing, in addition to Garaison, eight other centres of pilgrimages, with chapels dedicated to the Virgin, and all but one of these was in the diocese of Tarbes. Even the exception belonged to the neighbouring diocese of Bayonne. Lourdes was, as it were, a new star which had suddenly appeared in the middle of a circle of satellites.

This, however, was small consolation to the curé of Lourdes. Disgusted at the turn events had taken, he pulled down the church in which Bernadette had worshipped and began to build a basilica in rivalry with the one which was rising at Massabielle. But all the money brought by pilgrims was flowing to the Grotto, and he had to abandon his project. He died in 1877, a deeply disappointed man. Bernadette, far away in her convent at Nevers, followed him to the grave eighteen months later. Then the whole lay-out of the place was transformed. The course of the river was changed, valleys were raised and hills were lowered, and two huge ramps were constructed at the Grotto so that processions could start and finish at the basilica and never pass through the old town at all.

Something of the kind was, indeed, necessary, for the number of pilgrims grew greater every year. New hotels were needed, new shops, hospitals for the sick. The old town of Lourdes could never have accommodated a tenth part of the multitudes who came to be healed. When Zola visited it in 1892 he had the greatest difficulty in reconstructing the original scene, and Huysmans, ten years later, found more or less the Lourdes we see to-day.

At first the place staggered him. If 'the best proof of Catholicism is its art', what was he to think of Lourdes? He tells us, in a chapter which is surely one of the most savage pieces of vituperation in literature. The ugliness of what he saw was something more than natural. This plethora of baseness, this 'haemorrhage of bad taste' could only be explained by the personal intervention of the Evil One. The basilica was bad enough but what could be said of the Rosary, the dropsical circus whose bursting belly bulged beneath it? Its style was a mixture of romanesque and byzantine with suggestions of a casino and hippodrome, and with a touch of railway station thrown in.

The decoration was like that of a theatre, badly carried out, the windows were unspeakable, the columns were crowned with the plumed headdresses of savages: the whole thing reeked of the operatic exoticism of some provincial music hall. It was illuminated by hundreds of electric lamps, so that it was easy to imagine oneself anywhere in the world but in a church. An unscrupulous speculator and a delirious beadle must have conspired together to produce such a monstrosity.

But whoever had constructed this religious casino was a positive genius compared with the painters who had decorated it. One could not even call the pictures bad, for that implied some kind of standard. It was impossible to pass any judgment upon them at all; as works of art they were simply non-existent. One could only take refuge in the single panel that had been entrusted to a painter, a very mediocre painter to be sure, but one who at least knew the elements of his craft. In fact the chromolithographic-poster style displayed by M. Maxence might have looked well enough on a choco-

late box, and even here the nothingness of the paintings beside it made it seem almost real. What church rat, what
bishop afflicted with apoplexy could have been inspired by
the Powers of Hell to commission such things?

What about the painted cast-iron Virgin on the esplanade,
crowned with an aureole of electric bulbs and looking like a
madwoman escaped from an asylum! What of the Stations of
the Cross, just begun, with only one group yet completed!
Invective itself failed to find words when faced with such a
collection of dead dummies. A good priest had lamented that
money was still lacking to complete the series. He could, cries
Huysmans, be reassured. 'I know my Catholics well enough
not to doubt for a second that they will be ready to make every
sacrifice to finish such a work.' Without doubt such things
could only be due to the cunning of the Demon. They were
his revenge against the Queen of Heaven. He had created a
permanent blasphemy in inspiring thus the sacrilegeous
hideousness of Lourdes! Catholic readers must have reflected
ruefully when they came across this passage that the *immonde
Zola* himself had handled them much more gently than this
irascible convert to their Faith.

Having dealt with the architecture, Huysmans turns his
attention to the pilgrims. He describes the arrival of a troop
from Brittany, herded on by their priests like a flock of
sheep; he sees a crowd of Spaniards advancing, the women
waving their handkerchiefs, throwing kisses to the crowd
and 'roaring like hyenas'. They are eating oranges or bars of
chocolate; their priests (and this seems to have shocked Huysmans) are smoking cigarettes. He takes a particular dislike to
the English pilgrims, marching stiffly with a Union Jack.
'None of them sings, but a few of the women, with spectacles
and projecting teeth, croak!' Perhaps it is only fair to add that
Huysmans did not care for the English under any circumstances. It would even be true to say that he did not care for

humanity, at least in the mass. Certainly he viewed the crowds at Lourdes without indulgence.

The implacable *Naturaliste* spares the reader nothing. He describes the wounds and the ulcers of the patients, their cries, their groans, their pitiable faces. He makes us assist at the painful ceremony of plunging them into the sacred spring. And 'the water becomes a horrible soup, a kind of kitchen-grey slops, with bubbles, red patches and white clots floating on the tin-coloured liquid in which people continue to be immersed'. 'This' he cries, 'is the permanent miracle of Lourdes; they throw into these contaminated vessels sick people who have not yet digested their last meal; they immerse up to the neck women at a period when they are forbidden by the most elementary commonsense to take a bath—and often in such cases the water is suddenly changed into a pool of blood—and no one suffers from congestion or sudden chill. Antiseptic bandages, so vaunted by the surgeons, are here simply replaced by compresses soaked in the water of Lourdes, and no one is any the worse . . . Every possible outrage is inflicted on hygiene and orthodox medicine, and yet there is no infection, and if a malady is not cured, it is not made worse . . . How, if we do not believe in a divine inter-vention, can we explain this immunity, granted to Lourdes only and for as long as one is in the zone protected by the Virgin?' A reader unaware of the writer's orthodox convic-tions might be excused if he saw, in this passage, an elaborate piece of irony *à la Voltaire*.

And yet, as with St. Lydwine of Schiedam, the final effect, the total gesture of *Lourdes* is perhaps all the more impressive because the author was so difficult to please, so immune from the contagion of conventional piety. The cures he witnessed were few, pathetically few (and he grows almost angry with the Virgin for not answering more generously the supplica-tions of the faithful) but he makes them convincing. After all, it is well to remind ourselves that people *have* been cured at the Grotto, whatever sceptics may say. Huysmans did not waste his time at Lourdes.

During his stay there he had one strange, personal adventure. He met again 'La Sol', the passionate and eccentric Spanish woman who had so tormented him in Paris, with her importunities and her threats not only to practise black magic against him but to pursue him even into a monastery and create a scandal. He found her at Lourdes, but she too had undergone a spiritual evolution, and was now a nun in the Convent of the Carmelites.[1]

Had he a faint hope that he might himself be numbered among the *miraculés* of Lourdes? Certainly he had need of Divine intervention, for the medical profession could do nothing for him and his maladies grew worse and worse. In the summer of 1905 he suddenly lost his sight. After seven months of darkness, it was, as suddenly, restored to him on Easter Day, which caused him, says Descaves,[2] to be more than ever convinced of the superiority of liturgical to medical treatment. At the same period, he did a very strange thing: he replaced the Abbé Mugnier by the Abbé Fontaine as his spiritual director. The reasons are obscure. Possibly he felt that the Abbé Mugnier was too worldly, not indeed in himself, but in the company he kept. The Abbé Fontaine, on the other hand, was curé of the slum district of Clichy. Perhaps it was an act of humility on Huysmans' part, and although it gave great pain to the priest who had been responsible for his conversion, and had watched over him ever since, the two men continued to be friends.

Huysmans had recovered his sight, at least partially, but, as the year 1906 drew to a close, it became plain that he had

[1] Rancœur, *op. cit.*, p. 42, note.
[2] Lucien Descaves, *Deux Amis*, Paris (1946). See also the same author's *Les Dernières Années de Huysmans*.

not much longer to live. His sufferings were atrocious.
'It was', says Dom Dubourg, 'with a sentiment of religious
respect that, in his study on the fifth floor, so far from the
earth and so near to the heavens, I discovered our dear
friend in his usual surroundings, in the middle of the books
he could no longer read, having before him a page of manuscript he could no longer finish. His features were emaciated,
deformed by the malady from which he suffered, but illuminated from time to time by the sweet and limpid look which
he directed on his crucifix. In the middle of the agonies which
were tearing him to pieces . . . his lips never ceased to murmur their tireless *fiat* . . .

'To the doctors who wanted to give him morphia to ease
the pain, he cried: "Ah! You want to prevent me from suffering! You want to change the sufferings of the good God for
the evil pleasures of earth! I will not let you." As Lent drew
to its close, he said to me: "I have had a beautiful dream:
how I wished it could be realised!—I was on the cross with
Jesus. Ah! if my good Master would take me, as he did the
Penitent Thief, on Good Friday!" His wish was not granted.
He had to drink the cup of suffering to the dregs.'

Perhaps with a premonition of his own final agonies he
had already thought much on the subject of pain. There is a
strangely eloquent passage in *L'Oblat* in which, by a daring
flight of fancy, he personifies Suffering in the form of a
female genius, springing to life in Eden,—the first-born of
the sin of Adam. He pictures her, the curse and the accursed
of all mankind, waiting, like them, for the Redeemer who
should reveal her nature to be not wholly evil. For her too
He is the Bridegroom to Whom she can give herself completely, for only the Man-God is of a stature to endure her
full caress. His capacity for suffering was infinite; and that
night, in the Garden, when he assumed the sins of the world,
she hastened towards Him, embraced Him and grew gigantic.

The Mystery of Suffering

She was so terrible that He fainted at her touch. His agony was His betrothal to her, and the symbol of her betrothal, like that of all women, was a ring. But it was an enormous ring, at once the symbol of marriage and the symbol of royalty: a crown. She crowned His head with it, before ever the Jews had woven the Crown of Thorns, which she had commanded, and His forehead was circled with a sweat of rubies, adorned with pearls of blood, like a diadem . . .

And when the supreme moment of the marriage had come, while Mary, the Magdalen, and St. John stood in tears at the foot of the cross, she, like Poverty of whom St. Francis speaks, climbed deliberately on to the gibbet, and from the union of these two rejected of the world, the Church was born: she came forth in a gush of blood and water from the Victim's breast. And it was finished. The Christ, now impassable, escaped forever from her grasp. She was a widow in the very moment that she had been loved, and she came down from Calvary, set free by that love, redeemed by that death.

Rejected like the Messiah, she had raised herself with Him, and like Him, from the height of the Cross had dominated the world; her mission was now defined and ennobled; henceforward she was comprehensible for Christians, and to the end of the ages she would be loved by souls who would call upon her to hasten the expiation of their sins and those of others, and would love her in remembrance and in imitation of the Passion of Christ.

Day by day, Huysmans' sufferings grew worse. The roof of the mouth had been perforated by the cancer, and his very food was mixed with fragments of his own decomposing flesh. François Coppée was moved to cry: 'Huysmans! He described himself when he wrote of St. Lydwine.'

A picture of him when nearing his end is given by Madame Peaucellier, an *Oblate* of St. Benedict, writing to Dom

Micheau, one of the monks Huysmans had met at St. Wandrille. She describes a visit she had received from his confessor, Dom Fontaine, he whom the writer had humorously called 'the apostle of the rag-pickers.'[1] 'I was filled with wonder at what he told me . . . For a long time Huysmans has fasted all the year round, contenting himself in the morning with a very small cup of coffee and a morsel of bread. No one knew of his austerity for it did not prevent him from being very hospitable and offering his guests good fare, which he hardly touched himself . . . He has suffered martyrdom for the last eighteen months; his eyes, his ears, his teeth have, in turn, tortured him. Almost all his teeth had been extracted and his throat and mouth were nothing but a purulent wound.'

When the good Father sympathised with him he said: 'Do not pity me. I am far from being unhappy.' 'It was necessary for me to suffer all this in order that those who read my books should know that I was not just "making literature".' Certainly in his last days his faith was passionately sincere.

When he knew that his end was approaching he sent a message to Dom Besse to ask that he should be buried in the monastic habit. Dom Besse despatched from Belgium, where he was then living, the tunic and the scapulary. When they arrived Huysmans had very few days to live. He set about burning such of his papers as he did not wish to survive. He burned *La Faim*, one of his earliest works dealing, as we have already noticed, with the War of 1870 and the Siege of Paris, he burned an incomplete work entitled *La Comédie Humaine* written during his period of *Naturalisme*. He also destroyed a work on Notre Dame de la Salette, inspired by the Abbé Boullan. He received the Sacraments of the Church and he dictated the invitation to his funeral:

[1] The letter is dated October 16th, 1907: quoted in J. Decourt, *Les Débuts Bénédictins de J.-K. Huysmans*, St. Wandrille, 1950, p. 184.

The Mystery of Suffering

Vous êtes prié d'assister
aux convoi, service et enterrement de
M. Joris-Karl Huysmans
Homme de Lettres
Président de l'Académie des Goncourt
Officier de la Légion d'Honneur
decédé le   , muni des Sacrements de
l'Eglise en son domicile, rue Saint-Placide, No. 31.

He left the date blank, but he might almost have guessed it. On Sunday, May 12th, 1907 he felt well enough to get up for lunch. At four o'clock he smoked a final cigarette, went back to bed and shortly afterwards fell into a coma from which he never awakened.

On May 15th, the body of Huysmans, clad in his robe as *Oblat* of the Order of St. Benedict, and followed by a crowd of priests, monks and men of letters, was carried first to the Church of Notre Dame des Champs, where the Abbé Mugnier conducted the service, then to the Cemetery of Montparnasse, where the final prayers were said by the Abbé Fontaine. He was buried in the family grave. An unpretentious stone records his name: 'J.-K. Huysmans, Président de l'Académie Goncourt', and the names of those who lie with him: his father, Godefried Huysmans, 1815–1856, his mother, Vve Og, née Bâdin, 1826–1876, his maternal grandfather and grandmother, Jules Bâdin, 1800–1862, and Vve Bâdin, née Gérard, 1797–1876, his stepfather, Jules Og, 1823–1867, and *his* mother, Vve Og, née Breistroff, 1784–1870, and the mysterious Vve Alavoine, née Bavoil.[1]

Huysmans was gone but his friends were determined that he should not be forgotten. Every year, on the anniversary of his death, a mass was said for him by the Abbé Mugnier at St. Séverin which, in spite of his criticisms of the music there,

[1] See *ante*, p. 193.

had been, after all, one of his favourite churches. Later the service took place in the little chapel of St. Joseph-de-Cluny. At both sanctuaries the officiant was the Abbé Mugnier, and he continued this tribute to his dead friend almost to the end of his life. After 1935 he was almost blind, and it was a touching sight to see him groping his way through the service, and, when it was over, carefully descending the steps of the altar to breakfast in the sacristy with Lucien Descaves. He died in 1944, when he was almost ninety, having survived his penitent by nearly forty years. He was buried within a stone's throw of Huysmans' grave.

Huysmans' friends however did not confine themselves to religious ceremonials in his honour. The *Société Huysmans* began issuing its *Bulletin* in 1925 and a number of luncheons and dinners was held. The Abbé Mugnier and Lucien Descaves were the most faithful at these reunions, which often included also such men as Paul Valéry, René Dumesnil and Pierre Dufay. In 1934 the luncheon took place (appropriately enough, since Huysmans at his death had been President) in the room reserved for the Académie Goncourt at Drouant's restaurant in the Place Gaillon. The Second World War interrupted such meetings but it did not bring them to a close. The *Bulletin* went through a financial crisis in 1938 and the War seemed likely to end it altogether. However, it started again in 1946, and continues to be published.

Huysmans therefore still has disciples; his cult goes on, and even in the larger world of letters he seems to have maintained a more solid reputation than that of most of his contemporaries, with the notable exception of Verlaine. Zola, after a long period of eclipse, is beginning to emerge again, but the once enormous reputation of Anatole France has not, so far, revived, at least among the intellectuals. Huysmans has maintained his place; his books continue to be read, and commentaries on them appear with surprising frequency.

Some of the problems he raised and the questions he asked
are still 'live issues'. It is true that the general interest in
occultism has waned; no one seems any longer excited by the
existence or non-existence of the Black Mass in the heart of
Paris. But his conversion and his relationship to Catholicism
in general still provokes controversy. He was, after all, one of
the most surprising, if not one of the most spectacular, converts of the nineteenth century.

There have been many since: the poet Francis Jammes, the
former Protestant Jacques Maritain, the anti-clerical Péguy,
Psichari, the grandson of Renan; Rivière, Gheon, Dupouey,
Copeau, P. A. Laurens, Charles du Bos, René Schwob, Jean
Cocteau, Reverdy, Max Jacob.[1] But hardly any of these converts followed the road of aesthetic mysticism trodden by
Huysmans. None of these men would have echoed, whole-
heartedly, his dictum that the best proof of Catholicism is
its art. The general movement was of a quite different
character.

George Fonsegrive[2] has pointed out the astonishing change
that came over the intellectual climate of France between the
eighteen-eighties and the First World War. Renan, in the
oration with which he welcomed Victor Cherbuliez to the
Académie Française in 1882, referred to religion, in his suave
and deadly way, as the 'perfume of an empty vase'. And the
Academicians smiled and applauded. In 1913 René Bazin,
Director of the *Académie*, while distributing the *prix de vertu*,
spoke of 'the Master who brought Charity to earth, the
Friend of the Poor, the Consoler of suffering. He Who went
about doing good . . . our Lord Jesus Christ'; and his discourse was received with every mark of the warmest appro-
bation.

[1] Léon Pierre-Quint, *André Gide, Sa Vie, son Œuvre*, Paris, 1933.
[2] George Fonsegrive, *De Taine à Péguy*, *L'Evolution des Idées dans
la France Contemporaine*, Paris, 1917.

The Mystery of Suffering

The audience at such functions usually comprises the élite of French intellectual life, yet the phrases which would have excited ridicule in 1882, provoked nothing but approval thirty years later. The French intelligentsia had, in fact, emerged from the illusion of 'Scientism', which is not Science, but the 'contraband metaphysics' which too great a faith in Science implies. In the eighteen-eighties Taine and Renan held the field, and the reaction is all the more remarkable because the official policy of the French Government was, at least until 1914, aggressively anti-clerical.

It was not, however, a question of politics; it was a question of intellectual evolution. The notion that every department of human life and thought should one day be studied by the methods of the experimental sciences, and yield its ultimate secrets, was to the generation of Taine and Renan self-evident. But as the century drew to its close the idea began to be more and more questioned even by the scientists themselves; until in 1907 a savant of the stature of Henri Poincaré could say 'Formulæ are not true; they are useful'.[1]

Literary criticism showed a similar change of direction, and its progress can be summed up in the development of the most influential critic of his day, Ferdinand Brunetière, from the moment when, not yet a Catholic, he published in 1895 his article '*Après une visite au Vatican*', to the discourse which he pronounced at Besançon five years later, '*Ce que l'on apprend a l'école de Bossuet.*' What he had learned, he claimed, 'at the School of Bossuet' was the insufficiency of the scientific method.

In literature the supposed determinism of the scientific attitude had given rise to the doctrine of *Naturalisme* and this led inevitably to the adoption of one or other of two attitudes to life: to the dilettantism of a Renan, of a Rémy de Gourmont or of an Anatole France, or to the unrelieved

[1] Henri Poincaré, *La Science et l'Hypothèse*, Paris, 1907.

pessimism of the majority of French writers in the 'seventies and 'eighties.

Huysmans' temperament inclined him to pessimism but he tried to escape from this by a kind of æsthetic mysticism which is merely dilettantism under another name. It says in effect: let us concern ourselves only with the surface-pattern of life and let us concentrate our attention upon those parts of it from which æsthetic pleasure can be derived. This is the doctrine of art for art's sake, and, by proclaiming it, Huysmans became one of the founders of the whole Decadent School, both in France and England. Behind him, no doubt, stood Baudelaire who was the first to enlarge the borders of literary sensibility to include the sensations of taste and smell as well as those of sight and hearing.[1] But Huysmans was the first to make a systematic attempt to construct, as it were, an organ of the senses from which no stop was absent—unless by chance it was the stop called *Vox humana*; and the results of this attempt, as expressed in *A Rebours*, were still manifest well into the twentieth century. Indeed, as Francis Carco remarks,[2] he 'created a kind of personal hypnotism of which our generation was, consciously, the victim'.

Huysmans himself, however, passed to other modes of thought, and it is because he did so that he is still of interest to us today. We may not accept the solution he found, we may doubt (although it is very hard to do so) the sincerity of his convictions, but we cannot help being moved by his story, and inspired by the way in which he—the literary man in the very fibre of his being—transcended literature. 'Do not let them say', he cried in his agony, 'that I have only made literature.' Not his books but his life is our story, even although we are compelled to come to knowledge of his life, almost entirely, through his books.

[1] For a discussion of this point see Julien Benda, *Belphégor*, Paris, 1919.
[2] Francis Carco, *Bohême d'Artiste*, Paris (1940).

In reality Huysmans did not write novels, he wrote one novel the hero of which was himself. Proust of course did the same but, in *his* world, he was strangely uninvolved. Proust is static, Huysmans is dynamic. With whatever stumbles and back-slidings, he moves forward. Proust is the mirror of an epoch. Huysmans is an individual contemplating himself, and it is individuals that vitally interest us; for while we merely live in epochs, we *are* individuals. Proust is a suffering sensibility; Huysmans is a struggling soul. Mere contemplation cannot move us as participation moves us, and in Huysmans we are compelled to participate. For he is not a spectator; he is a pilgrim; in spite of the strangeness of some of his adventures one might call him the Universal Pilgrim; and his progress is the Pilgrim's Progress.

Like Christian he dwells long in the City of Destruction, and with difficulty escapes from Doubting Castle. If he wastes no more than a glance on Vanity Fair, he is well acquainted with the Valley of Humiliation and spends a considerable time in the Slough of Despond. Perhaps we should not press Bunyan's images too far, or Giant Pope might insist on taking his place in the picture. Let us be content to note that Huysmans came, in time, to the House of the Interpreter, and gained at last a glimpse of the Celestial City.

In spite of their difference in religious climate, how close the great allegories are to one another! Mr. Colin Still in his illuminating study of Shakespeare's 'Tempest',[1] points out the curious analogies in the stories of Bunyan's Christian, of Virgil's Æneas, of Dante, and even of the Children of Israel in Exodus. They all pass over a river, wander through a Wilderness and come to a Promised Land. And they do this because creative art, at its highest level, is the reflection of realities existing in the universal consciousness. It 'has but

[1] Colin Still, *The Timeless Theme*, London, 1936.

one essential theme, the Fall of the Human Soul and the means of its redemption'.

Such a notion, at least until the very end, probably never entered Huysmans' head. Yet he passes through each stage of the great journey with an almost pedantic accuracy. Concerning himself at first (or so he imagined) merely with the things of earth, he found nothing but misery and frustration in the world of physical facts. When he broke with Zola and discarded the doctrine of *Naturalisme*, it was only to fall into the mire of sensuality, Despond, Cocytus, call it what you will. And, struggling onward through the World of Water, he found himself enticed by the nymphs (which are 'the powers of Water in its Lethal sweetness') and assailed by the monsters (which are the 'powers of water in its Stygian bitterness'), and fighting forward yet into the World of Mist, the region of intellectual error, he was still followed by these hateful and alluring shapes, until they were concentrated into a single figure of love-loathing!—the comely, wanton witch, whose kiss was degradation and whose bed was sacrilege.

Then lifting up his eyes in despair he saw, far beyond him, in the World of Light, another Woman, and called to her for help. And it seemed to him, as he called, in broken accents, that other voices took up the cry, melodious voices, chanting in unison, and they put words into his mouth that he could never have found for himself:

> *Rosa mystica*
> *Domus aurea*
> *Turris Davidica*
> *Stella matutina*
> *Ora pro nobis.*

For, if the Woman of the Abyss is part of the universal mind, so also is the Queen of Heaven.

WORKS BY J. K. HUYSMANS

———————————— • ————————————

Le Drageoir à Épices, Paris, 1874.

Marthe. Histoire d'une Fille, Brussels, 1876.

Sac au Dos, Brussels, 1878.

Les Sœurs Vâtard, Paris, 1879.

Les Soirées de Médan (contains a revised version of *Sac au Dos*, together with contributions by Émile Zola, Guy de Maupassant, Henry Céard, Léon Hennique and Paul Alexis), Paris, 1880.

Croquis Parisiens, Paris, 1880.

En Ménage, Paris, 1881.

Pierrot Sceptique, Pantomime by L. Hennique and J.-K. Huysmans. Paris, 1881.

A Vau l'Eau, Brussels, 1882.

L'Art Moderne, Paris, 1883.

A Rebours, Paris, 1884.

La Bièvre, Amsterdam, 1886.

Un Dilemme, Paris, 1887.

En Rade, Paris, 1887.

Certains, Paris, 1889.

Là-bas, Paris, 1891.

En Route, Paris, 1895.

La Cathédrale, Paris, 1898.

La Magie en Poitou, Ligugé, 1899.

Pages Catholiques, Paris, 1900.

Sainte Lydwine de Schiedam, Paris, 1901.

De Tout, Paris, 1902.

L'Oblat, Paris, 1903.

Le Quartier Notre-Dame, Paris (1905).

Works by J. K. Huysmans

Trois Primitifs, Paris, 1905.

Les Foules de Lourdes, Paris, 1906.

Trois Églises et Trois Primitifs, Paris, 1908.

En Marge. Etudes et Préfaces réunies et annotées par Lucien Descaves, Paris (1927).

Pages Choisies. Introd. de Lucien Descaves, Paris (1918).

STUDIES OF HUYSMANS

———————————•———————————

Henri Bachelin: *J.-K. Huysmans. Du Naturalisme Littéraire au Naturalisme Mystique*, Paris, 1926.

Robert Baldick: *Huyimans and the Goncourt French Studies*, April, 1952.

J. Barbey d'Aurevilly: *Le Roman Contemporain*, Paris, 1902.

Dom A. Du Bourg, O.S.B.: *Huysmans Intime. Le Bloc Catholique*, Paris, 1908.

Gustave Boucher: *Une séance de spiritisme chez J.-K. Huysmans*, Paris, 1908.

J. Bricaud: *J.-K. Huysmans et le Satanisme*, Paris, 1913.

J. Bricaud: *Huysmans occultiste et magicien*, Paris, 1913.

E. de Bruyn: *Réflexions sur M. Huysmans*, Brussels, 1895.

Henri Céard et Jean de Caldain: *Huysmans Intime. Revue Hebdomadaire*, 25 avril, 2 mai, 9 mai, 14 novembre, 21 novembre, 28 novembre, 1908.

Gustave Coquiot: *Le vrai J.-K. Huysmans*, Paris, 1912.

Joseph Daoust: *Les Débuts Bénédictins de J.-K. Huysmans*, Saint Wandrille, 1950.

Lucien Descaves: *Deux Amis; J.-K. Huysmans et l'Abbé Mugnier*, Paris (1946).

André du Fresnois: *Une Étape de la Conversion de Huysmans. La Grande Revue*, May 15th, 1911, p. 340.

Rémy de Gourmont: *M. Huysmans, Écrivain pieux. Promenades Littéraires*, I. 10th ed., 1919.

Jules Lemaître: *Les Contemporains*, le. série, Paris, 1898.

A. Meunier (pseudonym of J.-K. Huysmans). *J.-K. Huysmans. Les Hommes d'Aujourd'hui*, Paris (1885).

M. C. Poinsot et G. U. Lange: *Les Logis de Huysmans*, 2nd ed., Paris, 1920.

René Rancœur: *La Correspondance de J.-K. Huysmans avec Madame Cécile Bruyère, Abbesse de Sainte-Cécile de Solesmes. La Pensée Catholique*, 13, Paris, 1950.

Ernest Seillière: *J.-K. Huysmans*, Paris, 1931.

Paul Valéry: *Durtal, ou les Points d'une Conversion*, Paris, 1927.

Paul Valéry: *Variété*, 2e série, Paris, 1930.

INDEX

Index

Index

Index